Agility
Start to Finish

DIANE L. BAUMAN

with Jessica M. Ajoux

Photos by
Bohm Marrazzo
Photography
unless otherwise
credited.

Alpine
PUBLICATIONS
Crawford, CO

Library of Congress Cataloging-in-Publication Data

Bauman, Diane L.
  Dog agility from start to finish / by Diane L. Bauman ; with Jessica M. Ajoux.
     p. cm.
  ISBN-13: 978-1-57779-091-4 (pb : alk. paper)
  ISBN-10: 1-57779-091-X (pb : alk. paper)
  1. Dogs--Agility trials. 2. Dogs--Training. I. Ajoux, Jessica M. II. Title.
  SF425.4.B38 2007
  636.7'0835--dc22

The information contained in this book is complete and accurate to the best of our knowledge. All recommendations are made without guarantee on the part of the author or Alpine Publications, Inc. The author and publisher disclaim any liability with the use of this information.

For the sake of simplicity, the terms "he" or "she" are sometimes used to identify an animal or person. These are used in the generic sense only. No discrimination of any kind is intended toward either sex.

Many manufacturers secure trademark rights for their products. When Alpine Publications is aware of a trademark claim we identify the product name by using initial capital letters.

Credits
Editing Dianne Nelson
Cover Design and Layout: Laura Newport
Photography: Cover photos and over 160 images created by Bohm Marrazzo
     Photography, www.bohm-marrazzo.com., with submissions also
     by M.Nicole Fischer, Tien Tran and Marian Hummel, as noted.
Diagrams by Jessica Ajoux

1 2 3 4 5 6 7 8 9 0

Printed in the United States of America.

TABLE OF CONTENTS

SECTION I: THE START

SECTION II: HANDLING

SECTION III: OBSTACLES

SECTION IV: THE FINISH

OTHER WORKS BY THE AUTHOR

Books written by Diane Bauman:

Beyond Basic Dog Training (Third Revision)
Beyond Basic Dog Training: the Workbook
Life with People
Bauman's Guide to Beginning Tracking

Videos/DVD by Diane Bauman:

The Obedience Retrieve for all Breeds
Scent Discrimination and the Directed Retrieve

ACKNOWLEDGMENTS

Agility: Start to Finish has been to date my most major literary accomplishment. It has taken years to organize, compile, illustrate and eventually write this book. With my incredibly busy schedule of teaching, training, and trialing, this book would still be a pile of pages on my desk if it were not for the help of some very special people.

The interesting thing about everyone who has helped bring this book to fruition is that they all share a special bond with me and a passion for the sport of Dog Agility. The pages that follow harbor the emotions and obsession that this sport ignites in anyone who participates in it long enough.

I would like to thank Jessica Ajoux, my good friend and agility partner for finally pushing this book to its completion. Jess' love for agility, unique insights, literary editing skills, and expertise on the computer has helped make this book a reality. I thank you Jess for all the times you threw your hands up in despair and exclaimed, "Ahhh! Don't worry, I will fix it!" and for all your poignant questions: "But, What If?"

The other irreplaceable person involved in this process is my dear friend Linda Bohm. In addition to the spectacular photography you see in the book, Linda took on the additional roles of editor and literary agent to deal with the publishing side of the project; something I had no time or talent for. Linda, for all you have done, I know not how to repay you.

A special thank you goes to Gerard Marrazzo, the other half of Bohm Marazzo Photography, who is the magician behind Linda. Thank you Gerry for waving your magic wand and making me look svelte in all the photographs!

Very special words of thanks to my good friend Karen Hoffman, always ready to help me whenever and wherever.

Another exceptional, behind the scenes person, without whom this book would not be what it is, goes to Jane Jeter, a long time friend and the person responsible for getting me my World Team Cocker Spaniel "Torville" and for introducing me to Jessica Ajoux. You are quite the match maker!

I would also like to thank all of my friends, friends of friends, students, and in some cases their spouses, who read early versions of the manuscript. Your ideas, suggestions and comments will benefit everyone. I know some of you don't think I own a Spell Check! Thank you Marilyn Abbott, Nancy Caswell, Jeff and Lynn Drogin, Jim Epperly, Linda Goldman, Ian Mackay, Lynn Pierson and many thanks to Niles Wolfson and Peter Mitchell for your time and creativity that gave this book its title.

Sincere thanks to all the people who allowed me to use pictures of their dogs in this book.

There are many wonderful people in the sport of agility willing to give seminars, teach lessons, write articles, offer suggestions and help others learn the sport in any way they can. I owe a great deal of gratitude to the professionals in the sport whose seminars and lessons I have attended. In this new evolving, fast growing world of agility, it is important to stay current and to continually grow and expand ones knowledge. I would like to thank all the people who have been and continue to be a part of my education in agility. Because of all of you, this book has become a reality.

A big "Thank you" to all my dogs who willingly took the off-courses I never intended to send them to. You patiently taught me how to communicate in your language. Now I can teach others.

And finally, "thank you" to all my students and their dogs. Without all your questions and mistakes, this book would not hold so many answers.

Photo by Tien Tran.

vi

PREFACE

It was in 1996, after decades of training obedience, that I first discovered the new and exciting world of dog Agility. This was a whole new world. Coming from an obedience perspective, I soon realized that in "obedience" training we teach dogs to understand English: in Agility training, we learn to speak "Dog." The dog's language is based on movement; dogs communicate through the motion of their bodies. A simple head turn, raising of tail, or stiffening of body carries with it a message that other dogs understand.

What does this actually mean to you as an agility trainer? When things go wrong on the agility field, it's usually the human who is not fluent in the language of "Dog" that causes the mistake. Learning this language is not as complicated as I had first thought. I now realize that I trained my first dogs in Agility much longer and harder then was necessary. I taught commands that were not essential, and ignored other commands simply because I did not realize they were needed. I had no idea of how long it should take a dog to learn a specific concept. At times, I became frustrated because I thought there was no progress. Not knowing what to teach first, I had no training plan. And, it was simple guesswork as to when a dog was ready to compete in a trial.

What was wrong? Why did I feel so confused? The answer is there was no comprehensive text about dog agility to reference.

THE GOAL

My goal for writing this book is to simplify agility for both my students and my dogs. *Agility Start to Finish* is an all-inclusive book; it touches on everything I know about agility at this time. It represents the culmination of years of devoted study, discourse, experimentation, and thought on the part of many individuals. It is not the first Agility book out there, nor will it be the last. It is however, the first book to cover Agility from different perspectives and multiple levels, and to present this information in a logical, progressive format.

I do not take credit for inventing all the methods, concepts and terms in this book. That information simply needed to be organized, labeled and arranged so to make it clear and understandable to everyone. By doing so I hope to help both first time students and seasoned competitors.

You will find as you go through the book chapter by chapter that one skill builds on another. There are frequent references to another section or another chapter. The purpose of this is to demonstrate the connection of skills used to solve agility challenges. My intent is to provide a single source that teaches all aspects of agility under one philosophy.

Agility Start to Finish suggests new ways of looking at fundamental concepts in agility and offers fresh new ideas. You will find the information presented in relaxed, simple language accompanied by

THIS BOOK IS RIGHT FOR YOU . . .

- if you own an energetic dog that needs a sport activity in his life.

- if you think it would be fun to encourage your dog to jump and run.

- if you want to learn how to teach your dog to weave through poles.

- if you have started taking agility lessons and feel confused.

- if you are seeking greater understanding and a cohesive picture.

- if training contacts is a mystery to you.

- if you fear sending your dog to difficult weave pole entrances.

- if your dog goes off course.

- if you are an instructor seeking new teaching options.

Whether you are an experienced, professional agility enthusiast or an absolute beginner, this book is for you!

diagrams, pictures and analogies. My hope is that this sport becomes clear and inviting for everyone who turns these pages.

My co-author, Jessica Marie Ajoux, has been a great help in reaching this goal. As soon as we started training together, ideas and techniques began to explode between us. Working together brought us both to a deeper level of understanding agility. Jessica's passion and high expectations for this sport along with her intuition and foresight, are exceptional. She challenges me and others to see the big picture, to look ahead at least three plays, feel the strategy and enjoy the energy. As soon as we began to collaborate on the book I knew that together we were onto something special.

AND FINALLY . . .

It is mind-boggling to experience the relentless efforts and clever solutions enthusiasts find when they make the commitment to excel in the sport of agility. My students and fellow competitors always surprise me with questions, challenges and examples of what I have taught them. I delight as I watch them take those challenges much further than I ever imagined. It is my hope that as you read this book, process the information and apply our techniques, that you, too, will experience the energy and excitement of agility and the sheer joy on your dog's face.

Diane L. Bauman
Sussex, N.J.

CHAPTER 1

AGILITY MAKES SENSE TO DOGS

A good dog and handler team can run a Standard Agility Course anywhere from 32 to 51 seconds. A fast run on a Jumpers with Weaves Course may last only 21 to 29 seconds! I have often asked myself, why do people drive hours and hours to spend less than a minute and a half in the ring with their dog?

People who do not understand the sport of agility often shake their heads at agility enthusiasts. What motivates these people to write check after check for entry fees, travel most weekends, and wake up at 5:30 A.M. or earlier to walk around a ring in an "obsessive walk through"? Anyone who has ever run agility with a dog, who enjoys the game, understands that the answer to these questions is really quite simple. We run agility for the tremendous thrill it brings to our dogs; the look in their eyes says it all!

To the dog, an agility course is like a hunt. While running with the handler, the dog is directed to jump over obstacles (jumps), duck into things (tunnels), run over planks of wood (dog walks) and weave in between poles (weave poles). This sport makes sense to a dog that could just as easily be jumping over logs, ducking under brush, running over rocks, and weaving between trees in the woods as he hunts for his prey. The dogs become energized and like their handlers, feel a rush of adrenaline which radiates from their faces. The simple fact is, we love to see our dogs exhilarated and having fun. This is why agility is one of the fastest growing sports in the world.

Agility is a man-made sport for dogs. Unlike obedience training where dogs are taught to understand verbal language, in agility, the handler must learn the canine language of using the body and movement to communicate. When two dogs meet, they speak to each other through their posture, ear positions, head carriage, tail positions, and general movement or non-movement. Dogs naturally focus on the movement around them as this is how they were originally able to hunt and survive. Dogs who have a high hunting (prey) drive are the most responsive to subtle handler movements.

> We run agility
> for the tremendous thrill it
> brings to our dogs;
> the look in their eyes says it all!

Photo by M Nicole Fischer.

When a handler runs with a dog, the dog is able to read and interpret the movement of the handler's body. He can anticipate where to run the same as he could while chasing prey during a hunt by reacting to shoulder, head, and ear movements. Dogs are born with this ability to read movement; humans need to learn to give the correct movements and motions in an effort to direct the dog around an agility course. We call this skill learning to "handle" a dog.

People and dogs have been known to get "addicted" to agility. Some dogs scream as they run a course, others pull to get into the ring, and many whine with excitement as they approach a training facility. People continue to acquire more and more dogs to train and run in agility, leading inevitably to the purchase of an RV or at the very least a "dog friendly" SUV or van needed to transport all the dogs to the trials. Vacations and holidays begin to center around where the agility trials are held. I believe there are good reasons why people and dogs are so crazy about running agility.

Have you ever heard of a "runners high"? The act of running releases chemicals into the brain that give a person or dog a sense of thrill and euphoria. Having experienced this feeling, dogs and people want more! When dogs are first learning the game of agility, many of them begin slowly. As time goes by, confidence grows, courses become more complex, and speed increases. You can actually witness the moment a dog gets hooked on the feeling of running an agility course; some call it "turning on" to agility!

This is a fabulous sport which we have the privilege of sharing with our closest companions. Agility makes sense to dogs, and this book will help agility make sense to you!

CHAPTER 2

A NEW APPROACH TO TRAINING

Any philosophy, whether it concerns training dogs, which religious deity to follow, or how the earth evolved, begins with certain facts that the philosopher believes to be true. Born from this foundation of beliefs are theories that grow and eventually mature into practiced methodologies. To explain how I have developed the training techniques I use to manipulate and create behaviors in dogs, I must begin by sharing with you what I believe to be true about our domestic canines.

DOGS ARE BRED TO WANT TO WORK WITH PEOPLE

Historically, dogs were bred to want to work with people, and some are still bred that way. Before the days of Conformation (breed shows) where dogs are judged only on how they look and move, dogs were valued and bred for their abilities to hunt, herd, guard, offer companionship, and a variety of other purposes. The individuals that did not perform well in their respective disciplines were not chosen by man to reproduce; through this process of selection, the working ability of the dog was enhanced. Some breeders today still strive to reproduce only dogs that can perform the jobs for which they were intended.

If you are searching for a dog to participate in any performance event (agility, obedience, herding, field, etc.), I would recommend buying a dog from a breeder who intentionally breeds for what dogs can do. Although the structure of the dog is important, you need to consider the entire dog and not just his parts.

Form is usually associated closely with function; that is, if a dog can do the job he was bred to do, he probably has the structure needed to get the job done. A Border Collie with poor physical structure will not be able to run very fast, nor can he work all day long herding sheep. Structure and good conformation are important in the sense that they allow dogs to perform the movements required for their work, yet it is still the work ethic that is of utmost importance. Owning and training a dog that wants to work with you is a true pleasure.

DOGS MAKE AN EFFORT TO COMMUNICATE WITH PEOPLE

Anyone who has ever spent time around dogs knows that dogs communicate in many different ways. Whining, crying, barking, and whimpering are their verbal attempts, but dogs do not have a verbal language of their own and rely on many other forms of communication. I'm sure you have had a dog nudge you with his cold, wet nose to ask to be petted, or a big, hairy paw has tapped you to get your attention. Then

there are dogs that speak with total silence and simply stare intently into your eyes with great expectation. They are not called puppy eyes for nothing! Dogs of all breeds and ages are freely communicating with humans all the time. Do people hear what their dogs are telling them? Training dogs is as much about listening to what a dog is saying as it is about issuing commands. Agility is a wonderful sport in which dogs teach people how to listen to them, and people learn to communicate with dogs in a non-verbal, canine fashion.

As you learn to communicate easily with a dog, a partnership is born. A dog is much more willing to work for a handler who is clear with instructions and takes the time to listen to his partner. Partnerships of all kinds are built on trust. Your dog must trust that you will tell him exactly what you want him to do and that you will not correct him unfairly for your mistakes. He must trust that you are willing to allow him to make honest errors along the road to learning, thus granting him "*the right to be wrong.*" You must trust that if you have taught your dog how to do something, he can do it on his own, without you right next to him.

For example, if you have taught your dog how to enter weave poles independently, there is no need to crowd him at the entrance. If you have taught your dog a "stay" at the start line, you should walk away from him with confidence and not repeat the stay command every few feet! A successful team relies on a partnership in which the handler does his or her part of teaching properly, and the dog does his part of performing correctly what he has been taught. The teamwork needed to succeed in the sport of agility requires two players, each trusting the other.

DOGS CAN SOLVE SIMPLE PROBLEMS

Have you ever watched a dog get a tennis ball out from underneath something? How about dogs who figure out how to open cabinets or get into the garbage? I have childproof locks on all of the doors in my kitchen. When a dog is motivated to figure something out, he has great problem-solving ability.

After years of observing dogs solve problems, I have learned that dogs remember best what *they* discover. Dogs that figure out how to get into the garbage rarely have to practice the skill to remember how to do it. With this in mind, much of my training is geared toward letting dogs discover on their own what I want them to know.

An example of this is placing a cookie on a low pause table and waiting for the dog to figure out how to get up onto the table. Another example is throwing or placing a cookie in the barrel of the chute and giving the dog time to figure out how to enter the barrel when the opening is not facing him. With the use of a treat, I am helping the dog discover that he can solve the problem of how to get on a table and how to find the hidden entrance to a chute. This prepares a dog to solve problems that he will encounter in the future as he learns new things.

As dogs work to solve a problem, they make many mistakes along the way. They try what does not work before they discover what does. I believe that dogs learn by trial and error. If you accept this theory, then you must be willing to allow dogs to make errors or you will stifle learning. Error-free learning is *not* my goal.

If a dog is corrected when he is wrong, he becomes afraid to be wrong and therefore afraid to experiment and try new approaches to solving his problems. This is referred to as a fear of failure, and a fear of failure hinders learning. (Many children suffer from a fear of failure, too, and it can become so emotionally devastating that they cannot even begin to take a test for fear that they might do poorly.) There are times in training when dogs should be corrected, *but never for honest attempts that just happen to be wrong.* Most of the time, if your dog offers the incorrect response, ignore it and begin again. By not drawing attention to the mistake, the dog will forget it and focus on the behaviors that seem to work to solve his problem. You never want to give your dog a list of things he should *not* do. It would be like me sending you to the grocery store with a shopping list of everything you shouldn't buy! How long would it take you to shop?

UNDERSTANDING CORRECTIONS

What is a correction? A correction is anything a dog would rather not have happen to him. A correction for one dog may not necessarily be a correction for another. For example, if your dog does not like it if you pull on his collar, that is a correction for that dog. If a dog does not care if you pull his collar, find something else to do if you are trying to give a correction. By the way, praise and reward are things a dog would like to *have* happen. If your dog hates to be touched on the head, stroking his head is not praise for this dog and might actually be considered by the dog to be a correction!

Before you can effectively correct a dog, you must understand not only *what* a correction is but *when* corrections are justified. Did you know that there are only four reasons why a dog does not respond correctly to a command? They are:

1. The dog is afraid.

2. The dog is confused.

3. The dog is distracted.

4. The dog feels he has a choice.

If your dog is confused or afraid, he should not be corrected but should be helped to understand what you are commanding him to do. If your dog is distracted (once he has been taught to pay attention) or feels that he has a choice, he deserves to be corrected. Honest errors are always the result of confusion and should never be corrected.

How do you know if your dog is afraid, confused, or distracted, or if he feels he has a choice? You must learn to "read" what your dog is thinking by watching his facial expressions and his head, tail, and ear carriage. It is also important to know what his body posture means. Some people read dogs very naturally; others must learn. The best way to learn how to "read dogs" is to work with an instructor who is good at it. It's like learning a new language, and sometimes just being around someone who speaks the language fluently is enough for you to learn it.

Being able to "read dogs" is what makes the difference between good dog trainers and people who only get results with "easy" dogs that learn in spite of what happens to them. Some dogs are very simple to understand, and others are much more complex. Take, for example, a dog that is sniffing the floor in response to a handler's command to get on the pause table. Is this dog really distracted, or is the dog confused or afraid? Many dogs when they are confused or afraid will act busy (sniff). It's a little like when you were in school and the teacher asked a question to which you did not know the answer. This was a perfect time to drop your pencil on the floor and reach to pick it up because everyone knew that the teacher would not call on someone who was bending down to pick up a pencil.

If you decide that your dog deserves to be corrected, always use the mildest correction that works. A sensitive dog is easier to train than one that does not notice a correction. Maintain your dog's sensitivity by trying gentle corrections before escalating to stronger ones.

What if you just don't know why your dog is not responding correctly? It is always safer to give the dog the benefit of the doubt and assume that he is confused or afraid. If you *help* a dog that actually deserves to be corrected, you will not make things worse. (You may not make anything better either!) If you *correct* a dog that is confused or afraid, you run the risk of losing the dog's trust. The dog may become afraid to be wrong, which is highly detrimental to learning. If you help the dog repeatedly and the behavior does not improve, you can always add corrections later.

Dog is Afraid Dog is Confused	Help
Dog is Distracted Dog feels he has a Choice	Correct

DOGS HAVE EXCELLENT HEARING AND CAN BE TAUGHT TO PAY ATTENTION AND REMEMBER

Scientists have proven that dogs have much more acute hearing than people do. If you accept this, then there is never a reason to shout commands at a dog. In fact, have you ever noticed that when people speak softly, those around them listen more intently?

Experience has taught me that most dogs can be taught to pay attention, and only a few do it naturally. Teaching a dog to pay attention involves giving him a reason why it is to *his* advantage to know where you are and what you are doing. In agility, you initially use toys and food to focus the dog's attention on you. Eventually, the movement and motions are what the dog looks for. Do not confuse attention with head position. A dog looking at you may not be paying attention (proven repeatedly in the Utility Signal exercise in obedience), and a dog whose head is focused straight ahead, looking for a jump, may know exactly where his handler is and what he is doing.

Dogs can be taught to remember what they are doing. I know this because in obedience, dogs are trained to remain in a sit position for three minutes and in a down position for five minutes when the handler is out of sight. If a dog cannot remember what he is doing, he will change position or get up and leave. The best way to get a dog to remember what he is doing is *not* to remind him. Put the responsibility of remembering how to do something on the dog. A good example of this is when teaching assumed contacts (see Chapter 14, All About Contact Obstacles, page 123). Partway through the contact training, stop verbally telling the dog that he needs to touch the contact. You expect the dog to remember this and do his job. This is called "assumed contacts," and the dog is expected to remember that he must hit the contact before going on to the next obstacle. As the dog makes mistakes at this new level of training, the concept of hitting the contact is strengthened. The dog chooses to remember what is expected of him in order to earn the reward of continuing on with the course.

WHEN LEARNING, DOGS OFTEN SLOW DOWN

Just like people, when dogs are learning new things, it is common for their actions to slow down. As they begin to understand and gain confidence, the speed increases naturally. If you are teaching your dog to do weave poles and the dog is rhythmical but not fast, do not be concerned. Some very fast dogs started out moving slowly. When dogs attempt to learn things at top speed, it often takes them longer to master the skill than a dog that slows down to learn. In the teaching phase of an exercise, do not encourage speed by tugging with a toy or running full out. On the other hand, don't try to slow a dog down. Allow the dog to learn at whatever speed is comfortable. Know that, once your dog understands, you can build more drive and speed into the task. Understanding and intensity of learning are not necessarily manifested through rapid movements.

Imagine if someone was trying to teach you to type at sixty words per minute. When you begin to learn to type, you push the keys slowly. As you gain experience, you increase your typing speed. Allowing you to type slowly in the beginning did not make you a slow typist.

BEHAVIORS PRECEDE LEARNING

Dogs do things long before they understand what they are doing. Just because a dog jumps over a broad jump as you run toward it doesn't mean that the dog understands he is supposed to jump a broad jump straight across regardless of the angle from which he approaches it. Dogs run through contacts correctly long before they understand what it means to hit a contact. It is important for you to realize that behaviors precede learning. Knowing this, you will not make unfair assumptions about what a dog knows and understands.

The only way to know whether a dog truly understands a concept is to proof it. *Proofing* is a technique used to test a dog's understanding of an exercise; it clarifies the concept while strengthening the dog's concentration and confidence. Proofing is an integral part of training, and every behavior and obstacle performance needs to be proofed. The dog must demonstrate that he can perform the skill in many different locations amidst a variety of distractions before you can consider the skill truly learned.

An example of proofing would be to place a tunnel opening very close to the weave poles to see if the dog truly

understands that all of the weave poles must be completed before another obstacle is attempted.

DOGS CAN LEARN TO MULTITASK

Multitasking is the ability to concentrate on multiple things at the same time. In agility, a dog must listen and know where the handler is while continuing to look for obstacles. In herding, a dog must listen for commands, know where the handler is, and not take his eyes off of the sheep. Both activities require the ability to multitask—something a dog can be taught to do with practice and experience.

THE POWER OF TIME

The "Power of Time" is one of the most effective ways to change behavior in dogs. It is important to realize that you, as the handler, control time by deciding when training begins and when it ends. You control a dog's life by dictating when he eats, when he relieves himself, when he rests, and when he works. How can you use this power in agility training?

Consider this example: A dog understands the command "down" and does not choose to lie down on the pause table. The handler commands "down," and the dog simply stands there. Now the handler waits for the dog to make a decision; either the dog will sit, lie down, or get off of the table. No dog will stay on a table forever. If the dog sits, the handler again commands "down" and waits. If the dog gets off of the table, the handler puts him back on the table and again instructs "table, down." When the dog realizes that life as he knows it does not continue until he lies down, he will eventually comply. Once a dog grasps the concept that you control time, you have passive power over even the strongest-willed dog. The key to tapping into the power of time is patience. Sometimes you can wait up to twenty minutes. Do not give in; you will always win, for you will outlive the dog!

TRAINING THAT MAKES SENSE

Training should make sense to both the trainer and the dog. Have a reason for why you teach something a certain way and for why you use a specific hand motion. If you are learning from an instructor, feel free to ask the instructor why you are being told to do something. Skills need to be broken down and taught so that you are confident that your dog understands what is expected of him at every level. Handling should be consistent and fair. Dogs should be corrected when they deliberately disobey ("feel they have a choice") or become distracted (once they have been taught to pay attention), but never for making honest errors.

In order to have a problem, you first must train the dog! In other words, any mistakes a dog makes while in the learning stages of an exercise are not "problems" but just a normal part of the learning process. I consider a "problem" to be an incorrect behavior that *not* every dog will exhibit during the course of training. For example, every dog will knock down bars while learning to jump; this is a learning stage. Not every dog stutter-steps in front of a jump; this is a problem. It is helpful in training for you to be able to recognize the difference between a problem and a learning stage because it keeps mistakes in perspective.

Not all dogs and people have equal abilities. You need to believe in yourself and in the ability of your dog.

If you and your dog want to become a successful team, you must trust each other.

Believe in yourself and the ability of your dog. Photo by M. Nicole Fischer.

To Click or Not to Click?

Clicker Training is an instructional method originally developed for training sea mammals at Sea World Marine Park performances. The Sea World trainers wanted a way to teach a dolphin, whale, or seal to perform tricks at the far end of the pool away from the trainer. To meet this need, they used a small, handheld device that made a clicking sound (much like the sound a dolphin makes when talking) and held it underwater so that the sea mammal could hear it. Before the clicker could be used in training, the animal had to associate it with something positive. This was accomplished by trainers who would click and then immediately throw the animal a fish. It wasn't long before the sound of a click meant a fish reward was on its way. Thus was born the "Click and Treat" method of training. Hearing of this new system, dog trainers started sponsoring seminars given by the professionals at Sea World. Soon, clickers could be found in Obedience, Agility, and Freestyle and became the focus of many new books and tapes. Clicker training has become so popular that some people act as if you cannot train a dog without it. The fact is, it is not possible to pick up a whale and put him on a platform. On the other hand, dogs can easily be led, guided, and lured, as well as shaped into a specific position when you are teaching them behaviors.

It is true that trainers get results using clicker training. Dogs are happy and willingly offer behaviors, demonstrating a desire to learn. While I have attended seminars and explored the use of clickers, I have never chosen to include them in my training. This is because I find it more practical and efficient to take advantage of the fact that you can guide and position a dog to help him understand what you want. My training methods have always produced happy dogs that are willing to work without the need for a mechanical device. How is this possible?

One value of the clicker is that it forces trainers to break down behaviors into small steps. It gives the trainer the patience to allow the dog time to think and learn by trial and error. Sound familiar? The clicker trainer ignores incorrect responses and only marks and rewards movements that will eventually lead to the desired behavior. Again, sound familiar?

The training philosophies you have just read about accomplish the same goals with the advantage of not having to remove an additional aid like the clicker mechanism. There is nothing you can teach with a clicker that I cannot teach without the clicker. Some dogs don't like the clicking sound, and the clicker is something else to juggle in your hands. Nor do clickers work well in group situations, where multiple people are clicking all at once. I have always promoted the idea of breaking down exercises into small pieces and allowing dogs time to think and learn. I have always given dogs "the right to be wrong" without penalty. I teach students to break down behaviors and focus on small successes, creating happy dogs that are willing to learn and offer behaviors. This can be accomplished with or without the sound of a clicker.

CHAPTER 3

BUILDING A SOLID FOUNDATION

Foundation training refers to the skills that dogs and puppies are taught before they begin to learn how to perform the various agility obstacles. This training includes some basic obedience commands, as well as reinforcing dogs for responding correctly to the movements of your body. Learning to play with toys, tugging with you, and becoming aware of how a "food tube" works are also included in early preparation for agility training.

LEARNING TO PLAY AND ESTABLISHING A REWARD SYSTEM

Teaching your dog or puppy to play with you is the beginning of building a long-lasting relationship, as well as establishing a reward system. Play helps focus a dog's attention on you, the handler, and can be used to stimulate a dog to run with or ahead of his teammate.

Dogs, like children, prefer different kinds of toys. Fortunately, there now are pet suppliers who have devoted pages and pages of their catalogues to unique dog toys. There are toys that roll, squeak, talk, rattle, light up, are attached to ropes, are

Tugging is a reward that builds drive and focus.

WHAT IF MY DOG WON'T TUG?

Not all dogs like to tug. Some just do it, some tug occasionally, and some can be taught to tug. Dogs will usually tug when they are excited. To get a dog interested in tugging, make the toy exciting. Tap into the dog's prey drive by wiggling the toy around, and try to get him to chase it. Sometimes it helps to growl at your dog as if the toy were alive. Do short sessions and quit before the dog has decided that the tug is not fun anymore. For the dog that is tentative about tugging, do not pull too hard or roughly. Adapt to the dog's pulling intensity and increase it as the dog becomes more involved and enthusiastic.

Remember that tugging can be a powerful game; it brings out the prey drive in dogs. Enthusiastic "tuggers" often start growling and pulling very harshly. It is important that the dog learns that the tugging game is on your terms. You should decide when it starts and when it ends. Although it is acceptable for the dog to win the game of tug sometimes, the more dominant the dog, the less often he should be allowed to win.

It is vital that the dog learn to respect a "release the toy" command (such as "give," "drop," or "thank-you"). For this to happen, remember that the dog wants you to pull on the toy. Therefore, trying to pull the toy out of his mouth is less than effective. Command "give," and simply reach down and hold the dog by the collar so that he can no longer pull on the toy. Then wait. The dog will realize that this is not a fun game (you holding the toy and his collar) and will eventually relinquish the toy. If the dog is still intent on holding onto the tug toy, push the toy further into his mouth as if to say, "If you won't give it to me, then eat it!"

filled with food, and even have fur on them. One of your first goals as a handler is to discover what kind of toys your dog or puppy likes and what the dog chooses to play with by himself and with a person.

Teaching a dog to tug on a toy with you is an excellent way to build drive and keep him focused in between training sequences and outside of a ring. Refrain from throwing toys away from you for the dog to retrieve because this encourages a dog to take his attention off of you. Throwing toys is a good idea only when you are trying to teach distance exercises. (See Chapter 10, Working from a Distance, page 81).

This is usually rather convincing. When the dog finally releases the toy, praise him and either give him a treat or reward him with another game of tug.

FOOD

Dogs have food preferences, and it is a good idea to know what your dog likes and what your dog really likes. Treats used in agility should be moist and easy to swallow. Some favorite rewards include chicken, steak, hot dogs, string cheese, chicken hearts, tortellini, beef jerky, and meatballs. Ideally, dogs should be willing to work for and be motivated by both toys and treats. If you rely on only one kind of reward, the dog is more likely to get bored.

Furthermore, toys and treats are more or less practical in some training situations than others. In general, food treats calm down a high-energy dog, while toys tend to excite them more. Keep this in mind as you train your dog so that you do not overly motivate him to the point where he can no longer learn. High-drive Border Collies do better when they are first learning things if they are rewarded with treats or simply praise, as they do not need a reason to go faster. (It is difficult to first learn to type at sixty words per minute!)

BASIC COMMANDS

The first command I teach a new dog or puppy is "here." My thinking is that if you teach a dog to come when he is called, he will be around later to teach the rest of the commands. The other foundation commands that your dog will need to master before starting agility training are "sit," "down," and "stay". (See Chapter 7, *Commands You Need*, page 37, to learn how to teach these behaviors.)

FOLLOWING BODY MOVEMENT AND STAYING ON ONE SIDE

Once a dog will come when called to a hand at the side of your body, it's time to teach him to follow your movement and to stay on the same side of your body until he is told to change sides. Command "here" and call your dog to your left side. Begin walking in a big circle to the right (clockwise). Holding a treat in your left hand (between your fingers so that your hand is open and your palm faces the dog) will help keep the dog focused. Every so often, praise your dog, then stop and let him take the treat from your open hand. While the dog is merely following the food at this point, he is nonetheless learning to stay at your side and follow your hand and body movements as you circle to the right.

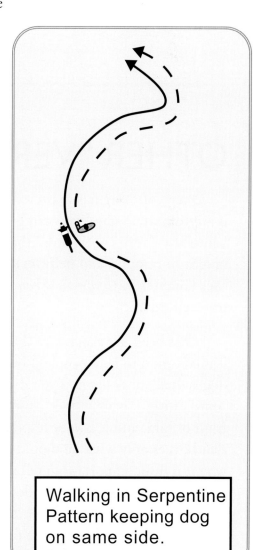

Walking in Serpentine Pattern keeping dog on same side.

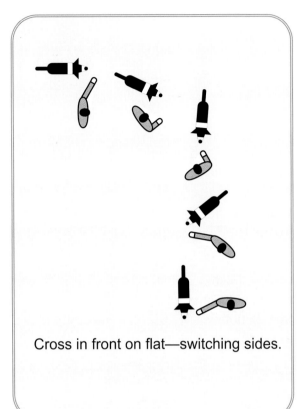

Cross in front on flat—switching sides.

Next, with the dog still on your left side, make a big circle to the left (counterclockwise). This will be more difficult, because the dog is on the inside of the circle and may try to get ahead of you. Help him learn to adjust his body and slow his stride in order to stay at your side by luring his head upward. When the dog lifts his head up to follow the food, he naturally shortens his stride. Finally, move in a serpentine pattern, keeping the dog on your left side regardless of where you turn. (Refer to Chapter 7, "Teaching the Here Command," page 41.)

When the dog is successfully following your movement and staying on one side, it is time to start teaching him to switch sides. To do this, start with the dog on your left, turn toward the dog, and extend your right hand so that he will now follow your right hand and will be on your right side. This is actually the beginning of teaching the front cross. (For more information on front crosses, refer to Chapter 8, in the section "Front Crosses," page 61.) The dog needs to be comfortable switching from your left and right sides and should not try to dart back to your other side as he switches.

The exercise must also be done with the dog on the right side. Repeat the circling process with the dog on the right side, and

OTHER "VERB COMMANDS"

Once your dog has mastered the basic commands of "here," "sit," "down," and, if appropriate, "stay," you can go on to teach the commands for "out" and "turn." These are additional "verb commands" that work to direct the dog around a course. "Turn" is easily taught to puppies and helps make them flexible while teaching a valuable agility command. (See Chapter 7, *Commands You Need*, page 37, for information on these behaviors and how to teach them.)

It has been my experience that dogs learn verbs long before they comprehend nouns. While it is common to hear people shouting "dog walk," "A-frame," "weave," etc., on a course, the dog actually does better if you direct him with the use of "verb commands" such as "here," "out," "turn," "back," and "close." This is because a dog will take the obstacles that he sees in front of him, and it is your responsibility as the handler to keep the dog on the correct path so that he sees only what he should take. Dogs take what they see in front of them, and that is why it is more important to tell them where to go than what obstacle to perform. It takes many years of training before dogs actually learn the names of the obstacles. Even when they do, dogs are not inclined to locate obstacles by name. This is why you can say "table," but the dog will still jump through the tire if that is what is in front of him.

switch sides from right to left. The final step is to run, with your dog making circles and serpentines in all directions, while your dog stays at your side. Eventually, you can use this exercise to run with your dog around agility obstacles and all over an agility course without letting the dog take any obstacles. It is just as important for a dog to learn which obstacles not to take as it is to perform obstacles.

WHEN TO TEACH "STAY"

Although the initial commands that a dog learns in the foundation training period include the stay command, I do not teach it to all beginning dogs. This is because high-energy dogs or dogs less than the age of six months find it very difficult to remain in one place. For these dogs, it would take too much correction and repetition to master a "stay" at a young age and would run the risk of dampening their enthusiasm. Agility is a moving game, and the more enthusiasm, the better.

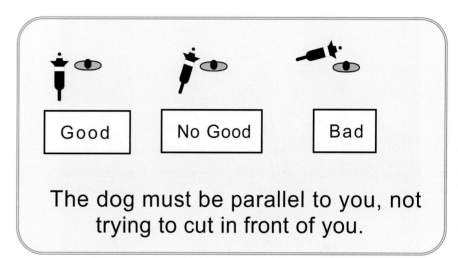

To avoid having to teach "stay" in early training, try to enlist the help of a friend or instructor to hold your dog as you move away when necessary. For some very high-drive dogs, "stay" may not be taught until after the dog knows all the agility obstacles. My basic philosophy is to get the dogs moving first and worry about the "stay" later.

LINING UP WITH THE HANDLER'S BODY

Dogs must be taught to align themselves with your body. They are instructed to move into a parallel sit position on either side, facing the same direction that you are facing, parallel to your body, and not trying to cut in front of you. This is a good exercise to include in foundation training.

The "lining up" skill becomes a valuable tool that is used to instruct the dog that your position and orientation dictate the direction in which he is going to be moving. This next maneuver is referred to as "call to heel" and "call to side" position training. When you refer to the left side of your body, you call it "heel" (borrowed from obedience training), and when you talk about a dog on your right side, you call it "side" (borrowed from freestyle training). The command used to call the dog to either side of your body is "here."

Begin with your dog in a sit at your side (either side is fine). Leave the dog in a stay about six feet away. Turn so that your dog is facing the side of your body.

CALLING DOG TO SIDE/HEEL

1. Dog is called "here" to hand with open palm.

2. Dog lines up his body with handler.

3. Dog sits next to handler.

With a piece of food or toy in the hand closest to the dog, command "here," and guide the dog into a sit at your side, parallel with you. Be sure to work this on both sides so that your dog can be called to either your right side or your left side in order to line up with your body.

The important part of this exercise is for your dog to learn to come to your side rather than in front of you. You want him to learn that he should never pass in front of you, as that is your space. A dog that does not understand and respect this concept will later be likely to cut in front of you or switch sides on course, which could result in a collision.

SET-UP POSITION

A "set-up position" refers to how a dog is positioned at the beginning of a course. In many courses it is an advantage to be able to position a dog exactly on a specific angle to take the first obstacle and see the second obstacle. You can set your dog at the beginning of a course in a sit, down, or stand position. There are advantages to each position depending on the particular dog. If you have a dog with no coat, such as an Italian Greyhound, a Whippet, a Hairless Chinese Crested, or a Min Pin, it might be a good idea to start him from a standing position so that if the ground is cold and wet, you are not asking him to sit in an uncomfortable position before beginning to run agility. If you have a very high-energy dog that has trouble containing his energy at the start of a course, perhaps a down position would help steady him. If you are not dealing with a high-energy dog or a hairless dog, leaving your dog in a sitting position is probably the best because usually a dog can move off of a sit into a canter stride faster than from any other position. The sit also allows your dog the best view of you, his handler, from over the bar or wing of a jump. (Photos page 18).

Regardless of the position in which my dog starts, I prefer a set-up position with the dog between my legs. At the beginning of a course, you may need to wait at the start line for some time as the dog before you is put on leash or the judge makes sure that the ring is ready. The most protected, safest place for your dog to wait is between your legs. (Of course, if your dog is so large that he cannot fit between your legs, you will need to make alternative plans!)

To teach a dog to move between your legs, begin with the dog on a sit stay. Stand in front of the dog, facing the same way he is facing, and separate your legs. Lure the dog with food or a toy between your legs and give a command that will mean "set up" (such as "through"), followed by a sit, down, or stand command. Eventually, the dog will assume the position of choice between your legs any time you give the command.

Another set-up option is to have the dog line up with your body in a heel or side position (see above). This technique is another way for you to position your dog on the desired angle.

CROSSES

Along with following body movement, you can begin to teach crosses and turns to your dog **on the flat,** meaning away from equipment. Any time you run with your dog on one side of you, turn toward the dog, and switch him to the other side of you, you have practiced a "front cross" (see Chapter 8, "Front Crosses," page 61). Eventually, this maneuver will be used to prompt the dog to change sides as the dog runs next to you over a jump or contact obstacle or through a tunnel or weave poles.

You can also teach a "rear cross" (see Chapter 8, "Rear Cross," page 66) on the flat as part of foundation training. Walk with your dog on a leash and buckle collar in a setting where the dog is likely to walk ahead of you. As the dog pulls ahead, change the leash from one hand to another as you walk from side to side behind the dog. See if you notice the dog turn his head to indicate his awareness that you have changed sides behind him. This is how you begin to get a dog to respond to a cross behind that will eventually take place before or after an obstacle while running a course.

These side switches help accustom your dog to seeing you on either side. It is extremely important in agility that the dog be able to work on both of your sides and not develop a preference for or dependence on one side. Be sure to practice everything with the dog on both sides, and switch sides often.

Dog sits behind handler

Handler lures dog through her legs.

Dog is commanded to sit between the legs.

A down position between the legs is taught the same way, but the dog is commanded to down as it comes through the handler's legs. The down position assures a safe, steady start position.

CHAPTER 4

PUPPIES IN AGILITY

It was the acquisition of two puppies the winter of l995 that plunged me into the sport of agility. My intention was to have only one puppy that winter, a black American Cocker Spaniel named Torville. The second puppy, a brindle Afghan Hound, arrived unexpectedly from an animal shelter at around the same time. Her name was Twyla. From the beginning, Twyla was such an exceptional puppy that I was intent on keeping her. So, against my better judgment, I found myself raising two puppies simultaneously. My plan was to train and compete with both dogs in AKC competitive obedience trials as I had done for the twenty years leading up to 1995. Little did I know how things were about to change.

Working to keep two puppies busy and stimulated without putting formal training pressure on them was the goal. Agility seemed like the perfect way to work with the pups in a fun, stimulating way, teach them some basic commands, and keep myself from getting too serious. After all, agility seemed like a game to me and therefore nothing to get very serious about.

It wasn't long before the world of agility—its puzzles, energy, and excitement— captivated me as it has so many others. While both Torville and Twyla ended up earning degrees in obedience, they were my last obedience titles earned to date. My focus is now agility. Twyla became the first Afghan Hound in history to earn a

Master Agility Dog (MX) title and a Master Agility Jumpers Dog (MXJ) title in AKC agility. There was no Master Agility Champion (MACH) at the time. Torville became the only American Cocker Spaniel and the youngest dog at the time to ever compete on the AKC World Agility Team, which she did for three years in a row—1998, 1999, and 2000. Torville was also the third MACH of any breed after the title was created and the first MACH American Cocker Spaniel.

Agility is a perfect place to begin any puppy's training, starting at eight weeks of age. I teach a program that is described to the pet owner as "learning obedience through agility." When basic commands are taught in the midst of agility, they make more sense to dogs and so the dogs learn more easily—often with little or no correction. For example, when a dog is taught to stay out of context, he sees no purpose in sitting still until you return to his side. When you teach a stay and follow it with a release to a jump, tunnel, or something the dog perceives as fun, he is more motivated to repeat the stay that earned him permission to play. If you teach a down on a table, followed by a happy release, the dog is more willing to assume the down position. And finally, dogs that learn to come when they are called in terms of agility are given permission to climb things, run through things, and play in an environment that easily resembles a doggie playground. This is fun!

As you may guess, I do not recommend teaching formal Obedience or Rally before Agility. This can stifle a dog's enthusiasm, because Obedience and Rally begin with the dog working on leash, close to the handler. Dogs learn to pace themselves in an effort to stay next to their owners. Obedience tends to calm dogs, while in agility, the goal is to excite them. In agility, dogs learn in an atmosphere of high energy and free expression, with no fear of failure. In this way, their natural drive and speed are not inhibited. Agility builds a close relationship between handler and dog as the dog learns to respect and obey commands off leash while running at top speed. Most owners call their dog to come when their dog is running away or chasing after something—not when the dog is sitting, waiting to be called! Agility training imitates real-life uses for commands and is therefore a better training choice for the average person who is initially just seeking control over an excitable pet.

TRAINING TOOLS

All puppies (and dogs) should begin agility training on a buckle collar. While

> As an activity, agility builds the confidence and coordination of dogs and puppies. They learn to move over different surfaces, crawl through tight spaces, and walk up and down inclines. Jumping up onto things and over things teaches them to coordinate their four feet. They are encouraged to bend, twist, and be aware of your presence as they negotiate other tasks. Whether the end goal for a dog is conformation, hunting, companion, obedience competitor, therapy dog, or agility competitor, agility training is the best way to get off on the right paw!

it is permissible to run a dog in agility without a collar, I like to have a buckle collar on the dog or puppy to help guide him when necessary. A lot of treats are used in agility training. Treats should be healthy, moist, easy to swallow, not require any chewing, and not be high in salt, sugar, or food coloring. Crunchy is not good, as the treat takes too long to eat. My favorite training treats are cooked chicken and meat (usually leftovers from my dinner) and string cheese.

DISPELLING MYTHS

In recent years, I have heard some very strange warnings about training puppies in agility. Students have informed me that breeders of their new puppies forbid them to jump their dogs until the dogs are a year old. Where is this all coming from? Is it true?

People seem overly concerned about letting young dogs learn weave poles. It seems to me that their bodies are quite flexible at young ages. Have you ever watched them rough-and-tumble with other puppies? Letting puppies bend never seemed to hurt them before the onset of agility. Personally, I do not teach weave poles to puppies because their bodies are going to grow so much that their stride will change and you will need to retrain them (see Chapter 22, *Weave Poles*, page 191), but not because it will hurt them to weave. So, what is going on?

In the book Peak Performance, author M. Christine Zink, DVM, PhD, writes:

It is important for the growth and development of puppies that they have proper exercise. Puppies that are prevented from exercising do not grow as large and are not as physically developed and coordinated as those provided with adequate exercise. An exercise program for a puppy should not, however, include strenuous exercises such as roadwork or full-height jumping. The growth plates, soft areas of the bone from which bone growth occurs, do not close or harden until the

Weave poles lying on their side teach puppies coordination.

Puppies playing and twisting. Photo by M. Nicole Fischer Photography.

puppy is about 14 months of age. (Copyright 1997, pages 125 and 126.)

Dr. Zink is certainly not suggesting that puppies be forbidden to jump at all until fourteen months of age—only that they not be asked to jump full height. She warns against excessive and strenuous jumping and exercise. Puppies frequently jump on their own when playing and running around and do not develop any problems unless they are injured by very rough or extreme activity.

When discussing puppies and when they should be encouraged to jump, there are many factors to consider. For example, in small-breed dogs, growth plates close faster. What about the surface on which the puppy is being asked to jump? Certainly, jumping on a soft, resilient surface produces less impact than landing on a hard surface.

GROWTH PLATES

With so much concern over growth plates and the effect of agility training on young dogs whose growth plates have not yet closed, I decided to consult with my husband, Robert Potter, DVM. Robert graduated from Colorado State University in 1978 and has been practicing small-animal medicine since that time. Here is what he had to say about growth plates and growth-plate injuries in puppies:

In my experience of almost twenty-eight years in small-animal practice, growth-plate injuries in puppies are extremely uncommon. When they do occur, they usually result from a significant fall or traumatic force, such as being hit by a car. There are two kinds of growth-plate injuries that we see. The first are compression-type fractures from falls off of high surfaces, such as decks, or small-breed puppies jumping out of a person's arms and landing on a hard surface. The second are shearing-type forces that cause the bone to fracture or break at the growth plate. Shearing forces are impacts from the side, across the bone, such as being hit by a car or impacting the side of the bone from a fall. In these kinds of injuries, the bone actually breaks into two pieces at the growth plate.

I think it's important that dog-sport enthusiasts have a basic understanding of what a growth plate is. In order for bones to grow, most mammalian bones have growth plates. To simplify matters, let's look at a long bone and imagine it with just two growth plates, one at each end. Each end of the bone is called the "epiphysis." The ends are separated from the shaft, or long part, of the bone by a band of cartilage referred to as the growth plate.

The epiphysis and the shaft are made of hard, mineralized bone. The growth plate is composed of cartilage and hence is the weakest point on the bone. Growth occurs through a complicated mechanism whereby the cartilage immediately adjacent to the epiphysis grows constantly, creating new cartilage. This pushes the epiphysis further away from the shaft. At the same time, from the shaft side of the growth plate, bone-forming cells lay down bone using the cartilage as a framework. Hence, the growth plate stays the same width while moving the epiphysis, leading to growth of the bone.

It has been known for years that some compression (end to end) across the growth plate is good for growth. This has been especially well documented in horses. Bones and cartilage are dynamic, constantly changing tissues that need to be used to stay healthy. If bones are not stressed in a normal physiologic way, they will actually have less mineral content and be weaker. Mammalian growth plates have evolved for millions of years to allow the young individuals of their species to romp, play, and grow to maturity. It is certainly normal for puppies to jump, twist, and run when they are playing with other puppies, and these kinds of stresses are not only tolerated by the growth plates but actually help to strengthen the bones.

Common sense (an endangered species) should be used when introducing puppies to agility or any other sport. Jumping over a reasonable-size jump, especially if the surface is soft and has good traction, is something that any normal puppy can do with no harm. The twisting motion in the weave-pole exercise is no worse than two puppies playing with each other. Where puppies stand a real chance of injuring their growth plates is by falling from a significant height. Extreme care must be exercised with obstacles that are high enough to fall off of, such as the full-height dog walk, A-frame, and seesaw.

EXERCISE AND PHYSICAL DEVELOPMENT

Human growth plates do not close until children are beyond puberty, sometimes as late as seventeen to eighteen years or more of age. It is not uncommon for students to still grow in college. Should we remove all playgrounds and sports from the school systems before the age of eighteen for fear of injury? Ban collegiate sports? Common sense tells us that this is an absurd idea; children need the activity and exercise to develop and grow their bones, muscles, and skeletons. Parents start their chil-

dren in competitive sports as young as four to five years of age, and these children grow up strong and healthy.

The benefits of exercise have been proven repeatedly by scientific research (Heaney et al., 2001), particularly the importance of stressing the young, growing skeleton. Bone mass refers to the mineral content and the density of the bone. More bone mass equals stronger bones. A person's peak bone mass, meaning the strongest a bone can become, is heavily determined in childhood and adolescence by the amount and type of physical exercise and stress the bones undergo (Bass et al., 1998). Weight-bearing or high-impact exercises, such as running, jumping, or gymnastics, have been shown to help develop bone mass more than non-weight-bearing exercise, such as swimming or biking (Heaney et al., 2001; Khan et al., 1998; Bass et al., 1998). This means that these activities, especially when performed by a young, growing body, are very beneficial and influential in developing ultimate bone strength.

The following passage comes from a study published in the *Journal of Bone and Mineral Research* that focused on children's physical activity and its effects on physical health:

Researchers at Oregon State University investigated the effect of high-intensity jumping on hip and spine bone mass in children. Eighty-nine prepubescent children between the ages of 5.9 and 9.8 years were assigned to a jumping group or a control group. Three times a week for seven months, the jumping group performed 100 two-footed drop landings off a 61-centimeter box, while the control group engaged in stretching exercises. After seven months, jumpers had significantly greater increases in bone mineral content at the lumbar spine and femoral neck than controls. The authors concluded that this simple jumping program is a safe and effective method for improving bone mass in prepubescent children and could be easily incorporated into physical education classes (Fuchs, Bauer, and Snow, 2001, as cited in Heaney et al., 2001).

Jumping helped the bones of these children become denser and thus stronger. It is therefore not the act of jumping that is harmful. Rather, the degree and intensity of the jumping have something to do with it, too. According to the findings of Heaney and colleagues, excessive exercise can cause injury to growth plates (2001). Furthermore, very strenuous weight-bearing, such as serious weight lifting, is also not desirable, as the excessive impact can stunt actual bone growth. Heaney and colleagues summarized that moderate to intense exercise, such as walking, running, and dancing for twenty to thirty minutes several times a week, produced positive skeletal benefits (2001). However, the exact exercise-program formula to optimize bone mass is still unknown.

While these studies apply to humans and not to dogs in particular, the information and findings are still relevant and worth considering when thinking about exercise and activities for puppies. Much information is first gleaned through studies of animals (like rats) before tests and ideas are shifted to human study. As stated earlier, the bone's ability to adapt to stress is much greater before maturity. In the wild, animals must have optimal bone strength (bones as strong as they will be) by the time they stop growing (Parfitt, 1994). This occurs naturally as young animals play, tumble, jump, run, and fight with each other.

Trainers need to use a lot of common sense when training puppies in agility. Too much of anything is never a good idea, but not exposing a young puppy to situations that he will face in adulthood is equally damaging. Puppies should never be drilled for long periods of time over jumps on hard surfaces, but jumping young dogs under good conditions does prepare them for future events.

WHAT CAN A PUPPY DO?

Most beginning training in agility on a young puppy falls into the category of foundation training. Foundation training does not involve obstacles of any kind but rather focuses on teaching a dog to pay attention and move with the handler's body. The puppy learns not to change sides until instructed to do so and what it means to stay, come, sit, down, and move out away from the handler. Foundation training also includes teaching a puppy to set up (the starting position for running a course) in the ring, follow hands, and turn away from the handler on command. All of foundation training can be started with puppies that are eight weeks of age or older. Begin by teaching a puppy to take food from your hand and then to follow the hand to get the food.

Puppies can be introduced to agility equipment. They can be started on the beginning steps of weave-pole training by learning to go through the open poles (Chapter 22, *Weave Poles*, page 191). Puppies can also learn the "four ways" of performing an obstacle over a low jump or tire, or on a low table. The table is also a good place to practice sits and downs. (See Chapter 6, *The Four Ways*, page 31, and Chapter 23, *The Pause Table*, page 217.) Introducing targets and touch boards is also a very appropriate exercise for puppies to learn. (See Chapter 17, *The Touch Method*, page 143.)

While it is perfectly safe and cute to teach a young puppy to run through an open tunnel, do not do it! Dogs and people tend to remember best what they learn first. If you teach tunnels to a puppy, he is inclined to choose them over other obstacles, causing what is referred to in the sport as "tunnel sucking." This is when a dog takes any tunnel he sees even if he has not been directed to do so. Tunnels are very easy to teach, so don't be in a big rush to do it. Work on teaching a new puppy how to walk on boards, deal with moving boards, and push through a closed chute, and allow him to learn all of the foundation skills that do not involve equipment.

WHEN TO PROGRESS

Personally, I like to let a puppy tell me when he is ready to progress in the training process. When I see confidence and a desire to run and perform, then I increase the difficulty of the task, either by raising the height of the jumps or making the sequences more difficult. I am much more protective of a young dog performing a full-height A-frame or dog walk than I am about allowing a young dog to jump. As mentioned earlier, a full-height A-frame puts a tremendous amount of stress on the shoulders and hips of any dog. A young dog that might fall off of a full-height dog walk runs the risk of a serious injury. I strongly recommend training puppies on very low dog walks and see-

saws. Teach the A-frame as the last exercise to a dog that has developed muscles in the rear and demonstrates a good degree of coordination.

SOCIALIZATION

In addition to teaching puppies about agility equipment and skills, puppies must be exposed to many different environments as a way of preparing them to feel comfortable in a trial atmosphere. All of my puppies learn to ride crated in my van and in the motor home. They also learn to respect the limitations of an exercise pen and are exposed to the sounds of a generator, a loudspeaker, and barking dogs. It is important for young dogs to learn to eat well while traveling and relieve themselves on leash in places away from home. Nothing is more frustrating than having a dog that works well at home but stresses from travel and new places.

PICKING A PUPPY

If there really was a way to tell what a puppy would grow into, we would all have chosen the perfect dogs. Breeders would always know which puppy to keep, and foundations that train dogs to assist the handicapped would not have such a high failure rate when choosing puppies to train. The fact is, picking puppies often involves a little knowledge and a lot of luck.

The best guideline for choosing a puppy, in my experience, is looking at the parents. If the sire and dam possess qualities that you like, chances are good that a portion of the puppies might inherit some of these desirable traits. Search for parents that appear enthusiastic about training and that have good structure and drive. When choosing from a litter, I usually focus on the smallest puppies or on the puppies with the least amount of bone. In general, lighter-weight dogs are more flexible and faster. If you like one parent more than the other, choose a puppy that looks like the favored parent. There seems to be a connection between physical and mental qualities—genetics perhaps?

Some of my best agility dogs were not puppies when I got them. Young adult dogs are often perfect candidates for agility prospects. Dogs with high drive that like to work usually do not make good pets for the average household. These dogs often find themselves in shelters or are given up because they have "too much energy," but they are perfect for homes where they are trained and given a job. Dogs can bond to their owners and be trained at any age. In fact, dogs that have been rescued from bad situations are often more giving and willing to please than are "perfect puppies."

References

Bass, S., Pearce, G., Bradney, M., Hendrich, E., Delmas, P.D., Harding, A., and Seeman, E. (1998). "Exercise Before Puberty May Confer Residual Benefits in Bone Density in Adulthood: Studies in Active Prepubertal and Retired Female Gymnasts." *Journal of Bone and Mineral Research* 13: 500–507.

Fuchs, R.K., Bauer, J. J., and Snow, C. M. (2001). "Jumping Improves Hip and Lumbar Spine Bone Mass in Prepubescent Children: A Randomized Controlled Trial.". *Journal of Bone and Mineral Research* 16: 148–156.

Heaney, R. P., Abrams, S., Dawson-Hughes, B., Looker, A., Looker, A., Marcus, R., Matkovic, V., and Weaver, C. (2001). "Peak Bone Mass." *Osteoporosis International* 11: 985–1009.

Khan, K.M., Bennell, K.L., Hopper, J.L., Flicker, L., Nowson, C.A., Sherwin, A.J., Crichton, K.J., Harcourt, P.R., and Wark, J.D. (1998). "Self-reported Ballet Classes Undertaken at Age 10-12 Years and Hip Bone Mineral Density in Later Life." *Osteoporosis International* 8: 165–173.

Parfitt, A. M. (1994). "The Two Faces of Growth: Benefits and Risks to Bone Integrity." *Osteoporosis International* 4: 382–398.

CHAPTER 5

THE STRATEGY OF HANDLING

Agility is a thrilling game of speed, dexterity, and strategy. For dogs, the challenges are running as fast as they can, turning sharply, jumping, weaving, ducking through tunnels, and balancing on boards, while at the same time always knowing the location of their handler. For the handler, agility demands physical stamina, coordination, timing, an understanding of dog training, and, most of all, mental planning.

Agility is a lot like the game of chess. When you start to learn chess, you must first learn how the chess pieces move. For example, the bishop moves only on a diagonal line, but as far as he wants to go across the board, while the king can move in any direction, one square at a time. In agility, you begin by teaching your dog how to properly execute the agility obstacles—but that's the easy part! In chess, you can understand how the pieces move but never be able to checkmate someone and win a game. In agility, you can have a dog that performs all of the equipment, but unless you can navigate him through the course, your team will not be successful. You must learn the moves and understand how to use them. It is the strategy of the chess game and the strategy of directing a dog around an agility course that makes both games intriguing.

Once I discovered the mental and strategic side of agility, I was hooked on the sport. I still find myself thinking about agility while driving, taking a shower, and

Agility requires both speed and dexterity. Photo by M. Nicole Fischer Photography.

lying in bed. I often run courses in my mind while looking at a course map on paper. Trying to discover alternate ways to negotiate the obstacles to save time and not risk sending the dog off course is the challenge. Handlers are always trying to find ways to get critical information to a fast-running dog in time for the dog to react appropriately.

MENTAL PLANNING

Once a dog knows how to perform all of the agility obstacles from all different angles and with you in all different positions (i.e., behind him, in front of him, on his left, and on his right), it is time to learn the art of handling. Handling is how you direct the dog where to go on the course through the use of your hands, arms, shoulders, body, movement, and voice. You need to focus on the path of the course as if it was a road on which you were driving. The fact that there are obstacles on the path is not as important as visualizing the direction a course takes. Generally, a dog will take what is in front of him, and it is your responsibility to make sure that the dog is on the path that will lead him to the approach of the correct obstacle.

To plan your strategy, you will need to consider the following:

- How fast can your dog turn on the surface on which he is running, and how do the existing weather conditions affect your dog's performance?

- Where will your dog land off of each jump?

- What will your dog see coming out of every tunnel, landing off of every jump, and coming off of the contact equipment (i.e., the course from the dog's point of view)?

- How fast can you run on the surface under the existing weather conditions?

- Which obstacle (if any) does your dog prefer?

- Are there any additional obstacle challenges, such as posts in the ring, unusable areas, or ring barriers? Is there any piece of equipment with which your dog is unfamiliar (e.g., a chute that looks like a dog house)?

- What is your dog's space (i.e., how close can you move toward your dog before he wants to move away from you)?

The objective in agility is to move the dog around the course, executing all the equipment correctly and in the specified order in the shortest amount of time possible. To plan your strategy, you will need to consider the following:

HANDLING STRATEGIES

The information gathered by answering these questions will help you determine the best handling strategy for the specific course. Before I go into the details of handling, techniques, and maneuvers, following is a brief overview of the strategies handlers may consider.

LEADING OUT

It is important to decide at which angle to position your dog at the start of the course and whether to run with the dog or to perform a lead out. A lead out is when the dog is told to stay, at which point you position yourself one, two, or even three jumps ahead. This approach gives you a head start. If the course has a very fast opening, a lead out may be useful and, in fact, necessary (see Chapter 11, *The Start of the Course,* page 89).

CROSSES AND SIDE SWITCHES

Deciding on which side of the dog you want to be is very important. You must plan how and where a cross will occur and what kind of cross it will be. Certain maneuvers are faster for the handler but riskier for the dog.

The dog's point of view: When you and your dog are running the same course, what you see is not necessarily the same. Consider your dog's point of view and what he can and cannot see. Some obstacles may look obvious to you, but from the dog's point of view, they are concealed. Furthermore, there are times on the course when the dog is completely blind, such as when he is in a tunnel or chute. You will need to know what the dog sees as he emerges from these obstacles to determine where you need to stand to direct him to the next obstacle in sequence. You can determine this by crouching down to the dog's eye level at the exit of tunnels and looking at the course from the dog's perspective.

TURNS

Moving a dog around a course involves getting the dog to turn. There are different ways to turn a dog. Some techniques are effective when the dog is far away. For others, you must be right near the dog for him to understand your body position and hand motion. You will eventually learn how to instruct your dog to make a sharp turn as well as a gentle, arcing turn.

When the surface is slick, you may opt to turn your dog more gradually, forfeiting speed for the sake of bringing the dog accurately and in a good, balanced position to the next jump in an attempt to avoid his knocking a bar. Whatever techniques you use, know how responsive your dog is. Some dogs are like sensitive race cars, while others seem to require the effort needed to turn a truck (see Chapter 8, *Ways of Turning a Dog,* page 57).

Dog performs the Seesaw while looking ahead for instructions from his handler.

Agility strategy combines the foresight of chess with the physics of billiards and then requires the reflexes, balance, and timing of figure skating. On all levels of expertise, the sport offers mental and physical challenges to both dogs and people. Good handlers usually start thinking and strategizing from the time a course is built or as soon as they have a copy of the course diagram. This can easily mean hours of mental concentration. When you consider that the average running time with the dog on course is well under sixty seconds, there is no doubt that agility is truly a mental sport!

FLOW OF THE COURSE

Certain parts of courses are open and flowing, giving the dogs the opportunity to pick up tremendous speed. Usually these open sections lead right into tight, controlling sequences with many traps or options. Analyze the flow of the course and give the dog instructions in time to prepare him to speed up or slow down.

CRITICAL POINTS

Critical points are places on the course where you must get to in time to direct your dog and prevent him from going off course. These points may be obstacle discriminations, tricky sequences, or sharp angles. Part of your strategy as a handler is deciding how to get to the critical point even if it means handling a previous sequence in a less efficient or riskier way. You may need to handle a part of the course from a greater distance, tapping into the send skills, in order reach a critical point later on the course.

ANTICIPATING

When you plan a strategy, you have an idea of where and how fast your dog will be moving. You can also try to anticipate where mistakes might occur. For example, you plan to turn your dog left with a rear cross. If the dog does not read the cross correctly, he will turn to the right. What are the repercussions of his turning right? What should be done to save the sequence if the dog mistakenly turns to the right? Part of strategizing includes analyzing all possible options so that you can anticipate and plan for potential mishaps.

CHAPTER **6**

THE FOUR WAYS

Each agility obstacle can be performed by a dog in four different ways:

- call-to
- send
- run-by right
- run-by left

Until you know the course, you cannot predict whether you will be ahead, behind, on the left, or on the right of the dog when approaching an obstacle. It is therefore important that your dog learn how to perform every obstacle in all four ways. A dog has not truly learned a particular obstacle until he can complete it in all four ways.

THE CALL-TO

In the call-to format, the dog performs an obstacle while moving toward you, his handler. The dog starts on the opposite side of the obstacle from you and, on a

1. Start of overhanded arm motion toward jump.

2. Continuation of overhanded arm motion toward jump.

3. Motioning to jump.

command and signal, takes the obstacle in the direction toward you. The call-to is frequently used when you start to teach obstacles such as jumps, weave poles, the table, and the seesaw because your position helps motivate the dog to move forward and toward the obstacle. Most dogs feel more secure when moving toward their handler.

THE CALL-TO SIGNAL

The hand signal used to indicate a call-to is an overhanded arm motion toward the obstacle (similar to an overhand throw), with the palm of your hand facing your dog. The hand motion is complete when your hand points to the obstacle. Either hand can be used to cue a call-to. The hand you choose will depend on which way you are directing the dog to go after the obstacle. If you want to indicate the next obstacle with your right hand, use the same right hand to cue the call-to.

I have chosen this specific hand signal for a good reason. When you are in front of your dog—for example, in a lead-out position—the dog is in a rush to get to you; he feels as if he has already been left behind. Dogs that rush jumps tend to flatten out, and bars come down. The overhanded signal motion works to back the dog slightly off the jump, reminding him to rock back on his hindquarters before leaving the ground, to not rush, and to jump roundly, not flatly. (See Chapter 12, *Jumping*, page 99, for a more indepth explanation.)

TEACHING THE CALL-TO

Begin with your dog sitting on one side of a very low jump, while you are on the other side of the jump. Hold a motivator (food or toy) in the hand that will give the signal. Give a verbal release command (for example, "okay") followed by a jump command (for example, " bar") as you give the overhanded hand signal pointing toward the jump. The verbal command, "okay, bar," along with the moving hand and motivator, should encourage the dog to go over the jump. If the dog does not get up, try lowering the jump, or move the dog or your hand closer to the jump. Do not lean forward. Stand up straight, and let the signal indicate the obstacle. If the dog is still inclined to go around the obstacle, move so close that your hand extends over the bar.

Special Cases

When doing a call-to through weave poles in the teaching phases, the call-to signal is modified. The arm is kept a "secret," and the hand is oriented so that the thumb is pointing toward the sky (the palm is not facing the dog). To keep the hand a "secret," slide your hand up close to your body until it gets above your shoulder; then extend your arm in the overhanded motion toward the poles. (Refer to Chapter 22, *Weave Poles*, page 191, for more information.)

THE SEND

If a dog can perform an obstacle moving toward you, he can and should be able to do it moving away from you. In the send, the dog leaves your side and executes the obstacle while you stay back at the beginning of the obstacle.

THE SEND SIGNAL

Sending a dog to an obstacle with a send signal tells the dog to drive ahead of you to the indicated obstacle. The cue for a send is an underhanded "bowling" hand motion coupled with a step forward in the direction of the desired obstacle. Always signal with your hand that is closest to the dog. The bowling motion sends the message of "forward" and simulates your tossing something forward, which is exactly how the send is initially taught.

The send signal gives the dog more information than simply which obstacle he is doing next. The implication of the send signal for a dog jumping a hurdle is that, since you are not moving with him, he should plan to jump short and turn immediately upon landing. To ensure a tight turn back, give a send signal pointing to the base of the jump. If you want the dog to jump and land far beyond the hurdle, continue the bowling motion higher in the air, and remain in that position until the dog has committed to the next obstacle. If you want your dog to continue moving forward, as opposed to wrapping back, you need to add a verbal command. I use the command "run" to mean, "Continue moving in a straight line and take the next obstacle in front of you while I am more than one obstacle away from you." (For information on how to teach the run command, see Chapter 7, *Commands You Need*, page 37.)

TEACHING THE SEND

The send is most easily taught over a jump or to a pause table. Placing a target or throwing a motivator to the other side of the jump or up onto the table focuses the dog's attention beyond the obstacle and encourages him to leave you while you remain immobile. The target is a reward and should be an object that the dog desires, such as a toy or a **food tube.** (See photo food tube, Chapter 10, page 82.) Make sure that your dog sees the motivator, and then, using a release command and a send signal, send the dog to the motivator. Once the dog has gone over the jump, hopped up onto the table, and reached his motivator, go to your dog, remove the food from the tube, and offer the reward to the dog. Do not call the dog back to you to reward him. Dogs are very aware of location. A dog has no reason to move away from you if the reward is always on you.

If the dog tries to duck around the obstacle or is reluctant to leave your side, move closer to the obstacle.

Send signal over jump.

THE RUN-BY

The final way a dog can perform an obstacle is while running next to you. The dog can either be on your left side (run-by left) or on your right side (run-by right). It is critical that the dog be comfortable working on both sides.

THE RUN-BY SIGNALS

The hand signal for the run-by is a lateral extension (like a push) of the arm directed to the line of approach of the obstacle. Your palm is facing the dog, and your fingertips should be pointed upward. Again, use the arm closest to the dog. The extension of the arm tells the dog not to turn in to you, but to continue moving forward toward the obstacle.

The line of approach refers to the path the dog must be on in order to take a particular obstacle. In order to give proper information, the signal should point to that path so that the dog can process his direction early enough to reach the obstacle.

The implication of the run-by signal for the dog is that he should jump big, while expecting to go on straight to the next obstacle. When doing a run-by past a series of jumps, give a small push-out motion for each jump, and don't look like you have become a fixed-wing airplane. (See the picture of the run-by signal.)

Handlers with experienced dogs often morph the palm run-by signal from an open palm into a pointed finger. The finger point is not as obvious and is usually more difficult for the novice dog to interpret.

The distance between you and your dog will vary depending on the sequence. Jumps with wings, tunnels under contacts, and other handler restrictions will force you further away from your dog. When you are running parallel with your dog, but at a distance, it is very important that the motivator be thrown in front of the dog to discourage him from turning toward you in anticipation of being rewarded.

TEACHING THE RUN-BY

Begin with your dog sitting in front of a low, wingless jump. Place a motivator beyond the jump. Leave the dog on a stay, and move to one side of the dog and slightly ahead of him. Give the run-by signal and verbal command, "okay, bar." If the dog allows you to run next to him and takes the jump, he will get to the reward. If you are successful, try adding a second jump with the motivator beyond the second jump. When your dog can successfully run parallel to you over two jumps and you can be on either side, try adding wings to the jumps. By adding wings, you will encourage your dog to move parallel to you but farther away.

What If?

- **What if every time you go to the side of the jump, your dog follows you around the jump?**

You can try placing the dog closer to the jump so that it would be easier for him to go over it than come around it. If this does not work, put up a baby-gate barrier next to the dog to guide him along the correct path to get to the jump.

Throughout this book, I will continuously refer back to the four ways. As you teach each obstacle, you should

1. Beginning of the run-by signal.

2. Hand is pushed toward the dog's path. Dog is looking at the motivator, not at the handler.

progressively teach each of its stages in the four ways; in most cases, start with a call-to and move on to the send, then finally teach both run-bys.

Remember . . . Strive to teach the dog to perform each obstacle independently. A dog that relies on your position or body motions to perform an obstacle does not truly understand that obstacle. Independent obstacle performance is necessary, as you may not always be able to get to a specific spot on course, and your dog must still be able to perform the obstacle without your assistance. Furthermore, speed comes with confidence, and confidence comes with understanding and practice. The dog with independent obstacle performance can anticipate his job, and thus his speed will not be compromised. By teaching a dog how to perform every obstacle in all four ways, the dog will have the knowledge and skill to complete each obstacle in any situation he encounters on the course.

Independent obstacle performance. The dog does not care where the handler is; he does his job.

COMMANDS YOU NEED

Dogs are not verbal creatures by nature. They have no verbal language to communicate with each other. While it is possible for a dog to learn verbal commands, the faster a dog is running, the harder it is for him to process verbal information. In agility, where dogs are moving at top speeds, dogs read body language before they interpret verbal commands. It is not uncommon for a handler to point to a tunnel, say "tire," and the dog will still take the tunnel. Body language overrides voice. Verbal commands become more important when you are unable to keep up and thereby cannot provide the necessary physical information. In agility, a combination of verbal and physical cues are used to direct the dog around the course. In some ways, you might think of it as "signing for the deaf," as everything is verbalized and choreographed.

How you say a command can be as important as what you say. Because dogs never really learn to spell, and rely only on what they hear, commands should sound distinctly different from each other. For example, giving the tunnel command in a low tone and the A-frame command in a higher tone helps the dog differentiate between the obstacles. Always make every effort to give clear, short, and consistent commands to avoid confusion.

In an effort to keep things simple, use as few commands as possible while still providing all necessary information. Experience has proven that "less is more," and what follows are the commands I believe to be essential. These concepts need commands, but you do not need to use the same words that I do.

Dogs are situational and learn in the context in which you teach, so be sure to teach each command with the dog on both your right and left sides. If you do an exercise teaching the dog to turn right, away from you, the next time, do it teaching the dog to turn left, away from you. When you teach a sit-stay with the dog on your left side, immediately follow it with a sit-stay on your right side.

This dog's hocks are not on the table, so it is not considered a "sit."

SIT

A sit can be used at the start line and is necessary on the table in some agility venues. A sit is also used to teach the dog to "rock back" for the "whoa" command (see page 52).

Some very driven dogs are reluctant to rest their hocks on the table and instead crouch or hold their head so low that their sit position becomes questionable. Judges have different requirements of what constitutes a sit. Personally, I like one judge's opinion that "a sit is more of a sit than a down!"

TEACHING THE SIT COMMAND

The key to getting a dog to sit is for him to raise his head up. Think of the dog as a seesaw: when the head comes up, the rear goes down. Use a toy or food in either hand to motivate your dog to raise his head. Once he assumes the sitting position, praise and reward him. Make a habit of stepping toward your dog when giving the sit command in preparation for pause-table training.

DOWN

A down position is generally considered a position of rest, with the dog's elbows and hocks in contact with the ground. A down is used on the pause table, can be used on the start line, and is sometimes used to help teach contacts.

TEACHING THE DOWN COMMAND

A down in agility should be taught from a standing position, never from a sit. Ideally, the dog will collapse from a stand into a drop on his haunches, ready to spring forward. The key to getting a dog to lie down is to get him to lower his head. Encourage the dog to lower his head to the ground and collapse backward by luring him with a toy or food placed between his front legs. Rest a hand on the dog's shoulder to prevent him from getting up. The dog should drop his front end first. Make a habit of stepping away from the dog when you give the down command in preparation for pause-table training.

Be sure that your dog can assume the sit and down positions with a verbal command only before you proceed to agility equipment. If you are still luring the dog into position with food and/or bending over, the command has not been taught!

An easy way to get a dog to lie down without bending over is a technique called a "foot drop." Put your dog on a six-foot leash and buckle collar. Stand with your dog at your side. Make a loop in the leash and command "down." If the dog does not respond correctly, gently place the foot closest to the dog on the snap of the leash, and pull up on the leash as you slowly step down on the snap to the ground. This pulls the dog's head to the ground. His rear may stay in the air for a moment, but if you wait, the uncomfortable position and power of time will convince him that it is in his best interest to lower his rear.

STAY

Handler steps into the "leash stirrup." This technique is used after the dog will perform a down. The handler now wants to be able to get the dog to lie down without needing to bend over.

"Stay" means: "Do not move out of position until released." It is used at the start line and sometimes on a lead-out from the pause table.

I prefer to use the term "stay" as opposed to "wait" to avoid confusion with dogs that are herding and learn the command "way-to-me."

TEACHING THE STAY COMMAND

The key to a reliable stay is consistency. Give the command only once and then gently enforce it. The dog must learn that a stay starts with the word "stay" and ends with a verbal release command, "okay," discussed below.

To teach the stay, begin with the dog on a leash and buckle collar. With the dog sitting at your side, bring the palm of your hand that is closest to the dog in front of his eyes and command "stay." Immediately step directly in front of the dog and face him. After a few seconds, return to the dog's side and give a release command to end the stay. If the dog gets up before he is released, reposition him by gently pulling up with the collar and leash; do not repeat the command. The dog must make the mistake of getting up before he can understand what "stay" truly means. Praise your dog immediately once he is back in position. Gradually increase your distance away from the dog and add a distraction to teach the dog under what conditions he must stay. Remember—dogs learn by trial and error. If the dog breaks the stay, always reposition him, praise him, and only then, release him. The reason why you do not reposition the dog with your hands is because he may confuse the physical contact with petting and reward. "Stay" can be taught in different positions (stand or down) but is easiest to correct when the dog is in a sitting position.

You will need to teach stay at a start line and stay on a pause table in specific situations. Do not assume that, because your dog understands a stay command in one set of circumstances, he will generalize it to all situations. Dogs are very situational, which means that they learn commands in the context in which you teach them. For example, if you teach a dog to do a sit-stay indoors, do not assume that he knows that he must do it outside as well. (For more information on stays at the start line, refer to Chapter 11, *The Start of the Course*, page 89. For more information on stays on the table, see Chapter 23, *The Pause Table*, page 217.)

For more in-depth information on teaching obedience, refer to my book *Beyond Basic Dog Training*, Third Edition, Howell Book House.

OKAY

"Okay" is a release command. That is to say, whatever the dog is doing at the time you say "okay," he is no longer required to be on command. He is "off duty." As soon as the dog receives an additional command, he is back on duty. For example, say that a dog is on a sit-stay and you lead out to the first jump. Your starting command is "okay" (releasing the dog off the sit-stay), "bar" (telling the dog to take the first jump). In this instance, the dog was only released for a split second. Sometimes a release lasts much longer, such as when you are finished training.

It is essential that, as you say "okay," your body does not move in any way. If there is movement associated with the "okay" release command, the dog does not understand whether he is responding to a verbal command or a motion. Since dogs comprehend motion more easily, they frequently focus on your movement and ignore the verbal "okay" command. This leads to a lot of confusion. You think that you are teaching a verbal release command, when, in fact, the dog has learned to move when you move.

"Okay" is used to release the dog off of stays at the start line and pause table and in some instances, off of a stopped contact. It is also used to release the dog off of the "close" command (see page 43).

TEACHING THE OKAY COMMAND

Remember to teach your dog to release on the word "okay" and not on your motion. To see if your dog understands that he is being released on the verbal command and not on your movement, give the command "okay" and wait for the dog to move first. After the dog moves, reward him with a treat or a toy. To avoid confusion later in training, such as when you need to move away from the dog (start line or table), the dog must understand that he is waiting for a verbal release command and not looking for a gesture.

Okay, if you are the type of person, okay, who uses the word "okay" every few words, okay, then I suggest you choose a different release word, okay? Here are some suggestions: "free," "freedom," "all done," "break," or "finish."

HERE

"Here" means: "Move toward me, line up with my body in the direction I am facing, and look for the next obstacle." If the dog is on your left side when you command "here," he should remain on your left side as he comes toward you. The same is true for the right side. "Here" is frequently used on the course to maneuver the dog onto the correct path.

TEACHING THE HERE COMMAND

To begin, put a piece of food between your fingers. Place your hand at your side, thumb against your thigh, pre-senting the palm of your hand with food to the dog's nose. Command "here" and lure the dog in the direction you are going. Make circles (in both directions), serpentines, and turns. Next, change direction by rotating your body toward the dog, presenting the other hand (thumb to thigh, palm toward the dog) with the food between your fingers. Command "here" as you make the change. Always present a clear direction when commanding "here." (See Chapter 3, *Building a Solid Foundation*, page 11.)

Teaching "here," thumb to thigh, with the dog following the food.

1. The dog follows the food in the palm of the handler's hand.

2. The handler turns toward the dog to change direction.

3. The dog follows the other hand in a new direction.

I prefer to use the command "here" as opposed to "come," for the latter can be confused with the "come-by" command in herding. Also, "come" is frequently used in obedience for the recall in which the dog is expected to end up sitting in front of the handler.

DOG'S NAME

Using a dog's name gets his attention. In agility, the dog's name is used to mean: "Turn your head toward me and pay attention, because it's not what you think it is." It is imperative that, since the dog's name is reserved for specific instructions, you do not use his name routinely before giving other commands. For example, the command phrase, "okay, Fido, jump," should never be used. "Okay, jump" is succinct, clear, and all that is needed.

"Dog's Name" is used on the course to create a sharp turn or when executing a reverse-flow pivot (see page 71). It is also used to warn the dog that things are not as they may seem and that careful attention is required. If your dog has a name with three or more syllables, you may want to shorten it for use on the course.

TEACHING THE DOG'S NAME COMMAND

Your dog will naturally look at you when he hears his name. If your dog does not look at you when you call his name, make a game out of calling his name. When he makes eye contact, throw a reward to him.

CLOSE

"Close" means: "Move toward my side and do not look at any obstacle until I release you." It is used to control a dog's path when he must run past obstacles and not take them. The command "close" is very useful in **Snooker classes,** and **threading-the-needle** sequences (see Figure 7-1), and when space is tight and off-courses are tempting.

It is necessary to release the dog from the close command with an "okay" before giving the command for the next obstacle. Otherwise, "close" will soon mean nothing more than "here."

TEACHING THE CLOSE COMMAND

Start by placing food in a closed fist at your side. Lure the dog past obstacles (tunnel openings, jumps, etc.) and command "close" each time you get to an obstacle. Reward after he passes a few obstacles. If the dog takes an obstacle, stop dead in your tracks and do nothing until the dog appears confused. Then begin again. When your dog is convinced that he should not take obstacles when you say "close," you are ready for the next step.

Circle in front of a jump two or three times, commanding "close" every time he passes by the

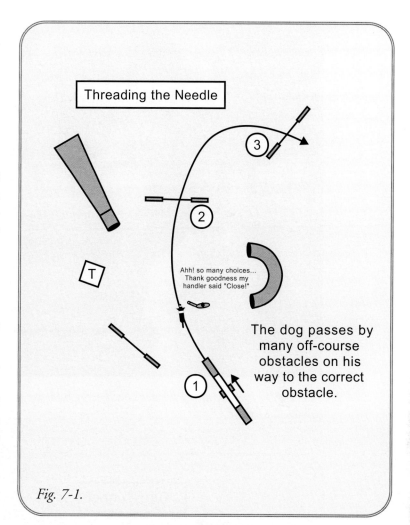

Threading the Needle

Ahh! so many choices...
Thank goodness my
handler said "Close!"

The dog passes by many off-course obstacles on his way to the correct obstacle.

Fig. 7-1.

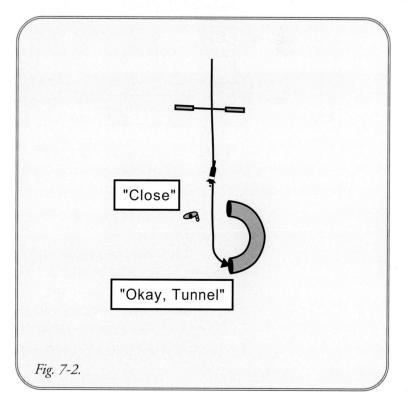

"Close"

"Okay, Tunnel"

Fig. 7-2.

Teaching the turn by luring the dog's head away from the handler with food.

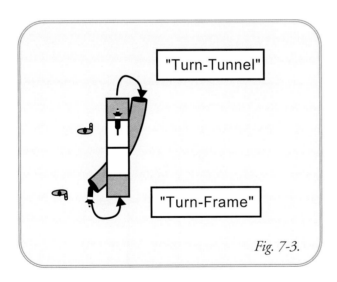

"Turn-Tunnel"

"Turn-Frame"

Fig. 7-3.

jump. On the fourth turn, tell the dog to take the jump with an "okay, bar" command. Alternate between not letting the dog take equipment and releasing him to that same equipment until the dog demonstrates an understanding of the difference.

TURN

Turn means: "Turn 180 degrees away from me and look for the next obstacle." If the dog is on your right side, "turn" would get him to turn to his right. If the dog is on your left side, he would turn to his left.

"Turn" is used to turn a dog from a contact obstacle into a tunnel directly next to it, but it can be used for any tight 180-degree turn away from you. A trained dog becomes so proficient at this that you can actually give a "turn-tunnel" command when he is halfway across a contact obstacle and he will look to duck into the tunnel at the end of the contact. (See Chapter 9, the section "Teaching Turn-Tunnel," page 77.)

TEACHING THE TURN COMMAND

Start with the dog at your side and a piece of food in the hand closest to your dog. Command "turn," then, with a downward motion, lure the dog's head away from you until he completely turns his body around and is facing the opposite direction. Then reward him. Be sure to alternate the directions of your turn. "Turn" should always be cued with the arm and hand closest to the dog.

When the dog can do turn on the flat, try putting an obstacle so that, once he turns, he is set up to take it. Now your commands are "turn," turning the dog 180 degrees away from you, and then "tunnel," directing the dog to the next obstacle.

Remember—the turn command implies that the dog should make a sharp and complete 180-degree reversal of direction before taking an obstacle. It is not used when you are trying to cause a gentle change of direction on the course.

BACK

"Back" is a command that tells the dog to change leads and arc away from you. When a dog is running (cantering or galloping) on an arc to the right, he is on his "right lead." His front right leg, called the lead leg, is extended out further than the front left leg. In contrast, when the dog is running on an arc to the left, he is on his "left lead" and his lead leg is the front left leg. (See Chapter 12, the section "Leads," page 101, and Chapter 8, *Ways of Turning a Dog*, page 58, for a photo of a dog on his right lead.)

Fact: A dog that lands over a jump on his right lead will turn to the right. A dog that lands on his left lead will turn to the left. In order for a dog to change directions, he must change leads. Because a dog naturally arcs toward you, his handler, he is often on the lead closest to you. If you want the dog to arc away from you (i.e., change direction), you must instruct the dog to change leads. If you are on your dog's right side, he will have difficulty turning left if he does not change leads.

A dog naturally changes leads before turning, but if he does not know that a turn is coming, then you must cue the turn with a "change leads" command (i.e., "back"). Ideally, you instruct your dog to change leads both verbally and with body language. The command "back" is used to prepare the dog for a turn that will occur after a rear cross (see page 66). While the back command is often coupled with a rear cross, use the back command whenever your dog must make an arc away from you. In the event that you are too far away from your dog for body language to be clearly interpreted, the verbal command is still effective.

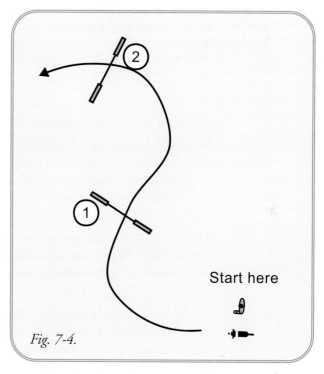

Fig. 7-4.

Start here

TEACHING THE BACK COMMAND

Before teaching the back command, be sure you have taught the turn command. This will ensure that your dog can bend equally in both directions. It is not uncommon for a dog to favor turning in one direction over the other. This is because, like people, most dogs are right-handed (pawed), some are left-handed, and a few are ambidextrous. When a dog is very right-handed, he

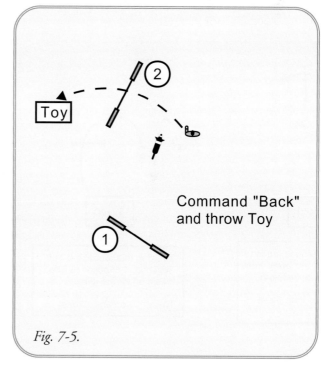

Toy

Command "Back"
and throw Toy

Fig. 7-5.

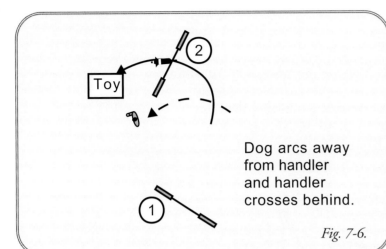

Toy

Dog arcs away
from handler
and handler
crosses behind.

Fig. 7-6.

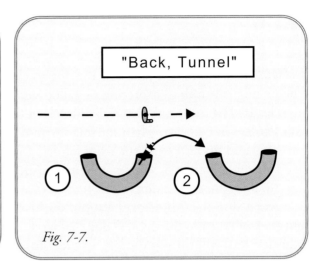

"Back, Tunnel"

Fig. 7-7.

may resist or have difficulty turning onto the left lead. Therefore, it is important that the dog be comfortable running and jumping in a circle in both directions before you teach him the back command.

To teach the back command, set up the jump sequence in Figure 7-4 using low jumps. Run with the dog on your left side over the first jump while holding a toy or food tube in your left hand (the hand closest to the dog). As the dog lands off of the first jump, throw the toy in an arc over the second jump as you command "back" (Figure 7-5). The toy should lead him on a path over the jump. Once he has turned away from you and commits to the jump, cross behind him and let him get the toy (Figure 7-6). Be sure to work the back command in both directions.

As the dog starts to understand that the sweeping-arc motion of your hand closest to him means to turn away, you will want to delay the throwing of the toy until he has turned, and eventually until he has turned, jumped, and landed on the other side of the jump. The toy starts out as a lure and fades into a reward.

Back	Turn
The dog changes leads to make a 90° arc away from the handler to the jump.	The dog has to make a 180° reversal of direction before taking off for the jump.
The handler then Rear-Crosses.	There is no Rear-Cross.

Fig. 7-8.

If you are having problems getting your dog to turn away from you, ask for a complete spin away from you before the second jump to emphasize the turning concept. Once the dog is spinning easily, go back to asking for a "back" over the jump.

If the dog goes around the jump chasing the toy, use a jump with bigger wings and shorten the distance between the dog and the jump. Try to time your throw so that the dog follows the toy over the jump.

Do not worry about the dog's jumping form at this point. It is common to see dogs jumping awkwardly at this time, as they are learning something new and are more focused on the toy than the jump. They will figure it out.

You can teach the "back" concept with obstacles other than jumps. Set up two tunnels, as in

Figure 7-7. When the dog exits the first tunnel, command and signal "back" to arc him into tunnel two.

The Difference Between "Back" and "Turn"

"Turn" and "back" may seem similar but are, in fact, both separate and necessary concepts. "Turn" cues a sharp, 180-degree reversal of direction away from you, while "back" cues a lead change that tells the dog to arc away from you but continue on in the same forward direction. See figures 7-8, 7-9, and 7-10.

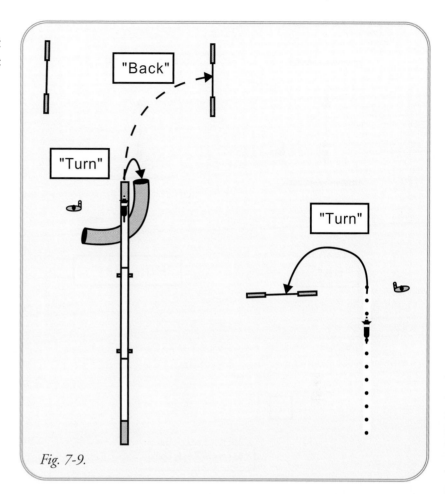

Fig. 7-9.

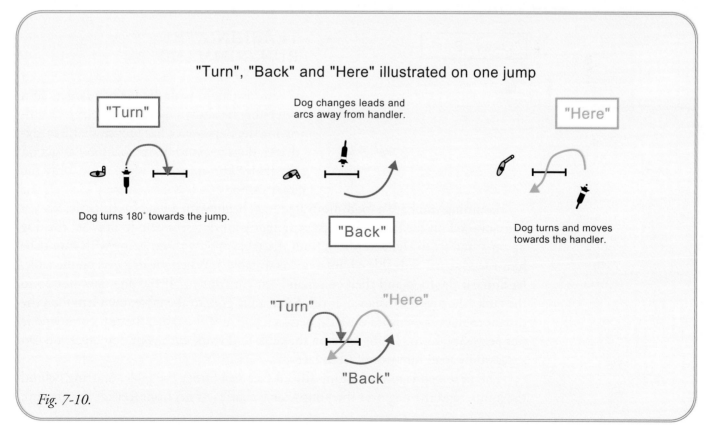

Fig. 7-10.

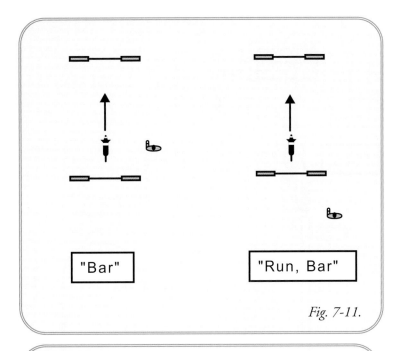

"Bar"   "Run, Bar"

Fig. 7-11.

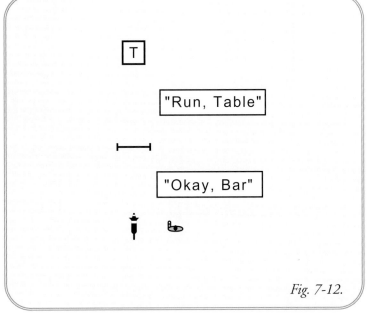

T

"Run, Table"

"Okay, Bar"

Fig. 7-12.

RUN

"Run" is the command that means: "Continue in a straight line and take the next obstacle you see even though I am at least one obstacle behind you." "Run" is used to get the dog to continue moving straight forward as you fall farther behind. It is frequently used in the closing sequence of a course, in Gamblers classes and in distance handling. I prefer to use the command "run" to "go" because many handlers say "go" as encouragement on poles or as general conversation with their dog. If "go" falls out of your mouth too easily, do not use it as a specific send command.

NOTE: "Run" is used only when you are at least one obstacle away. When you wish to send the dog ahead to an obstacle and there is nothing between you and that obstacle, "run" should not be used; the send signal and obstacle name suffice. If you use "run" or "go" for every send (e.g., "go-weave" or "go-tunnel"), the command will lose its value when you send the dog ahead for distance work.

TEACHING THE RUN COMMAND

"Run" is taught with the use of a target. This can either be a toy, a food tube, a target board, or a table. Experience has proven that less toy-driven dogs respond better to a food target on the table. The approach is the same, only the target varies.

Assuming you have a food-motivated dog, begin with a send to the table. Place a piece of food on the table and make sure that your dog sees you do this. Set the dog up on a stay six to eight feet back from the table and, without going with him, give him a send signal and table command ("okay, table"). When the dog gets on the table, let him eat the food and then command "sit" or "down." If the dog does not go to the table, shorten the distance. If the dog readily goes to the table, then lengthen the distance. Since there is no obstacle between you and the table, the run command is not necessary. Keep placing food on the table and work with your dog until you can successfully send him from fifteen feet away.

The next step is to put a jump fifteen feet away from the table. Starting behind the jump, send the dog over the jump ("okay, bar"). As his front feet hit the ground, give another send signal and command "run, table." When the dog can do this successfully, add another jump. Build on this exercise by adding multiple and diverse obstacles until you can send your dog to the table up to 100 feet away. Remember—the command "run" will be used before every obstacle except the first one.

When you are using the table as a target, require your dog to sit or down once he has eaten the piece of food. If he jumps off of the table, place him back on the obstacle and insist on the correct position. Be sure to always release him off of the table. (For more information on teaching the table, see Chapter 23, *The Pause Table*, page 217.)

As mentioned earlier, a toy or **food tube** can be used as a target instead of the table. (See food tube, Chapter 10, page 82.) If you are using a toy or food tube, remember to release the dog with an "okay, get it!" as he approaches the target. This is important, because in a training situation, a dog should only grab at a toy that he has been instructed to take. By grabbing a toy, the dog is rewarding himself, and you want to make sure that you are in control of all rewards. In the event that the dog cheats and runs around the jump to get the toy, have a helper step on the toy so that the dog cannot get it.

Remember—I use the word "run" as opposed to "go" or "go on," because these words are used too frequently by handlers trying to motivate their dogs to run faster. "Let's go" or "go, go, go, go!" start to resemble encouraging chatter and not a command.

OUT

"Out" cues the dog to move laterally away from you and to look for the next obstacle. It is the opposite of "here." If the dog is on the right side and you command "out," the dog should move laterally to the right. If the dog is on the left, he should move laterally to the left. How far out away from you the dog moves depends on the height of your hand signal. The higher in the air the hand signal, the further the dog should go. "Out" is used for obstacle discriminations, distance handling, layering, and often in Gambler classes.

The response to an out command is for the dog to move laterally away from you while continuing in the same forward direction.

The dog will only understand the out command when you are at his side (but not necessarily close to him). You cannot push a dog out if you are behind him. If you are behind the dog, a back command to turn the dog away from you will do the trick.

Sometimes "out" is used to maintain the distance between you and your dog. For example,

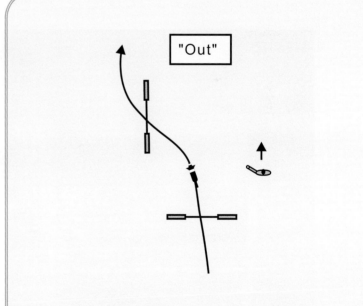

"Out" moves the dog laterally away from the handler but does not include a turn. The dog should continue moving in the direction the handler is moving. Notice that the handler is even with the dog as he makes the lateral movement.

Fig. 7-13.

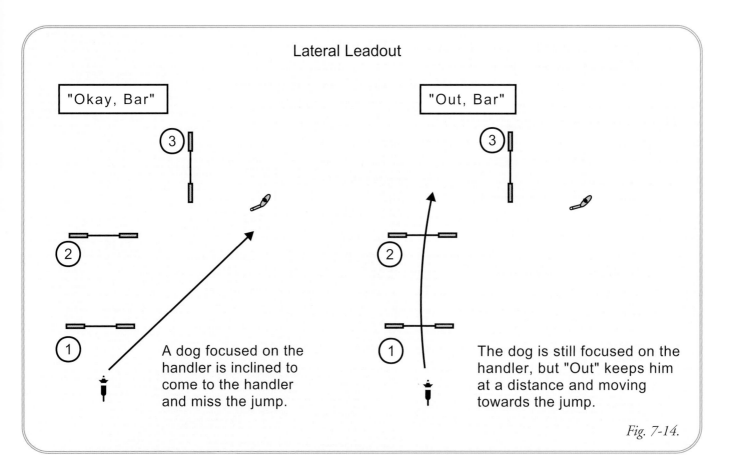

Lateral Leadout

"Okay, Bar"

A dog focused on the handler is inclined to come to the handler and miss the jump.

"Out, Bar"

The dog is still focused on the handler, but "Out" keeps him at a distance and moving towards the jump.

Fig. 7-14.

Foot and hand move together to give the out signal.

in a lateral lead out (see page 50), the dog may be inclined to come toward you, but the "out" command will direct him to stay away and take the obstacle in front of him. The out command lets the dog know that even if you are far away and/or off to the side, he should stay out there and not move in toward you. In the case of a lateral lead out, the "okay" is omitted, and the first thing the dog hears is the out command. This lets the dog know that his first movement is away from you. See Fig. 7-14.

THE OUT SIGNAL

To indicate to the dog that he should move laterally away from you, extend at shoulder height the arm that is closest to your dog. The palm of the hand faces the dog and the fingertips are pointed up toward the sky. You must give the out signal in the direction of the dog and the path he is on, not in the direction of the next obstacle.

TEACHING THE OUT COMMAND

Place two traffic cones approximately four feet apart. Start with the dog on your left side in a sitting position, facing the midway point between the cones. Put a piece of food in your left hand and lure the dog out around the cone on your right while saying "out." As the dog comes around the cone, switch the food to your right hand and call your dog to your side with a "here." Now begin again in the opposite direction. With your right hand, lure the dog around the cone on your left, using the command "out." Once he has gone around the cone, switch the food to your left hand and call the dog to your left side with a "here." The dog is moving, but you remain stationary.

Once the dog is confident moving out around the cones, place a low jump next to each cone. Continue to focus on the cones and repeat the exercise, but include the jump command after your out command. For example, you will now be saying, "out, bar" and then "here" as the dog comes around the first cone and over the jump back to you.

Teaching "out" with traffic cones.

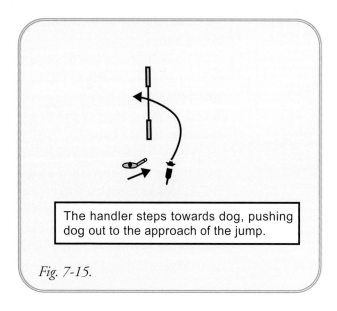

The handler steps towards dog, pushing dog out to the approach of the jump.

Fig. 7-15.

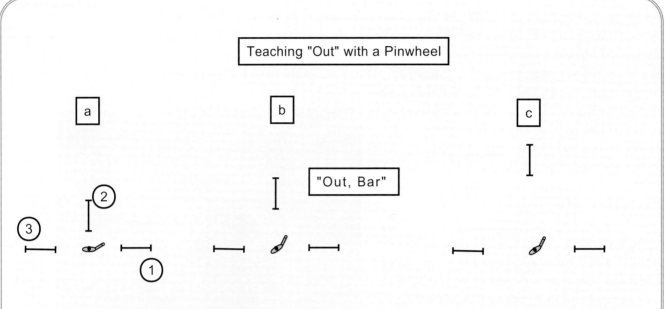

Gradually move #2 jump further and further away. Since this is to teach "Out", the handler should remain in between jumps #1 and #3.

Fig. 7-16.

Now start to introduce the concept of "out" with only the obstacles and no cones. Begin with a low jump. Position yourself facing the jump stanchion as in Figure 7-15. Start the dog on your right side. Command "out," then step into the dog with your right foot as you give the out signal to the line of approach of the jump. The point of this is to get the dog to move laterally away from you so that he can jump.

You will now work to push the dog out further and further. To accomplish this, set up a pinwheel (see Figure 7-16a). Stand in the center of the three jumps (between jumps 1 and 3). With the dog on your right, direct him over 1-2-3. Repeat in the other direction (dog on left, 3-2-1). Make sure that you give a run-by signal for each jump. Next, move jump 2 farther away from the other two jumps (see Figure 7-16b). Standing in the same spot, direct the dog over the jumps but include the word "out" before jump 2. Be sure to give a pronounced out signal and take one step toward the dog as he lands off of jump 1. Work both directions. Continue to move jump 2 farther and farther away. You may also have to spread jumps 2 and 3 farther apart to maintain a gentle jump circle (Fig. 7-16c).

WHOA

The command "whoa" tells the dog to shorten his stride. It is used in jumping and for up contacts. In jump sequences where tight turns are required, it is useful to prepare the dog for a tight turn by telling him to shorten his stride and plan to land close to the jump. By not jumping long over a jump, he saves distance and avoids a wide turn to the next obstacle.

Dogs with long strides can easily miss the upside contacts of the dog walk and seesaw. A shortened stride increases his chance of hitting the up contact without him having to drastically slow down or stop.

TEACHING THE WHOA COMMAND

"Whoa" must be taught in two directions—one with the dog coming toward you and the other with the dog running with you. Start by teaching "whoa" with the dog coming toward you.

Leave the dog on a sit-stay on one side of a low jump and position yourself facing him on the other side. Stand approximately two and one-half to three feet back from the jump, allowing your dog just enough room to land with his front feet and tuck his rear into a sitting position. Call the dog over the jump using a call-to signal and command "okay, whoa, bar." As soon as the dog's front legs hit the ground, command "sit" and raise your hand (holding a moti-

Jumping into the handler, "whoa-sit."

vator) to encourage the dog to lift his head. The dog should end up sitting directly in front of you within the space provided.

The purpose of this exercise is not only to teach the dog to rock back on his hindquarters before jumping (allowing him to land short), but also to teach him not to jump past you. When you are standing close to the landing side of a jump, the dog does not have much room to land, and if he doesn't shorten his stride and jump small, he will either jump past or collide with you.

Work this exercise until the jump is at full height and the dog can comfortably land sitting directly in front of you, even when he is given plenty of room on the approach to pick up speed. The estimate of two and one-half to three feet is for a medium-size dog. The distance may need adjustment depending on the dog's size. Do not ask for the impossible, but the distance should be short enough that the dog lands into the sit, without taking a stride.

If your dog continually runs past you, lower the jump and put a baby gate behind you. This will prevent your dog from running past you. This is also the foundation training for teaching a front cross. (See Chapter 8, section on "Front Crosses," page 57). Once the dog understands that you are asking for him to jump, the word "bar" can be dropped, leaving just the hand signal and the command "whoa."

Next you will learn "whoa" with you and your dog running together. Begin with the dog at your side and a single bar jump fifteen feet ahead of you. Run with the dog toward the jump. About five to six feet in front of the jump, turn toward the dog, raise your hands over his head, and command "whoa, sit." When the dog sits, reward him. Repeat this sequence until the dog is very willing to sit before a jump. At this point, the dog has not been asked to jump, only to shorten his stride and rock back into a sit in front of a jump.

The next step is to run with the dog and turn toward him with a "whoa, sit" command before the jump. This time, as soon as the dog sits, turn back toward the jump and send him over it with the command "whoa, bar." This "whoa" can also be used just before contact equip-

ment to ensure that the dog steps into the up contact. Be sure that the dog is in a full sit before you release him to the next obstacle.

Once the dog is responding accurately and quickly to the "whoa, sit" and the "whoa, bar," the final step is to eliminate the sit command. Approach the jump with the dog. About six feet before the jump, turn toward the dog and command "whoa." Before he can sit, give a send signal with the command "bar." If the dog does not break his stride in response to the whoa command, go back to insisting on a sit. Be sure to work the dog off of both your right and left sides.

A good practice exercise for teaching the dog to "whoa" at a distance away from you involves the use of bounce jumps (see Chapter 12, the section on "Bounce Jumps," page 107). Set up a series of four or more jumps at a low height spaced so that there is only enough room between the jumps for the dog to land and immediately take off for the next jump. The best way to discover this distance is to start with jumps ten feet apart and see if the dog puts in strides between the jumps. If he does, shorten the distance until there are no strides. Run the line of jumps until the dog is comfortably "bouncing" the entire sequence. Gradually raise the jump to full height, adjusting the distance when necessary (as jumps go up, dogs will need more space).

Next, set up a line of three jumps that are eighteen feet apart, followed by two jumps that are close enough to create a bounce. See Fig 7-17.

Run with the dog, who will probably get ahead of you. Command "whoa" as the dog lands off of the second jump. This prepares him for the upcoming bounce jumps by telling him to short-

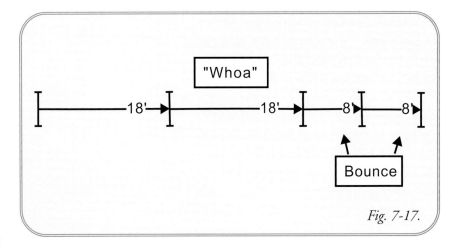

Fig. 7-17.

en his stride. If the dog does not respond, he will self correct by knocking down or avoiding one of the bounce jumps.

Repeating this procedure and alternating sides will help your dog to eventually learn to take the whoa command seriously.

NAMES OF OBSTACLES

It is my experience that dogs associate words with actions, not nouns. It is much easier to teach a dog "here" and "out" in relation to the handler than it is to teach a dog to search for an obstacle by name. Some beginning handlers attempt to direct their dogs through a course by telling them what obstacle to look for, when they should be directing them along the path leading to the obstacle. In agility, dogs tend to take what is in front of them. It is your responsibility as a handler to put the dog on the correct path. Over time, some dogs eventually learn the names of obstacles, but directional cues are much stronger and more reliable. Nevertheless, every obstacle needs a cue word, even though this is often more helpful to you than it is to the dog.

I use a different verbal command for each contact obstacle. It is important that the dog differentiate between each contact, particularly between a seesaw and dog walk that can look very similar. I use the command "walk-on" for the dog walk, "frame" for the A-frame, and "seesaw" for the seesaw. Other popular words for contact obstacles include: "climb," "scramble," "up," "walk it," "teeter," "A-frame" or "A,"

and "plank." If you are using a "whoa" or "lie down" to ensure that the dog hits the up contact, then "lie down, walk on" or "whoa, seesaw" almost becomes the command for the entire obstacle.

Spread jumps and the tire are distinguished from other jumps by separate names. I use "big" to indicate a double, triple, or broad jump and "tire" to indicate the tire jump. All other jumps are called "bar." It is necessary to warn the dog of a spread jump because he will need to stay in the air longer. The tire has a separate name simply because it looks very different from other jumps. Other popular words used for jumps include "jump," "over," "hup," "triple," "big jump," and "hoop."

Tunnels and chutes should also be distinguished from each other. I use the command "tunnel" for open tunnels and "chute" for closed tunnels. Other popular words are "through," "push," and "get in."

The table and weave poles also need their own commands. I use the word "table"; another popular word is "box." For weave poles, I use the term "weave." Another common command is "poles."

When you are choosing commands for agility, opt for short words that can be said easily, quickly, and distinctly. On the agility field, you are at liberty to utilize any words you wish (other than foul language, of course!). Some handlers even train their dogs in foreign languages. Be creative, but be logical. If the word does not "roll off your tongue," there may be a better option.

To prevent confusion, make sure that your commands do not rhyme with your dog's name. I learned this when I realized that my dog named Jaq was confused with the command "Back!"

Use a low sound when saying, "Tunnel" to distinguish it from other obstacles.

Looking for the next obstacle.

CHAPTER 8

WAYS OF TURNING A DOG

As you and your dog proceed through a course, it will be necessary to instruct him to turn and change direction. Your responsibility as the handler is to communicate the direction and the degree of sharpness of the turn. The dog's job is to know where you are at all times and to respond to your body and verbal cues.

There are different ways to change a dog's direction. The handling maneuver needed will depend on:

- How sharp a turn is desired.

- How far away you are from the dog.

- Which side of the dog you want to end up on following the turn.

You must always strive to turn the dog efficiently between obstacles to minimize yardage. This is best accomplished by giving the dog an early warning of a turn so that he may adjust his stride appropriately before the obstacle. Dogs do not have wings! They cannot change direction in midair (and those who try usually knock down bars). Dogs must prepare for a turn by knowing on which lead to land, before they launch.

If you send your dog straight over a jump with the intention of telling him about the turn after he lands, the end result will be a wide turn and a frustrated

Dog on his right lead.

dog. Suppose you are driving in a car and you do not know where you are going. The person in the backseat does know and is giving you directions. How would you feel if your friend suddenly screamed, "Turn Right Now!" as you sailed into the intersection?

LEADS

Turning is all about leads. In order for a dog to change direction (turn), he must change leads. A lead refers to the front leg that is extended the farthest in a canter stride or when the dog lands off of a jump. A dog on his right lead will have his right front leg extended the farthest and can only turn to the right. A dog on his left lead will have the left front leg extended and will turn to the left. To change directions, a dog must change leads.

Dogs naturally tend to curl toward their handler. If you are on the dog's right, the dog is most likely on his right lead and is able to turn to the right. Be aware of which lead the dog will be on when approaching a turn. Spins in the wrong direction are usually a result of a dog landing off of a jump on the wrong lead because you did not give the turn information early enough.

SIGNALING TURNS

When running agility, dogs are naturally inclined to turn in the direction of their handler. This means that if you are on the dog's right and you send the dog over a jump, giving no other information, the dog will generally land and turn to the right to come back to you. This is valuable information, for it allows you to anticipate which way your dog is likely to turn if he is left alone. If this is not the desirable direction, you must give your dog more information and instruction to tell him where, how far, and in what direction to turn.

To alert your dog of upcoming turns, make use of shoulder rotation, voice, arms, and movement.

SHOULDER ROTATION

Dogs naturally follow shoulder movement. Their instinctive hunting abilities give them the knowledge to predict where their prey is going to run next by watching body movement; the turn of the prey's shoulder depicts a change in direction.

Dogs read human body movement the same way; wherever the shoulder points, the dog goes. To visualize this concept, imagine you have a flashlight taped to the outside of your shoulder. The direction in which your shoulder turns and the light beam points is the direction in which the dog will move. This innate ability of the dog is enhanced by teaching the "here" command.

When you turn away from the dog, the dog follows with you; when you rotate sharply toward the dog, the dog then turns toward you.

VOICE AND ARMS

The commands to signal turns include "here" (to get the dog to turn and move toward you), "turn" (turn 180 degrees away from you), and "back" (to get the dog to switch leads and turn or arc away from you). The appropriate arm signals should accompany the verbal cues. (For more information on these commands and signals, refer back to Chapter 7, *Commands You Need*, page 37.)

MOVEMENT

A dog responds to changes in your movement as his handler the same as he would react to changes in the movement of prey that he chases. When you speed up, the dog drives forward. When you slow down, the dog slows down in anticipation of change. This is important information because it means that you can cue the dog of an upcoming change of direction by adjusting your speed.

Your position relative to the obstacle can also be indicative of a turn. If

A flashlight demonstrates where the shoulder is pointing.

you run straight toward an obstacle, with your shoulder facing forward, and you signal with the hand closest to the dog, your body language is telling the dog to power straight forward. However, if you move away from the obstacle as the dog commits, you draw the dog to that side. This maneuver, of moving forward but gradually away from an obstacle, is called "peeling off," and it lets the dog know the direction in which he will be going next as he approaches the obstacle. See Fig. 8-1.

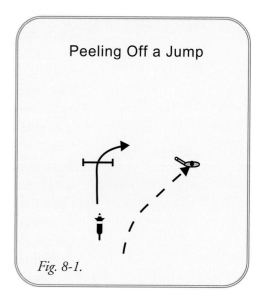

Peeling Off a Jump

Fig. 8-1.

WHY NOT LEFT AND RIGHT?

Some trainers attempt to teach their dogs the commands "left" and "right" in an effort to communicate which direction they want the dog to turn. I do not use this system of handling for a number of reasons. After years of teaching obedience to people and dogs, I know how many mistakes humans make when they are instructed to go to the left or right—and these people are not running at full speed while trying to decipher verbal information! Commanding a dog that is moving toward you requires the opposite cues from a dog that is moving away from you. Are you going to be able to keep it all straight? I have observed too many left and right mistakes in the rings, by both handlers and dogs, to justify the hours and hours of training that are required to supposedly teach "left" and "right."

Then there is the issue of how far left "left" is and how far right "right" is. I once heard a handler command "right" and then "hard right" to his dog. I'm sorry, but I think that this goes beyond the capability of the average canine. Many people think that their dogs know right from left when, in fact, the dogs are just following the handler's body. It would be an interesting test to have the handler turn one way and verbally instruct the dog to go the other way! Many dogs may also interpret "left" or "right" to simply mean switch leads. So now, you have two words that the dog understands as meaning the same thing. I prefer to teach a single command to instruct the dog to change leads and arc away from me (i.e., "back" or "switch").

Some people will argue that Border Collies learn the directional commands "way to me" and "come by" in herding and therefore should be able to learn "left" and "right." As a person who trains herding dogs, I assure you that it is not even close to the same concept. "Way to me" is a flanking command that means to circle the sheep in a counterclockwise direction, while "come by" instructs the dog to circle the sheep clockwise. The difference here is that the livestock provides a constant picture. In agility, there is no constant reference point other than you. If you use yourself as the reference point, then all that is needed is a command that means turn toward me ("here") and a command that means change leads and turn away from me ("back"). This is much simpler for both you and your dog. By the way, when Border Collies feel the pressures of a field and/or are running full out, they often respond incorrectly to flanking commands.

While it may be possible to teach certain dogs the meaning of left and right, when it comes to running agility, changes in direction are much more effectively accomplished by all dogs using a directional system that turns a dog toward or away from the handler.

CROSSES

Whenever you hear the word "cross" in agility, it means that the dog is moving from one side of the handler to the other. For example, if your dog is on your left side and you execute a front cross, at the completion of the front cross, your dog will now be on your right side. In agility, front crosses, rear crosses, and blind crosses are used.

FRONT CROSSES

In a front cross, start with your dog on one side (on his left, for example), then rotate by turning toward the dog. You will end up with the dog on the other side (on the right).

The front cross is very important, for it is the foundation of other handling techniques, including the reverse-flow pivot (RFP), the lead-out pivot (LOP) (see Chapter 11, *The Start of the Course*, page 89), and the lead arm.

The front cross is used to create tight turns and/or to allow you to change sides while staying ahead of your dog's path. It can be used before or after any obstacle.

Beginning handlers arrive at the common misconception that front crosses require them to cross directly in front of the dog. If you run directly in front of your dog, you are asking for a collision! It would probably be more accurate to describe the front cross as "a cross at the side, while you see the front of the dog," because you are actually off to the side of the dog while in transit to the next obstacle. A front cross takes place ahead of the dog, but not in front of him.

To minimize yardage, a front cross should be executed just beyond the dog's ideal path between the two obstacles and where the turn occurs. In Figure 8-2, you and your dog's ideal paths are delineated. An easy way to help visualize where to execute a front cross is by drawing an imaginary line between the stanchion of the jump from which you are coming to the stanchion of the jump to which you are going. In Figure 8-3, this line is drawn in red. The ideal location for a front cross is just beyond the intersection of the dog's path and the imaginary line.

Executing a front cross after a jump.

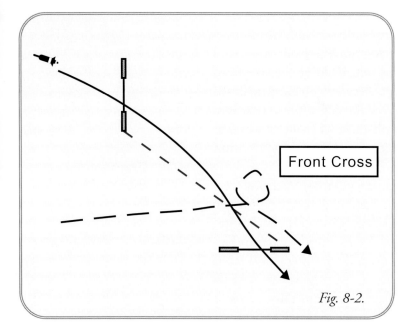

Front Cross

Fig. 8-2.

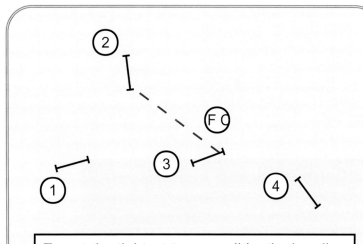

To get the tightest turn possible, the handler should excute his front cross just beyond the dotted line and closer to the next obstacle in sequence.

Fig. 8-3.

In order for a front cross to be possible, you must be even with or ahead of the dog. This is more easily accomplished than you would think, even with fast dogs and slower handlers. Sending a dog out away from you buys you the time to get where you need to be in order to successfully cross in front. See Fig. 8-4.

An added benefit of the front cross is that, when taught correctly, it allows you to use your body to dictate the jumping path of the dog, thus preventing wide turns. The front-cross maneuver can be tricky; it requires some footwork and pivoting ability, and you must remain upright. Many handlers bend down to the dog's eye level. Since your body acts like a wall to delineate which path the dog must take, the dog cannot visualize his path clearly if you bend over.

When you execute a front cross, it is easy to become disoriented after turning. To avoid disorientation, find a visual marker to let yourself know exactly where to make the turn. Be sure that the marker point is something that you can see without taking your eyes off of your dog. An example of a marker point would be the wing of a jump, the point where a bar meets an upright, or the leg of a jump.

Teaching the Front Cross

The first cue for a front cross is when you raise your outside arm (the one farthest from the dog) and then turn toward the dog. A dog that understands these cues knows that when he sees them, he must plan to turn toward you. Consistency is essential for the dog to learn to read your cues. Always use your outside arm to instruct the dog to turn toward you. Use the arm closest to the dog to indicate that he should continue forward or turn away.

Getting the Dog to Understand Not to Pass You

The first goal of teaching the front cross is to teach the dog that he must never jump past where you are standing. You can accomplish this by teaching the dog to jump into a sit directly in front of you.

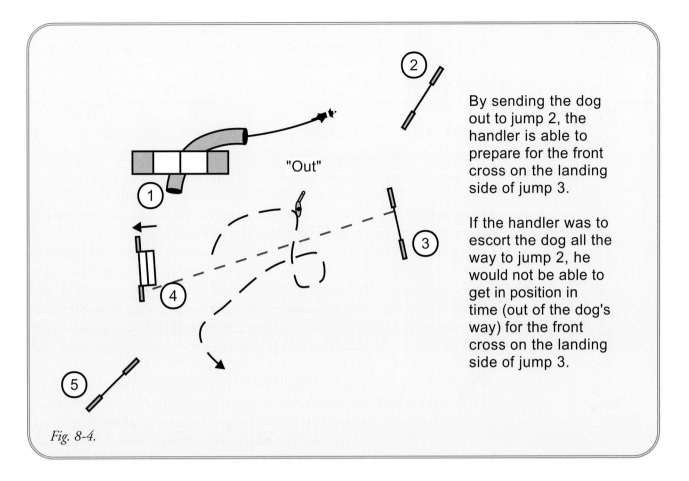

"Out"

By sending the dog out to jump 2, the handler is able to prepare for the front cross on the landing side of jump 3.

If the handler was to escort the dog all the way to jump 2, he would not be able to get in position in time (out of the dog's way) for the front cross on the landing side of jump 3.

Fig. 8-4.

Begin with the dog on one side of a low jump and you on the other side. Leave the dog on a stay and go to the other side of the jump. Turn to face the dog and give a call to signal as you command "okay, bar." The dog is expected to clear the bar, and as soon as his front feet hit the ground, he should fold into a sit. The training is the same as that required for teaching the command "whoa" when the dog is coming to you. (See Chapter 7, *Commands You Need*, page 37, for more information.)

It is important that you be close enough to the jump so that the dog only has room enough to land and immediately fold into the sit position. Set the dog far enough back from the jump to allow for only one or two strides before he takes off. Initially, a dog may be uncomfortable jumping into a limited space in front of you. To help him un-

derstand that he does indeed have room to land, set the bar as low as necessary. Raise the bar as the dog gains confidence and is successful.

To help the dog assume a sitting position, hold a motivator over the dog's head as soon as his front feet hit the ground. This brings his head up and his rear end down.

If the dog attempts to run past you, abort the activity and begin again. If lowering the jump does not seem to help and the dog repeatedly passes you, you can position a baby gate or wall directly behind you to convince the dog that he must learn to control his stride in order to stop in front of you.

Continue working on this exercise until the dog can clear a full-height jump and land into a sit in front of you. Next, try calling the dog over two jumps while you stand close behind the second one. This exercise promotes good jumping form. It teaches the dog to run to the base of the jump, rock back, and execute a correct arc over the jump instead of taking off too early, jumping flat, and knocking bars.

Teaching the Dog to Understand Your Directional Body Cue

As part of the dog's foundation training for agility (see Chapter 3, *Building a Solid Foundation*, page 11), the dog should understand how to come into a heel position on either side of you. The exercises of "call to heel" (left side) and "call to side" (right side) are used to teach this. You can now incorporate this concept into jumping as a way of communicating to your dog that a turn is imminent.

Begin by using a lowered jump, with your dog on one side and you on the other side. This time, stand close to the jump but turn your body so that your left or right shoulder is facing the dog. With the hand that is closest to the dog, give a "call to" signal and a verbal "okay, bar." As soon as the dog commits to the jump, bring the signal arm behind your leg, encouraging the dog to land and move up into a sit position next to your hip. A motivator in your hand will help the dog focus on the right place. See photos page 65.

If your left hip is facing the dog, the dog will sit at a heel position; if your right hip is facing the dog, the dog should sit in a side position. Do not command "heel" or "side." You want the dog to learn to interpret your body position.

As you continue to work this exercise, be sure to alternate the direction you face, and gradually raise the jump up to full height. Once the dog can negotiate the higher jump and turn to land in a heel or side position, begin moving further away from the jump, as shown in Figure 8-5.

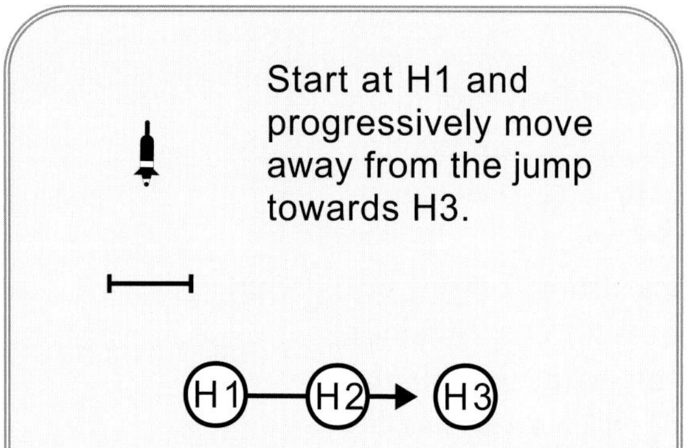

Start at H1 and progressively move away from the jump towards H3.

Fig. 8-5.

1. The dog notices the handler's position.

2. The dog begins to jump.

3. The dog turns to line up with the handler.

4. Dog ends up aligned with the handler's body.

WHAT IF? *What if the dog never seems to line up properly with my body?*

Some dogs have more difficulty bending their bodies than others. If your dog is reluctant to flex enough to get into a sit at your side, parallel with your body, try placing a traffic cone between you and the jump so that the dog must go around the cone on his way into a heel or side position. A few repetitions of bending around the cone will usually help the dog understand how to move appropriately.

With practice, a dog will learn to anticipate, based on your body position, when he needs to turn, and he will actually begin the turn before jumping. Now this is a good way to tighten turns!

The dog now understands that the direction you are facing is the way in which he will be moving, and he knows that he must land off of a jump and not run past you. These are the fundamental skills that a dog needs in order to understand the cue for a front cross.

REAR CROSSES

Rear crosses (also referred to as "cross behinds," "hind crosses," or "back crosses") occur when you start out on one side of the dog and end up on the other side while running behind the dog. The rear cross is cued by your movement, by a hand signal, and by a verbal command.

Your Movement

Rear crosses are effective in altering a dog's direction, because dogs tend to look and move toward their handlers. When changing sides behind the dog, you can get the dog's head to turn, which will result in a change of direction.

Assume that you are on the dog's left while approaching a jump, and you want the dog to turn to the right upon landing. To signal the turn, send the dog forward to the jump, move behind the dog, and then end up on the dog's right-hand side. See Fig. 8-6. Noticing your movement, the dog will land and turn to the right toward you. If you do not change sides before the dog lands, the dog will expect to see you on the original side, and he will land turning the wrong way. This will result in a spin as the dog realizes that you are on the other side.

1	2	3
Handler on dog's left. Send to jump.	Handler behind dog before dog jumps.	Handler on dog's right. Dog turning towards handler.

Three Part Rear Cross

Fig. 8-6.

In order to execute a rear cross, the dog must be ahead of you. Therefore, on the approach to an obstacle, you must either be behind the dog, or you must send the dog ahead.

The Special Signal for the Rear Cross

The dog is sent to the jump with the hand closest to the dog. Sometimes I explain the signal as a "send signal with a hook." One of my friends sees it as a backhanded swing of a tennis racket. The hand closest to the dog moves in an arc across your body and back in the direction in which you want the dog to land. Another way to perfect the signal is to try throwing (underhanded) an object over the jump and have it land where you want the dog to land. You will need to create an arc to throw the object sideways. With one student, I drew the dog's path in the dirt floor as the dog approached the jump and explained to the student that her hand signal should follow the path she wanted the dog to take. This seemed to help this student give the correct arc for the rear cross signal.

Verbal Cue

In addition to moving your body at the right time in the correct direction, and using the special hand signal, a verbal command is added to indicate a rear cross. The verbal command is "back," which instructs the dog to change leads. The advantage to also using the verbal command is so that the dog understands that he is changing direction long before he takes off for the jump. This allows you to cue a rear cross from farther away. When you send the dog to a jump and want to rear cross, use only the back command. It is not necessary to say "bar" or to give any other jump command, as the word "back" implies that the jump is to be taken.

Once a dog learns that "back" means to change leads, you can make

Executing the rear cross.

use of this information on the flat as well as over a jump. This becomes very useful if your dog is running straight ahead of you and you need him to arc gently away from you.

Takeoff or Landing Side?

Usually, handlers think of doing a rear cross as a dog takes off for a jump. This is called a rear cross on the "takeoff" side of a jump. It is also possible to do a rear cross on the "landing side" of the jump, after the dog has landed. Some people call this a rear cross on the flat, since it occurs between obstacles and not while the dog is executing the obstacle. As mentioned before, you cannot execute a rear cross unless the dog is ahead of you. If you get to a jump, expecting the dog to be ahead of you and he is not, you can always run past the jump and cross behind the dog on the landing side. The same rear cross hand signal and verbal command "back" would apply.

Front Versus Rear

Part of course-handling strategy is deciding whether to use a front cross or a rear cross. Some handlers prefer one

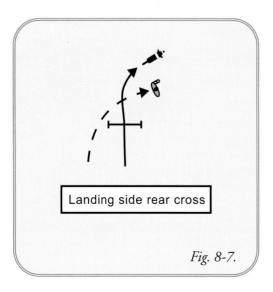

Landing side rear cross

Fig. 8-7.

kind of cross over the other because they find one easier to perform. Personally, I have been known to get disoriented following a front cross and will opt for a rear cross if possible. Some dogs also seem to prefer one cross to the other, although this is often correlated with the handler's proficiency in executing the maneuver. A competent agility team should master both the front and the rear crosses so as not to needlessly limit their options. Your decision regarding how to indicate a turn should be based on the sequence in question, and not on your preference.

You are now well aware of the fact that the dog must be ahead of you in order for a rear cross to occur. This rule never changes. In order to execute a front cross, you must be able to get ahead of the dog's path (but not necessarily in front of the dog). As you decide how to negotiate a turn, you must predict how fast your dog will run and where he will be in relation to your position. This information is vital in determining which cross is most appropriate. If you cannot get ahead of your dog's path, do not plan a front cross!

As a rule of thumb, if you have begun a sequence using rear crosses and the dog is moving at a constant speed (i.e., not stopping for a contact or a table), the likelihood that you can somehow end up ahead of the dog to execute a front cross is slim. Think about it: How do you go from a position behind the dog to suddenly in front of his path? The reverse scenario is not a problem. As long as you start out ahead of the dog, you can always slow down, let the dog drive ahead of you, and be in position to rear cross.

In some instances, it does not matter which kind of cross is used—preference and expertise help make the decision.

Blind Crosses

When you execute a "blind cross," it means that the dog will change sides and you will not see this happen, because the change occurs behind your back. There are advantages and disadvantages to using the blind cross. One advantage is that you can continue running forward and are therefore less likely to become disoriented on the course. A blind cross is usually faster than a front cross, which means that if you are trying to beat a dog out of a tunnel, this would be a good option.

Blind crosses following a contact obstacle are useful because they allow you to change sides in front of the dog without the dog seeing your face. This is helpful because if the dog sees your face as you cross in front of a contact obstacle, it might cause him to lift up his head, lose his balance, and bail off of the contact.

I do not like to use blind crosses for anything other than when a dog is in a tunnel or coming off of a contact. There is a big disadvantage in taking your eyes off of your dog while running a course. When a blind cross is used between jumps, the timing must be exact, and the dog must totally understand the signal for the change of side. Blind crosses while running are risky because it is difficult for you to save an imminent mistake if you cannot see your dog.

To teach the dog to read the blind cross off of a contact obstacle, target the contact and run slightly ahead of the dog. As the dog begins to descend the ramp, slide in front of the bottom contact with your back to the dog until you

have changed sides. The dog should be focused on the target and not pick up his head until you have completed the change of side.

You do not need to teach a dog a blind cross in a tunnel because he cannot see you anyway. Simply run past the opening of the tunnel with your back to the tunnel until you have changed sides. Be sure to drop your hand (the one now closest to the dog) down to pick up the dog on the new side.

THE CONNECTION BETWEEN FRONT CROSS, LEAD ARM, AND REVERSE FLOW PIVOT (RFP)

Once your dog has an understanding of the front cross, he will also be able to interpret the "lead arm" and the "reverse flow pivot." This is because these two handling maneuvers are derivatives of the front cross. Once you teach a front cross, you get the other two for free!

When you raise your arm that is farthest from the dog (the lead arm), the trained dog sees it as the beginning of a front cross; his response will then be to begin to arc toward you. If you raise your arm that is farthest from the dog and begin to rotate your body toward the dog (RFP), the dog's response will be to turn more sharply and move toward you, still in anticipation of a front cross. If you raise your arm that is farthest from the dog and fully rotate, you will execute a front cross and end up on the other side of the dog. The lead arm cue and RFP are just varying degrees of a front cross.

The Lead Arm

Using the "lead arm," sometimes referred to as a "pre-cue," keeps a dog turning toward you in a gentle arc, or it lets a dog know which way he will be turning after a jump, before he jumps it. I call it the "lead arm" because it tells the dog which lead he should be on for the next obstacle. The lead arm is always the arm farthest away from the dog. The maneuver can be thought of as the beginning of a front cross that never happens. If you have taught your dog a front cross, he already has the foundation for understanding the meaning of the lead arm.

For example, if you are running down a straight line of jumps with the dog on your left, and you need to turn the dog to the right after the last jump, you would send the dog to the last jump with your lead arm (right arm). This tells the dog that he is to jump and turn to the right (toward you). By having this information early, the dog knows that he is not to continue straight ahead; this allows him to prepare for the turn by collecting his stride before the jump, thus avoiding a wide turn.

Practicing the Lead Arm

Begin with the dog on your left side, facing a single bar jump. Hold a motivator in your right hand. Now, think about this . . . if you send the dog over the jump with your left arm, all you have told the dog is to move forward and take the jump in front of him. If you send the dog over the jump with your right arm (requiring a slight turn of your body toward the dog), you have told him to move forward, take the jump, and plan to land on his right lead for an immediate turn to the right.

So, you are starting with a low jump, a motivator in your right hand, and the dog on your left. Give a send signal with your right arm. The dog should jump, turn to the right, and come to your right side to get the motivator. Work on this until you can do it without a motivator in your hand, then lengthen your distance. Remember—the right arm means land on your right lead, and the left arm means land on your left lead! Amazingly, this is automatically understood by the dog once you teach a front cross. The secret is to realize that the dog comprehends this cue, and you can use it to your advantage!

Try setting up a pinwheel of jumps and direct your dog around the pinwheel with the lead arm cue. Do you get a tighter turn when using the lead arm than you would if you used the arm closest to the dog?

Lead Arm on the Flat

Another situation in which the lead arm cue is very useful is when the dog is faced with many

"Lead arm" over a single jump.

"Lead arm" through the pinwheel.

choices. In the sequence in Figure 8-8, the handler is faced with having to bring the dog past the A-frame and tunnel opening on his way to a 180-degree turn after jump 2. By using the lead arm after jump 1, the handler is instructing the dog to stay on his right lead and arc toward the handler, thus ignoring the off-course tunnel and the A-frame. Furthermore, if the handler keeps the lead arm up to indicate jump 2, the dog knows that he is turning to the right after the jump and not continuing straight to the off-course jump 8. The lead arm keeps the dog on course and creates a tighter turn.

The Reverse Flow Pivot

The Reverse Flow Pivot (RFP), or "false turn" as it is sometimes called, is

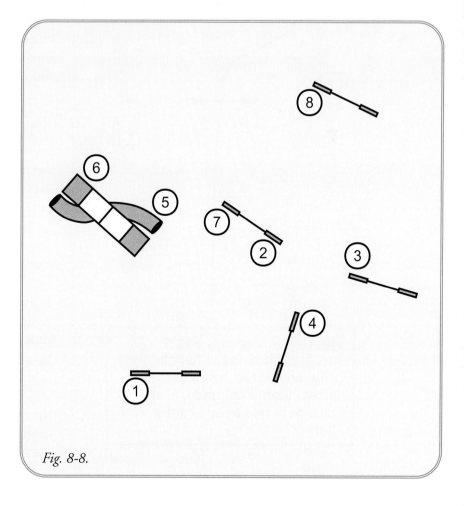

Fig. 8-8.

a way of changing a dog's path without having the dog change sides. The name is derived from the fact that the handler is reversing the flow of the dog's path by pivoting his body. It is used frequently when approaching an obstacle discrimination or when changing a dog's path to ensure that the dog enters the correct end of a C-shaped tunnel that he may not be heading directly for.

Referring back to Figure 8-8, to get the dog into tunnel 5, the handler may need a stronger indication to pull the dog toward him. This can be accomplished with the use of a reverse flow pivot. In this maneuver, you begin a front cross (you turn and rotate your body toward the dog while raising the arm that is farthest from the dog), but you never complete the rotation. Instead, once the dog has acknowledged your cue and has begun to move toward you, you then turn back to continue in the original direction. A reverse flow pivot can be thought of as "getting the dog's head" and attention. Your quick rotation and arm movement draw the dog's head sharply toward you, thus instructing the dog to move toward you.

The RFP is based on the principle that if you run, a dog will usually chase you, and if you suddenly change directions and run in the opposite direction, the dog will suddenly change directions with you. Dogs quickly understand that when you change arms and rotate your body, they should change leads. Keep this in mind as the RFP is described in more detail.

Think of the RFP as you start to do a front cross. Once the dog has turned toward you, you change your mind and continue in the original direction. The RFP adjusts the dog's path without causing the dog to change sides. It is more dramatic than the lead arm and can be used when the lead arm is not enough.

The RFP maneuver is useful for obstacle discrimination or to indicate the correct choice between two options. In Figure 8-9, the handler uses an RFP to get the dog into the correct end of the tunnel. See photo of RFP, page 79.

To execute an RFP, begin by running with the dog on your left side. Command "here" (or your dog's name) as you take off with a toy in your left hand. Now, turn suddenly toward the dog, command "here," and switch the toy to your right hand. Take only one step in the new direction and then switch the toy back to your left hand, again commanding "here," and continue in the original direction.

Some people think of the RFP as a "fake-out," since you are making the dog think that you are changing directions but then you do not. While the reverse flow pivot is a very useful handling

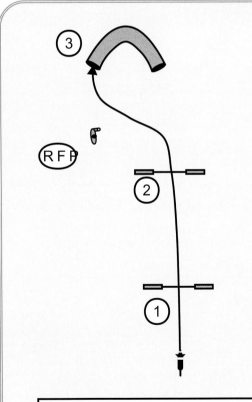

The RFP draws the dog's attention towards the handler who can then redirect him into the correct tunnel entrance. The dog's path has been slightly altered.

Fig. 8-9.

Handler demonstrates a shoulder pull.

technique, be careful not to use it excessively. If you continually fake a dog out, it will slow down his forward motion. Some dogs may also become frustrated with too much sudden change of direction. There are other ways to alter a dog's path that should be used whenever possible. Save the RFP for situations when nothing else will suffice.

OTHER TURNING MANEUVERS

Shoulder Pull

The shoulder pull is a very simple maneuver. You turn your shoulders and the dog follows in the direction indicated by your shoulders. Remember the flashlight analogy discussed at the beginning of this chapter? This turning technique is good for instructing a dog to turn in a gentle arc but is not effective when a sharp turn is needed.

The shoulder pull is more useful on small dogs and dogs that do not have a herding instinct. A herding dog often reacts by kicking out away from you if you attempt to pull him sharply with your shoulders. (For more information on this, refer to Chapter 27, *Border Collies in Agility*, page 241.)

Big, fast dogs and dogs that have large strides tend to move wide in response to a shoulder pull. Their ability to cover ground quickly makes it difficult for them to change direction if they do not turn their heads abruptly. The shoulder pull does not cause a dog's head to turn sharply. Therefore, when you want to create a wide or gentle arc, the shoulder pull is exactly the handling maneuver of choice.

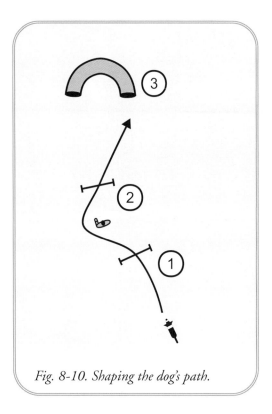

Fig. 8-10. Shaping the dog's path.

Shaping

Shaping is a term used to describe gentle adjustments to a dog's path as he proceeds around a course. Dogs can jump a jump from many different angles. In an effort to keep a dog on the proper path of the course, you can alter the angle at which the dog approaches any obstacle. You can accomplish this by standing in a strategic location and forcing the dog to alter his path so as not to collide with you. See Fig. 8-10. An extreme version of shaping is called "setting the V" (see Chapter 11, *The Start of the Course*, page 89).

Turning and changing direction is critical in agility. Much time can be gained or lost depending on your ability to cue turns and the dog's responses to them. Early communication and a consistent system will put you on the correct path.

Looking for the next jump. Photo by M Nicole Fischer.

CHAPTER 9

HANDLING SEQUENCES

After years of running agility courses, I have noticed that certain obstacle sequences are repeated frequently. Both dogs and handlers can learn to recognize these familiar patterns and develop what I call "course sense." This "sense" helps handlers remember the course, and dogs learn to recognize familiar sequences. Some dogs develop course sense faster than others, but all eventually learn the game. While there are an infinite number of possible sequences, it is worth practicing the common patterns.

What follows are some sequences that occur frequently in agility courses and techniques for teaching and handling them.

TUNNELS NEXT TO CONTACTS

In this country, tunnels are often positioned under contact obstacles. This creates three unique situations. The dog is either on the contact and must dive directly into the tunnel, is in the tunnel and must turn to climb up the contact, or is running toward the two obstacles and needs to discriminate which obstacle to take.

75

Turn-tunnel.

"TURN–TUNNEL"

In order to dive into an adjacent tunnel from the A-frame or dog walk, the dog needs to recognize the situation while he is still traveling over the boards; otherwise he will have a wide turn or risk a refusal. Dogs with moving or running contacts will need to be given the command before they complete the contact obstacle, while dogs with stopped contacts must be released and then immediately directed to the tunnel.

The command to tell the dog to turn away from you and duck into the tunnel directly off of the contact obstacle is "turn–tunnel." While dogs have been taught the command "turn" (turn sharply 180 degrees away from me) and the command "tunnel," this scenario appears so frequently on agility courses that it is worth teaching dogs to recognize it. Dogs become so familiar with the phrase "turn–tunnel" that they will start looking for the tunnel when they are coming over the dog walk or apex of the A-frame. Since they are able to anticipate where they are going next, their speed increases.

The exact placement of the tunnel next to the contact makes a difference as to when you can give the turn–tunnel command. If the tunnel is positioned right next to the contact, it is almost impossible for a dog to miss the contact if he is trying to get into the tunnel. In this situation, the command can be given as the dog is traveling down the descent ramp. If the position of the tunnel is such that the dog could miss the contact by jumping off of it and turning into the tunnel (such as when the tunnel is three or four feet away), then you must wait until the dog is in the contact zone before giving the turn–tunnel command. (See Fig. 9-1.)

TEACHING TURN-TUNNEL

Begin with the dog standing on the board at the bottom of the contact (dog walk or A-frame), while you are at the side of the dog. The tunnel is on the side of the dog away from you. From a stationary position, command "okay, turn–tunnel," and motion with your hand that is closest to the dog in an arc away and toward the tunnel (a turn signal). The dog should get off of the obstacle, turn 180 degrees away from you, and enter the tunnel. As the dog comes out of the tunnel, praise him and reward him by throwing a motivator ahead of him.

The dog may initially be confused and might curl in to look at you. Make sure that the dog does the turn, and then direct him into the tunnel. With a few repetitions, the dog will start to realize that you want him to go into the tunnel, and he will begin to turn tighter and aim directly for the tunnel.

When your dog is successful, begin again, and this time, position yourself slightly behind him. You want him to learn to look for the tunnel on his own. Give the signal and command "okay, turn–tunnel." The release command is being used only because the dog is starting from a stationary position at the bottom of the obstacle. When the dog is traveling over the contact obstacle, only the command "turn–tunnel" will be necessary (unless the dog has stopped contacts, for which you do need to re-

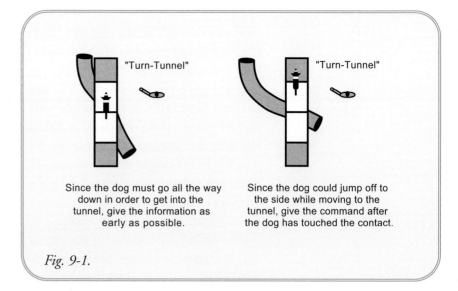

"Turn-Tunnel"   "Turn-Tunnel"

Since the dog must go all the way down in order to get into the tunnel, give the information as early as possible.

Since the dog could jump off to the side while moving to the tunnel, give the command after the dog has touched the contact.

Fig. 9-1.

lease him before directing him into the tunnel).

Dogs generally like this game and, after a few repetitions, are very ready to dive into the tunnel. Before long, you can run the entire piece of equipment and experiment with when you can give the command. Once you have taught the turn–tunnel skill on both sides of both the A-frame and dog walk, be sure to go back to doing a straight run off of the dog walk and A-frame so that the dog does not think that he is always going to dive into a tunnel after a contact if the tunnel is positioned next to the board.

The phrase turn–tunnel always refers to a turn away from you and into the tunnel. If you are on the side of the tunnel and the dog must turn toward you off of the contact and into the tunnel, then the command is "here–tunnel." As you command "here–tunnel," you should also begin to pivot slightly toward the dog and raise your lead arm.

"HERE–WALK/FRAME"

The opposite of "turn–tunnel" is "here–walk/frame." Suppose the dog is first sent through the tunnel and, upon exiting he must immediately turn toward you and scale the contact obstacle (the dog walk or A-frame). The dog will have a tighter turn and will look for the contact if he is given the information before shooting straight out of the tunnel.

While the dog is still in the tunnel, turn toward the tunnel and face the contact obstacle (as in a front cross). Command either "here–frame" or "here–walk," depending on the obstacle. With practice, dogs can learn to do this when you are standing halfway down the side of the contact obstacle, ready to move in the new direction.

OBSTACLE DISCRIMINATION

A challenge often seen on agility courses is when obstacles are positioned side by side. This is called an "obstacle discrimination," as the dog must understand which of the obstacles the handler is directing him to. While obstacle discriminations can be created with any obstacles, they are commonly created with tunnels placed next to contacts or jumps, or even a table with a tunnel wrapped around it.

While it is true that after years of running agility, some dogs do learn the names of obstacles—and rely on the verbal cues in obstacle discriminations—this is rare and generally not reliable. Remember—dogs are not verbal creatures and do not comprehend nouns (the names of obstacles) as direction to move toward something. If you want to tell your dog to move, you need to use verbs such as "here," "out," "back," and "turn." These handling commands imply motion and can be used to put the dog on the proper path so that he will see the next obstacle he is to take. It is much more effective to tell the dog where than what.

"Here–frame."

When a dog is faced with obstacle discrimination, it is your responsibility to move the dog onto the correct path for the next obstacle as quickly as possible and then say the command for the obstacle name. The dog either needs to move toward you to take the obstacle closest to you or move out and away to take the obstacle farther away from you. The lead arm or RFP are effective strategies for directing the dog to the closer obstacle, while an out command and signal will move the dog to the farther obstacle.

Try this experiment: Take your experienced agility dog into the center of a course. Stand still, do not face any obstacle in particular, and give an obstacle command (e.g., "weave," "table," "frame"). What happens? Most dogs do not think of moving to find an obstacle based on the obstacle's name. Now try giving a verb command, such as "turn," "out," or "back." Did the dog do the behavior?

The dog's path and focus are toward the A-frame. The RFP pulls the dog's focus and path toward the handler, who then redirects the dog to the tunnel.

LAYERING

Sometimes a sequence on course is set so that an obstacle is in the way of the handler's preferred path. In these situations, you must decide which side of that obstacle to go on. It is often advantageous to direct the dog where to go next from the far side of an obstacle.

This position of handling the dog with an obstacle separating you and your dog is called "layering."

When layering, you will need to use the out command to tell the dog not to move toward you. Layering is part of distance handling, discussed in Chapter 10, *Working From a Distance,* page 81.

Dogs are intense when running agility.

CHAPTER 10

WORKING FROM A DISTANCE

Dogs have four legs, we only have two. It is therefore understandable that they are capable of running faster than we are. Since the sport of agility is a timed event, the faster a dog moves the better it is, and no handler should ever work to slow his dog down. There is no such thing as a dog that is too fast in agility, only one who has not yet learned to pay attention, do his job, and take direction at soaring speed.

Someone once asked me how I got my World Team American Cocker Spaniel to run so fast. "Simple," I replied, "I never slowed her down!" I believe that fast dogs are born, not made, but you can certainly take a fast dog and make it slow with poor training. Once you slow a dog down, it's almost impossible to speed him back up to what he could have been. If a dog slows itself down in the learning process, do not worry, because once learned, the speed will return with confidence.

If you are learning to do agility and find that you cannot keep up with your dog, this is a good thing! Dogs can be taught to work away from you which often increases their speed and limits the amount of running the handler needs to do.

I never met a dog that would not leave its handler, only handlers that will not leave their dogs for fear the dog will make a mistake. Once you realize that mistakes are a necessary part of learning, and you allow your dog the *"right to be wrong,"* you have an opportunity to teach your dog to work away from you.

REWARDS

Agility trainers who want their dogs to work away from them must have a way of rewarding the dog for moving away. If all you ever do is feed the dog from your hands, why should he ever leave you? The key to teaching distance is rewarding the dog while he is still *away* from you.

Rewards can take the form of toys, food tubes (description to follow), and targets. Throwing a toy that the dog likes, following the completion of a short sequence, motivates the dog to continue moving forward to reach the toy.

If a dog is taught to touch a target (butter lid, round disk, etc.), the target can be placed beyond the last obstacle to motivate the dog to go forward and touch it. Once the dog has touched the target, *then* the handler can come over and put a piece of food on the lid (giving the dog a treat from your hand draws his focus away from the target and to your hands). It is not a good idea to bait a target with food because if the dog does not complete the sequence, he can still steal the reward!

To prevent a dog from rewarding himself, I suggest the use of a food tube as a motivator. A **food tube** is a clear plastic cylinder that holds food which is only accessible to the dog when the handler opens it. It is the same item that is used to hold nails for carpenters and can be found in hardware stores or online web sites that sell agility target training products.

Dogs should first be taught that when they run to a food tube and touch it, the handler will open it and let the dog get the food out. It is important that the *dog* gets the food out of the tube and not the handler, as this keeps the dog focused on the tube. The advantage to using the food tube is that if the dog makes a mistake but still runs to the tube, he cannot extract the reward himself. The handler remains in control of when the dog is being rewarded.

Food tubes are usually introduced when we begin to teach the "send" command over a jump. (See Chapter 6, *The Four Ways,* page 31.)

A typical "Food Tube."

DISTANCE HANDLING

Teaching a dog to work at a distance away from the handler takes two different forms. The dog may be asked to work away from the handler at *vertical distances and/or horizontal distance,* (also called lateral distances.) These are taught separately. I usually teach the vertical distance first because it is easier for the dog to learn.

VERTICAL DISTANCE

Vertical distance refers to getting a dog to move ahead and away from you, as in a very long "send." The handler has a dog running ahead of him and wants the dog to continue running straight in this direction.

The dog should already have been introduced to the command "run" (please refer to Chapter 7, *Commands You Need,* page 37). To teach vertical distance, we make use of a baited pause table as a point of focus. The food placed on the table encourages the dog to move forward to the obstacle.

- Place a treat in the center of the table and use a "send signal," to send the dog to the table. (As long as the dog must get onto the table to reach the food, a food tube is not necessary.)

- As the dog ascends onto the table and shows interest in the food, give a positional command of "sit" or "down."

- Once the dog has assumed the correct position the handler may go to the table and reward the dog again, this time for assuming the correct position.

Reward the dog for a down position by putting the food on the table and for a sit position by making him reach up to get a treat out of your hand. If the dog eats the food (which is a reward for the send) but does not assume the correct position on the table, repeat the command. If the dog responds correctly, go to the table and give the second reward for the sit or down position. If the dog jumps off the table, send the dog again, this time standing right next to the table.

Next place a jump 15 feet from the table. Stand behind the jump and give a send signal as you command, "Okay, Bar, Run table." If there is food or a food tube on the table, the dog should be inclined to run to the table. If the dog does not run to the table, shorten the distance between the jump and the table and begin again. NOTE: This is the same way we teach "run."

Gradually add more bar jumps before the table. Now as you send the dog, your commands will sound something like "Okay, Bar, Run Bar, Run Bar, Run table." While both words are important, vocal emphasis should be placed on the word "RUN." (To understand the use of the "RUN" command, see Chapter 7, *Commands You Need,* page 37.)

To wean the dog off of having food on the table, begin again with the dog 6 feet from the table and no jumps in front of him. Send the dog to the table and command "Down" remembering to move back. (See Chapter 23, *The Pause Table,* page 217.) As soon as the dog gets into the correct position, go up to the table and reward the dog by putting a piece of food on the table. The dog is now being rewarded from you for having left your side and getting on the table. Gradually add more distance and eventually try it from behind a jump.

Even though the dog may know that you have food with you, he must learn that he does not get it until he moves away from you, jumps onto the table, and assumes the correct position.

T

"Run, Table"

"Run, Seesaw"

"Run, Bar"

"Bar"

Say next command as dog finishes preceeding obstacle.

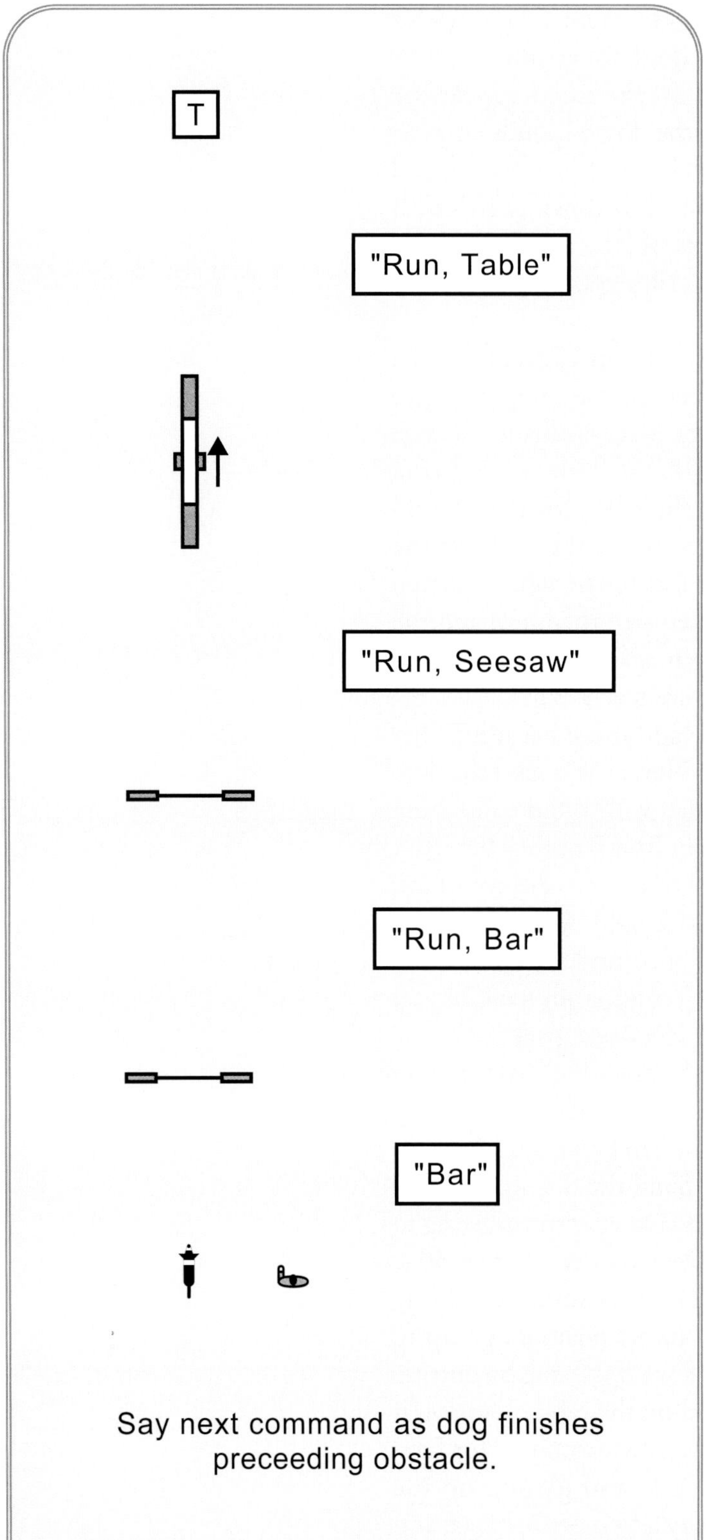

Fig. 10-1. Sample of Other Obstacles.

If the dog will not move away from you because there is no reward awaiting him on the table, shorten the distance between the dog and the table until you find a distance where the dog is willing to jump onto the table. As soon as the dog ascends the table, go to him and give him a reward. Gradually, begin backing away from the table and repeat this process.

Other Obstacles

Jumps are not the only obstacles that can be used in this vertical line to the table. Once you have taught a "send" on the other obstacles (see Chapter 6, *The Four Ways*, page 31) try incorporating those other obstacles into the line. Now your commands might sound something like, "Okay Bar, Run Bar, Run Seesaw, Run Table." See Fig. 10-1.

One of the most difficult obstacles to send ahead to is the chute. This is because as dogs exit a chute, they are momentarily disoriented and tend to curl back towards their handlers. It takes a few seconds for them to regain their senses so that they can listen to what you are telling them to do next. Practice "Chute, Run Bar."

Removing the Table as a Destination

Set up a series of jumps 18 feet apart with a table at the end. Now place a jump off to the side of these jumps creating a box. See Fig. 10-2.

• Begin by sending the dog in a straight line over the jumps and onto the table. Do not become discouraged if the dog suddenly takes one of the jumps on the side. If this happens, shorten the distance from the table and begin again. When you can send the dog ahead vertically to the table and he will ignore the jumps on either side, it is time to move on in your training.

• Send the dog over the first jump and on to the second jump with a "Run Bar" command.

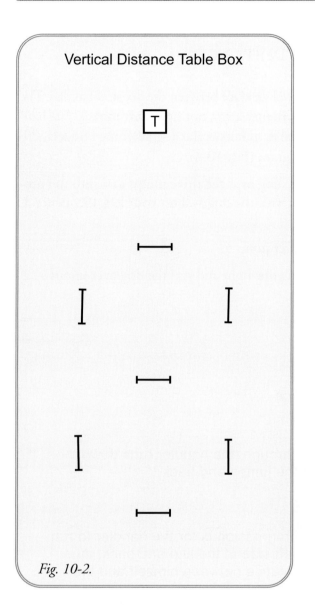

Fig. 10-2.

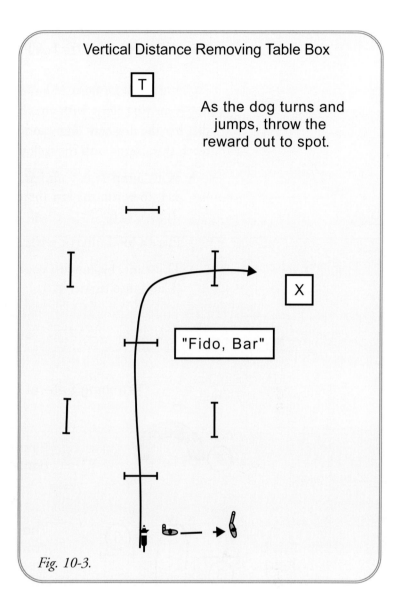

Fig. 10-3.

- After the dog lands off the second jump, call the dog's name or command, "Here." If the dog turns towards you, move off to the side and give the dog a command to jump one of the side jumps. See Fig. 10-3.

- Reward the dog with a food tube or toy thrown in front of him. Practice this exercise on both sides and occasionally go back to sending to the table. You may need to say "Out Bar" after calling the dog's name or saying "Here" to get the dog to take the jump after the turn. This is also the beginning of teaching Horizontal Distance!

After a few sessions, the dog should be willing to move ahead whether or not there is a table out there since his destination is no longer only the table. It is important that the handler continue to reward the dog for moving forward by throwing the reward out in front of him as he takes the final jump.

HORIZONTAL OR LATERAL DISTANCE

Horizontal Distance refers to the lateral distance between the dog and handler. The dog is moving along with you, but is a distance away, not right next to you. The handler has the dog stay "out" and run parallel to him as the dog takes the obstacles. To teach this, begin with the following diagram (Fig. 10-4).

- With jump 1 on your left, run the dog over the three jumps and into the tunnel, then run the last three jumps with the dog still on your left. (Sequence 1, 2, 3, 4, 5, 6, 7)

- Place a food tube or reward just after jump 5.

- This time, begin with your dog on your right and run the dog over jumps 1, 2, 3, and into tunnel 4.

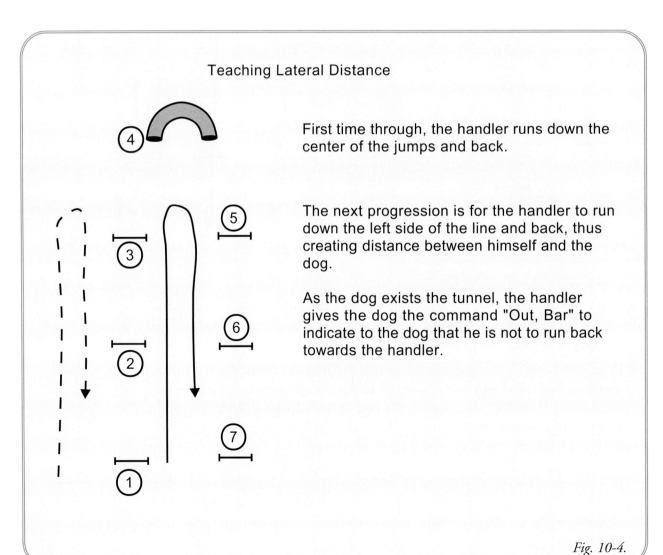

Teaching Lateral Distance

First time through, the handler runs down the center of the jumps and back.

The next progression is for the handler to run down the left side of the line and back, thus creating distance between himself and the dog.

As the dog exists the tunnel, the handler gives the dog the command "Out, Bar" to indicate to the dog that he is not to run back towards the handler.

Fig. 10-4.

- As the dog comes out of the tunnel, stand up between jump 3 and tunnel 4.

- Facing the direction the dog will be running, give the command and signal for "Out, Bar." If the dog understands, he will exit the tunnel, stay out away from the handler, jump 5 and immediately find his reward.

Move the reward to between jumps 6 and 7. Begin again by running parallel to the dog and maintaining the distance between you and him.

Eventually, put the reward beyond jump 7. You should now be able to run the dog over jumps 1, 2, and 3, into the tunnel, and staying close to your original path, direct the dog over jumps 5, 6, and 7. You will need to use the "out" command before each jump command.

Eventually you can combine vertical distance and lateral distance. Try the sequence in Fig. 10-5.

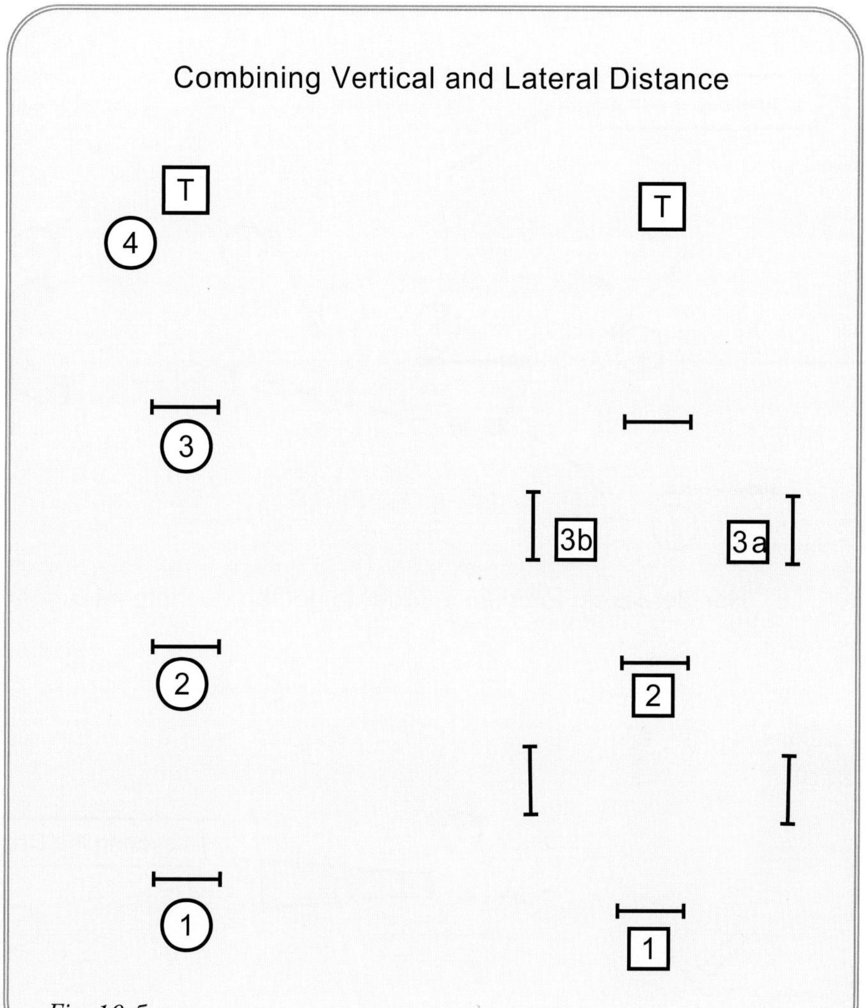

Other Obstacles

Try replacing the jumps with other obstacles. Incorporate a tire and a seesaw or A-frame into the horizontal distance exercise. Remember to target with a food tube or other reward the first time you change to a different obstacle. See Fig. 10-1.

Combining Vertical and Lateral Distance

Fig. 10-5.

LAYERING

Layering is a term used to explain a situation when the handler is moving so far away laterally from the dog, that there are actually other obstacles between the dog and the handler. When a course encourages the handlers to layer obstacles, it is a sneaky way for the judge to see if the dog has mastered the skill of working at a distance away from the handler. While courses cannot require layering, sometimes it is the only logical way to direct a dog through a sequence.

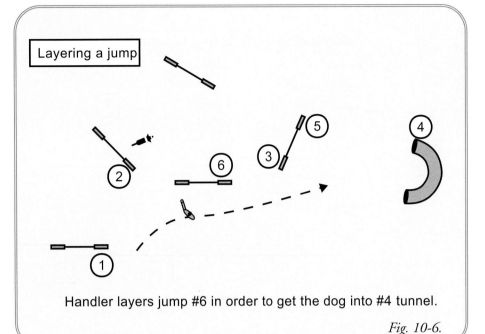

Handler layers jump #6 in order to get the dog into #4 tunnel.

Fig. 10-6.

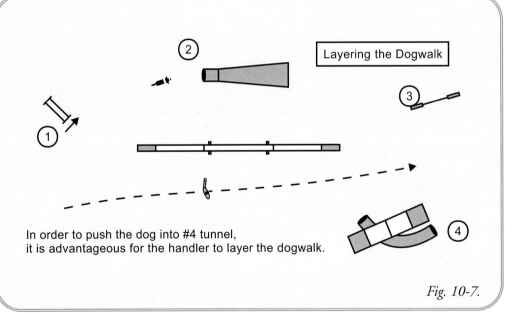

In order to push the dog into #4 tunnel,
it is advantageous for the handler to layer the dogwalk.

Fig. 10-7.

Let's look at some sequences that would best be handled by layering obstacles. See Fig. 10-6 and Fig. 10-7.

SUMMARY

Any dog can be taught to work away from its handler. Teaching a dog to work ahead of the handler encourages the dog to increase his speed since he does not need to wait for his handler to catch up. Distance handling is absolutely necessary for agility teams of fast dogs and slower handlers, as well as game classes that require distance handling (i.e., Gamblers and FAST).

In practice I train my dog to work far away from me, but in the ring I stay as close as I can to the dog's path. This approach minimizes mistakes, makes the dog confident, and affords me the option of using distance handling when necessary. There will be certain course designs that require my dog to work independently and away from me, to allow me to get to where I need to be, to give clear instructions to the next obstacle (i.e., critical points).

During the process of teaching a dog to work away from its handler, the dog is going to make many mistakes. These are good mistakes for they will help the dog learn that it is okay to work away from his handler. Continue to work with rewards thrown ahead of the dog and when necessary, shorten the distance you are asking the dog to move. Do not resort to running with the dog to avoid mistakes, for this will not build confidence, speed or teach a dog to work independently away from you.

THE START OF THE COURSE

An agility run actually begins before the dog has ever taken the first obstacle. Each course has a delineated start line that marks the point at which time starts ticking. Start lines and finish lines can be drawn between two cones placed just before the first obstacle or, with the advent of electrical timing, can be the plane of the first jump, chute, or tunnel. In competition, you and your dog must stay behind the start line until the official indicates that you may begin your run. At this point, you have the option to move out onto the course and position yourself while leaving your dog behind the start line, or you can run with your dog. There are a variety of handling maneuvers used specifically at the beginning of a course, all which require the use of a stay command.

Start lines and the beginning of the course are important as they set the tone of the entire run. You want your dog focused and attentive as you bring him into the ring and position him in front of the first obstacle. Your starting position should give the dog as much information as possible about the first few obstacles.

STAYS AT THE START LINE

Teaching a dog to stay at the start line until he is released is a valuable agility skill. It allows a lead-out advantage (discussed below), giving you a head start on the course. In addition, it helps focus a dog's attention. (To teach stay, see Chapter 7, *Commands You Need*, page 37.)

It is more difficult to teach a dog to stay on a start line in agility than it is to teach a stay in everyday life. This is because most dogs get extremely excited at the prospect of running agility. Additionally, the problem is compounded by handlers who want so much to run the course that they become inconsistent. They end up rewarding dogs that break stays at the start by allowing them to run the course. When inconsistency leads to disaster, some handlers abandon the "stay" skill completely and thereby limit their handling ability.

Any dog can be taught to stay at the start line. Stays simply require consistency and maintenance—the same as any other agility skill. You must make the commitment to consistency and uphold start-line criteria under all circumstances.

What If?

- **What if the dog breaks his stay?**
  Most dogs break a stay because they are anxious to run agility. The worst thing you can do when a dog breaks a stay is to move; this teaches the dog that he can get you to start moving. When a dog breaks a stay, you need to freeze. Allow the dog to do whatever was his intent. When the dog notices that you are doing nothing, he will eventually come over to see what is wrong. Now is the time to take the dog by the collar, gently bring him back, and reposition him at the start line. Once he is in position, repeat the stay command and leave again.

My attitude when a dog breaks a start line and actually takes equipment is, "Apparently you have some course in mind, so I will stand still and watch, since you seem to have a plan and don't need me." I have never had a dog whose plan went very far. Upon realizing that you will not follow them, most dogs become very embarrassed and are willing to stay at the start line to see what you have in mind. This "freeze-and-do-not-continue" approach will only work if you are 100 percent consistent *in and out of the agility ring*. Expect to lose three to four runs as you invest in your dog's agility future. No stay, no play.

- **What if the dog stays in the position you left him but starts "creeping" forward?**
  Creeping is the stepping stone to broken starts. A dog that creeps forward is aware that he must stay, but he is trying to cheat. If ignored, creeping will soon lead to breaking stays, or the dog will end up too close to the first jump to clear it. There are two different approaches to dealing with this problem, depending on whether you have a sensitive dog or an insensitive dog. A sensitive dog truly cares about being wrong; an insensitive dog needs to be convinced that "crime doesn't pay." In both cases, it is imperative that you pay close attention to the dog in order to catch him in the act of creeping.

When the sensitive dog creeps forward, stop, turn to the dog, and ask in a questioning voice, "What are you doing?" While the dog will not understand this phrase, it will interrupt his behavior and bring his focus back to you. Over time, the phrase will serve as a reminder to the dog that he should stay. If the dog does not stop when you say, "What are you doing?" then walk back and reposition the dog. This phrase can be used in the ring as well as in practice.

An insensitive dog requires a more dramatic approach. When an insensitive dog creeps forward, remove the bar from the first jump and gently toss it on the ground in front of the dog's feet. This will surprise the dog. When the dog reacts, return, reposition the dog in a stay, and replace the bar. By using the bar as the correction, the dog views the first jump as a reminder that he should stay and not creep forward.

- **What if the dog has good start-line stays in practice but breaks in competition?**

Remember—the key to stays is consistency; no stay, no play. You must always react the same way whether you are in or out of the ring. Dogs learn to differentiate between practice and competition. They learn that rules in practice do not always apply or are not enforced in competition. *You must not let this happen.* The way to get consistent behavior is to utilize consistent rules. If the dog decides to get up before you release him at a trial, in practice, in a **fun match**, or on the moon, you must let the dog know that this is unacceptable by refusing to continue. While you cannot toss a bar at a dog in competition, find a fun match where you can walk through the jump by "accident," causing the bar to roll toward the dog, and then escort the dog out of the ring.

If the dog has already learned, and takes advantage of, the difference between trials and practice and has been allowed to get away with broken stays in the ring, do not despair—it can be fixed, although it may take some time. You simply must decide that the "stay" at the start is more important than the run.

RELEASING

As with any stay, the release from the stay is an integral component of the exercise and behavior. *You must release the dog from the stay in the same way, each and every time.* Vary the length of the stay time. Many broken stays are the result of confusion on the release; the dog is not sure of the release criteria and starts guessing. This causes stress and, with a sensitive dog, can lead to a dog that decides not to start at all because he is unsure and does not want to be wrong.

When you are teaching a release, be sure that the dog understands that he moves only when he hears the verbal command (e.g., "okay"). To accomplish this, you must be frozen still at the time the verbal release command is given. The only thing that should move is your mouth! If you make a hand motion, or a head-bob, or walk at the time of the verbal release, the dog will not be sure if the cue to get up is a movement by you or a verbal command.

The Start-Line Game

To help your dog learn that the cue to begin moving is a verbal command and not motion, teach him the Start-Line Game. You will need to locate a very large field in which to play this proofing game. Position your dog as if he was on a start line. Give the stay command, and as you leave your dog, swing both arms and walk away 150 feet or more. Stop every 50 feet or so, face the dog, praise him for staying, then turn and continue walking. When you finally get a sizable distance from the dog, stop moving, stand still, turn back to look at the dog, and, in a loud voice, release him with an "okay." Then, and only then, start running away. Your dog will undoubtedly come running toward you and will eventually catch you, at which time you can celebrate, reward him, and play with him.

Push your limits; see how far you can get! Working with such a great distance between you and your dog teaches the dog to focus on *listening* for a command and not watching for a movement. If the dog breaks the stay at any time, walk back, reposition the dog, and begin again. In the beginning, you might need to walk back many times, but think of the bright side—you are proofing a stay, gaining a start line, and getting a workout all at once!

OTHER START-LINE ISSUES

STARTING SLOWLY, THEN PICKING UP SPEED

It is not uncommon for experienced agility dogs to begin a course tentatively and then finish the run with gusto. There are different reasons why this might happen. This problem can only be fixed once you have determined why the dog is cautious at the start of the course.

Pay attention and notice if the dog's speed increases after the completion of a particular obstacle. If, for example, the

dog's speed increases after weave poles, you might conclude that the dog is not confident with his weave-pole performance and that he relaxes after the completion of the stressful poles. I have observed many dogs relax and run faster after executing the seesaw. For these dogs, the concern over the seesaw performance is likely the reason for the slow start on the course.

If a dog lacks confidence on a specific agility obstacle, re-teach the obstacle until the dog demonstrates full confidence and speed in his total performance. The obstacle causing anxiety needs to be dealt with before the dog returns to running full courses.

———

What If?

- **What if the dog is slow on the beginning of every course and picks up speed in the end regardless of the order of obstacles?**

This pattern is usually seen in very sensitive, young dogs. These are the dogs that are highly intelligent and hate to be wrong. They have a fear of failure and become tense and stressed before a run. However, once they start and progress through the course, they relax, and their speed increases as if running helps them to relax. This problem may not surface until the dog has progressed to the more advanced courses where there are many more chances for errors.

To fix this problem, you need to find a way to break the dog's tension before the run begins. The technique with which I have had the most success is to get the dog to bark before the run begins. This requires that the dog learn to "speak" on command. Some handlers use the phrase, "Are you ready?" to prompt a bark response, while others simply command "speak" or "say it."

With the dog in a sitting position, teach your dog to bark on command away from agility. This is most easily accomplished at a time when your dog is likely to bark anyway—for example, when company comes to the door. Give your speak command as your dog is barking, then reward him. Eventually, your dog should start to bark on command to earn a reward.

This technique works because dogs need to be relaxed in order to bark on command. Therefore, if you can elicit a bark on command at the start line of an agility course, you can break the tension and begin the course with speed. The dog learns that you will not begin a run until he responds to you verbally, thus demonstrating focus and a readiness to begin working as a team.

As you first begin to retrain your dog at the start line, asking him to bark, it may take a few minutes (which will feel longer) to get him to bark. This is normal, and you must be patient. A dog cannot remain tense forever. Eventually, *time* will allow the dog to relax, and he will be able to respond to the speak command. At this point, the agility run may begin.

• **What if the dog will not bark on the start line, even though he will successfully respond to the speak command in other places?**

This behavior indicates that the dog is still too stressed to start running. To help the dog, remove him from the start line and get a correct response to the speak command in another location. If this is a training environment, you may then return to the start line and try once again to elicit a bark. If the problem occurs in a ring situation, you must forfeit the run and invest in the dog's agility future. Once a dog learns that the course will not begin until he relaxes, this knowledge will actually help him to relax. The dog will no longer feel pressured to begin something for which he is not ready.

OLDER DOGS STARTING SLOWLY

If an older dog begins a course slowly and then picks up speed, you need to consider that the older dog might be stiff and require more stretching and warm-up before entering the ring. These older dogs often have a harder time moving in cold, wet weather, since their arthritis is aggravated. Some of us "older" handlers can relate to these feelings with firsthand experience!

A dog should run agility with enthusiasm and confidence. If you feel like you are dragging your dog through a course, find a way to break the tension and relax your dog. Back up in your training, work on shorter, easier sequences, or discover which obstacle your dog is worried about and master it.

START-LINE HANDLING TECHNIQUES

When planning how to handle the beginning of a course, you have many options available to you, because it is easy to predict where the dog will be before he has picked up a lot of speed. Assuming the dog has learned to stay at the start line, you have the option of

Executing the lead-out push.

leading out from the starting position of the course to give yourself the advantage of getting ahead of the dog at the beginning of the run. A **lead out** involves you leaving your dog behind the start line while you place yourself in a strategic position within the course. There are different types of lead-out maneuvers that can be used to direct the dog at the start of the course, including the lead-out push, the lead-out pivot, and setting a "V."

The Lead-Out Push

A lead-out push is used in situations where a sharp turn is required within the first few obstacles. As in any lead out, you leave your dog on a stay at the start line and position yourself at the point where the course makes a turn and the dog's path is to be adjusted. Your feet point in the direction the dog is to move. You then rotate your upper body to indicate the first few jumps. As the dog approaches the last obstacle before the turn, rotate your upper body back in the direction your feet are facing.

From the initial work done while teaching the dog the front cross (see Chapter 8, *Ways of Turning a Dog*, page 57), the dog knows by your position which way he will be turning and exactly where to proceed on course. Because your feet are stationary and only your upper body moves, this technique requires a lot of training and good timing.

Executing the lead-out pivot.

THE LEAD-OUT PIVOT

In this scenario, leave your dog in a stay and move past at least one jump. As the dog begins the course, run ahead of him and execute a front cross at the point where the dog needs to turn. This technique works better for smaller dogs than it does for large, fast dogs, as the information to turn is given later than it is in the lead-out push. The advantage to doing the lead-out pivot is that the timing is not as critical as it is for the lead-out push.

THE LATERAL LEAD OUT

The term "lateral lead-out" refers to a situation at the beginning of a course in which you move ahead a few jumps *and* off to the side by a jump or two. The dog is taught to jump what he sees in front of him, then turn toward you to take the next jump. See Fig. 11-1.

SETTING A "V"

In this technique, position yourself between the first two obstacles where the dog needs to begin a turn. The dog is forced to run around you before taking the obstacle,

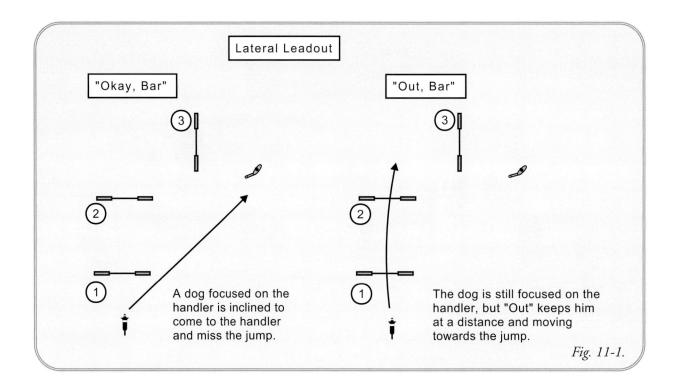

Lateral Leadout

"Okay, Bar"

"Out, Bar"

A dog focused on the handler is inclined to come to the handler and miss the jump.

The dog is still focused on the handler, but "Out" keeps him at a distance and moving towards the jump.

Fig. 11-1.

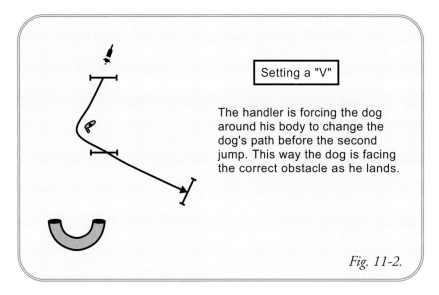

Setting a "V"

The handler is forcing the dog around his body to change the dog's path before the second jump. This way the dog is facing the correct obstacle as he lands.

Fig. 11-2.

thus changing his path. In this maneuver, you are shaping the dog's path at the start of the course. Because you must wait for the dog to pass you in the new direction, you end up being behind the dog, which may or may not be an advantage. See Fig. 11-2.

KEEP PRACTICING

Changing a dog's direction while running an agility course requires thought, timing, practice, coordination, and an understanding of how dogs follow movement. Beginning handlers should keep in mind that what may initially seem complicated will, one day, become very automatic. Handling in agility is a lot like learning to drive a car. After a while, you do not have to think about what you are doing and can concentrate on your passengers and where you are going.

1. Positioning for the "V."

2. Starting the movement.

3. Wrapping the dog around the handler's body to make a "V."

4. Directing the dog over the next jump with a different trajectory.

Photo by M. Nicole Fischer.

CHAPTER 12

JUMPING

The sport of agility requires more jumping than any other canine activity. It is extremely important for every agility dog to learn to jump from all angles and on different surfaces. In all levels of agility, a knocked bar constitutes a fault, and no qualifying score can be awarded. This puts a lot of pressure on you to teach your dog to jump not only quickly, but carefully.

Some dogs are naturally better jumpers than others. Jumping aptitude is determined by both a dog's structure and his attitude. I have known many dogs that had good jumping structure but were timid and fearful, making them poor jumpers in competition. In contrast, I have owned dogs with poor structure for jumping that had so much drive and heart that they more than made up for their physical handicaps. All dogs can learn to jump, although some are innately more careful about not touching bars than others.

If your dog is a natural jumper, leave him alone! However, not all dogs are natural jumpers, and some must be taught *how* to jump without knocking down a bar. Early in your dog's agility career, pay attention to how naturally your dog jumps. This helps determine how much time you will need to spend on teaching jumping skills. Regardless, all dogs—natural jumpers or not—should be exposed to many different jumping experiences and jump configurations.

There is no one correct style of jumping. Photo by M. Nicole Fischer.

JUMPING FORM AND STRUCTURE

Dogs use their bodies in many different ways when jumping. There is no one correct style of jumping. Some dogs extend their hind legs, while others hang their rear legs. Some tuck their hind legs, and some partially tuck their hind legs and then kick out as they descend over the jump. Some dogs stretch their front legs out, while others tuck their front legs up. There are dogs that jump with their heads high and others that jump with their heads low; the combinations are endless. The dog's jumping style is usually a product of his structure.

Good jumpers are almost always balanced dogs with good reach. This is to say that their front angulation and rear angulation are somewhat equal, and they are capable of raising and extending their front legs past their chin. Dogs with short upper arms have limited reach, and their jumping style usually reflects this handicap. These dogs tend to push more off of their rear to raise their front end enough to clear the jump. For more complete and in-depth information about structure and its correlation to jumping, please refer to Dr. Christine Zink and Julie Daniel's *Jumping A to Z; Teaching Your Dog to Soar* (Canine Sports Production, 1996, pages 10-12).

In an effort to build coordination, confidence, and body awareness, I like to start puppies walking over bars on the ground. As puppies grow, the bars are gradually raised and the jumping experience begins. Exposing dogs to jumping early on helps build their confidence and coordination. Young dogs, like children, have no fear of getting hurt. Children who are taught to ski at an early age usually pick up the sport easily and without fear. I think that the same concept can be applied to puppies in encouraging them to jump. I do not believe it is harmful to jump puppies low, on a soft surface (grass or dirt). (See Chapter 4, *Puppies in Agility*, page 19, for more complete information about puppies and jumping.)

THE PERFECT JUMP

Think of the dog's trajectory over a jump as an arc. When a dog jumps correctly, the apex of the jump should be in the

> All dogs can learn to jump, although some are innately more careful about not touching bars than others.

center of the arc. Good jumpers clear a jump by only a small margin of space. If a dog is "over jumping," he is not jumping efficiently. The exact shape of the arc depends on the dog's speed and approach to the jump. At a higher speed, a dog tends to extend his body over the jump: he takes off earlier and his jumping arc is flatter. A rounder jumping arc occurs when the dog takes off closer to the jump. An extended jump trajectory is faster but not desirable for sharp turns. Each has its place, and a dog should learn to jump both extended and collected. In the perfect jump, regardless of whether the dog jumps in a flat or rounded trajectory, the dog should be clearing the bar at the highest point of the jumping arc.

Dogs need to be relaxed and confident in order to jump efficiently. Photo by M. Nicole Fischer.

LEADS

A lead refers to the front leg that is extended the farthest in a canter stride or when the dog is landing off of a jump. If a dog lands with his right front leg extended, he is said to have landed on his right lead. If a dog lands with his left front leg extended, then he has landed on his left lead. In order for a dog to make a right turn off of a jump, he must land on his right lead. To turn left, he would need to land on his left lead. Whenever a dog lands off of a jump and spins in a circle, it is because he is confused and landed on the incorrect lead for the direction he needed to turn. Certain handling techniques are used to instruct the dog which way he will be turning before he lands (see Chapter 8, *Ways of Turning a Dog,* the section on the Lead Arm, page 70) so that he lands on the appropriate lead.

WHY DOGS KNOCK DOWN BARS

Dogs knock down bars for different reasons. If a dog launches for a jump and takes off too early, he is likely to hit the jump with his hind feet on the descent. If a dog gets too close to a jump before taking off, he will hit the bar with his front feet. A dog that attempts to turn in midair, in response to a handler's here or come command, drops his legs or hips, which results in a knocked bar. A dog with a long coat and a long tail may also drop a bar if he does not make allowance for this "extra baggage" in his jumping technique.

Surfaces play a big part in how successfully a dog jumps. A dog that slips on a wet surface on takeoff will most likely bring a bar down. A dog needs to learn to adjust his power and stride in order to successfully master jumping uphill, downhill, at different angles, and over spread jumps. Furthermore, as a dog's speed increases, it is normal for him to knock bars down. It is almost as if he needs to relearn how to jump and handle his body at each new speed.

If agility courses involved only straight lines or mild turns with plenty of space for all dogs to move and stride in between jumps, fewer bars would fall. However, jumping sequences often involve small spacing between obstacles and demand that dogs jump into and make adjustments in crowded conditions. Couple this with the fact that you may need to move into those spaces as well, and it can make for very tight conditions.

A dog that does not feel he has enough room to jump and land will often take down bars or refuse to jump. Some dogs become nervous when they feel that their handler is running into their space. They try to change their stride at the last minute but often fail to get over the bar successfully. All dogs initially have a different sense of space. It is important to teach a dog that he can jump toward you or toward a barrier, into limited space, and still clear the jump. (See Chapter 8, *Ways of Turning a Dog*, page 57, and Chapter 7, Commands You Need, page 37, for more techniques to get your dog comfortable jumping toward you.)

It is not uncommon for experienced jumpers that have competed for years to start hitting bars. This can happen when a dog becomes so accustomed to jumping a single height that he no longer looks at the jump before taking off and just assumes that he knows how high to jump. Fixing this problem is easy; you just need to change the picture. Start practicing with bars at all different heights and with some bars resting on an angle so that one end of the bar is higher than the other. Watch how fast the dog starts paying attention to the jumps and see if his jumping performance improves. This is also a good exercise for a good jumping dog that seems to knock down one bar per class!

WHAT TO DO WHEN THE DOG HITS A BAR

I have never known a dog that intentionally tried to hit a bar. I have known many dogs that did not appear to care if they hit a bar or if it fell. It is my belief that if a dog has the skills and ability to clear every jump at top speed, he would choose to do this every time. With this in mind, I do not correct a dog for knocking down a jump. Instead, I work to help him learn how to keep the bar up. Teach the dog what it is he needs to do with his body to clear a particular jump by placing bars on the ground before or after the jump to adjust the dog's take-off point.

THE REASON FOR GROUND BARS

If a dog takes off too close to a jump and hits the bar with his front feet, place a bar on the ground in front of the jump to suggest that he take off earlier. The exact placement and distance of the ground bar vary with the height of the jump and the dog's jumping style; you will need to experiment.

The goal is to create a jumping trajectory so that the bar of the jump is at the apex of the jumping arc.

If a dog takes off too early and hits the bar with his hind feet on the descent, put a bar on the ground after the jump. As the dog approaches the jump and realizes that he must clear both the bar and the pole on the ground, he will adjust his stride and take off closer in order to travel farther over the jump.

Whenever a dog knocks down a bar, you will want to stop and place a ground bar on the problem jump. Once you have determined which side of the jump to place the ground bar, simply repeat the sequence you were running. The ground bar should prompt the dog to adjust his stride and jump in a manner that allows him to clear the bar. If the dog still takes down the same bar, you might need to adjust the ground bar and try again. If necessary, make the task easier by starting closer to the problem jump so that the dog has less speed. Once he successfully clears it, try the full sequence again.

Ground pole after a jump for dogs that take off too early.

Remember—do not correct, yell "no!" or command "lie down!" when a dog takes down a bar. You do not want the dog to become nervous or fearful about jumping. Dogs need to be relaxed and confident in order to jump efficiently. The dog did not choose to knock down the bar; he needs help to learn how to physically negotiate this particular jump in this specific setup.

TEACHING JUMPING

Other than the very first jumping lesson, I never ask a dog to jump with a leash on. In addition to being potentially dangerous, I feel that the leash inhibits a dog's movement and discourages him from accelerating over a jump. If you cannot take your dog off leash for fear you will lose control, work on "here" before you worry about teaching the dog to jump!

Introducing Jumps

Dogs should be encouraged to jump without luring. You may use food or a toy to motivate the dog forward over a jump, but don't put food in front of the dog's face to lead him over the jump. The dog must learn to negotiate jumps by looking at the jumps—not at food or the hand in front of him. Place rewards beyond the jump so that the dog inevitably looks at the jump and beyond to get to the motivator.

To first introduce jumps and let the dog see that he can pass in between standards and over a bar, start with a jump that is low enough so that the dog cannot go underneath it. With the dog close at your side and on a leash and a buckle collar, walk briskly toward and over the single bar jump (yes, you are going over the jump as well). Do not stop or hesitate. Praise the dog as he goes with you over the bar. Because the dog is on leash, you can ensure that he passes between the standards and over the jump. Do not pull the dog. Simply do not allow him to go around the jump. Given no other option, the dog will eventually go over the bar.

Be sure to practice with the dog on both sides of you. When the dog is moving willingly at your side and over the bar jump, start adding your jump command as you head for the jump. As soon as possible, see if the dog will go with you off leash.

ALL FOUR WAYS AND RAISING THE BAR

Now that you know the dog will jump a low jump with your help, it is time to teach him that he can jump on his own. Starting with the call-to, teach the dog to negotiate the jump in all four ways. (See Chapter 6, *The Four Ways*, page 31, for instructions on teaching each format over a jump.)

Gradually add more jumps and raise the height of the bars. Watch for signs of jumping problems (discussed at the end of this chapter). If your dog starts ducking under bars, add an additional bar to eliminate the space, or lower the jump.

With a full-grown adult dog, progress to full height as quickly as possible. This means that as soon as the dog is jumping confidently, raise the bar. If your dog is still growing, keep jumps slightly above the height of the dog's elbow for training, and always use resilient surfaces with good traction for jumping.

SPREAD JUMPS

In agility, some jumps are broader and larger than single bar jumps. The broad jump, the double, and the triple are considered spread jumps or extended spread jumps. When a dog jumps a spread jump, he must plan to stay in the air longer than if he were going over a single bar jump. It takes training and practice for a dog to learn to recognize the look of a spread jump. To help alert the dog that one of these "special" jumps is coming up next, use a different command, such as "big," instead of the normal jump command. With experience, a dog learns to notice the appearance of a "spread" and anticipates that he will need to extend his jump. Spread jumps should be incorporated into jumping practice and sequences.

The double, triple, or extended spread jumps are taught in the same way as a single bar jump but begin off leash. Start with the jump low and in call-to format. Gradually raise the height of the jump, then introduce the run-by and the send. Plant a motivator beyond the jump for the run-by and send to encourage the dog to look forward, extend, and stay in the air longer.

Small Dogs and Triple Jumps

The design of the triple or extended spread jump creates additional challenges for the mini- and midi-sized dogs. At eight, twelve, and sixteen inches, the bars of the jump do not extend to the beginning of the stanchions, and for a proper takeoff, the dog must actually move inside the stanchions. This does not occur on a spread set at twenty, twenty-two, twenty-four, or twenty-six inches, as the bars reach the front of the stanchions. This distinction is important, because with practice, small dogs can learn to focus on the bars of the jump and not on the sides. One way to help the small dog focus on bars is to accentuate the sides of the triple by adding baby gates to extend the length of the sides of the jump.

Triple set for large dogs.

BROAD JUMP

The broad jump is different from every other jump that you will teach your dog. Since the broad jump is low and flat, a dog doesn't always see a reason to jump it. The agility broad jump has four poles delineating the four corners of the jump. To convince a dog to jump up over a low, flat jump, attach a string (high enough to encourage a dog to jump) between the front two uprights. When the dog sees the string, he will automatically rock back and jump up over the boards of the broad jump. Keep the string on the jump until you have successfully taught the jump all four ways and practiced crosses.

Begin to teach the broad jump with two boards for a large dog or one board for a small dog. Work in a call-to format until the jump is at regulation size. Working in the call-to position, the dog learns to jump and stay in the air long enough to clear the jump and reach you. To teach a run-by and send, put a motivator beyond to keep the dog's focus forward.

Triple set for small dogs.

Gates used to teach small dogs to focus on jump bars.

Broad jump with string.

Electric timer on a triple jump.

What If?

• **What if the dog does not jump straight across the broad jump but cuts the corner?**

This is a common problem when the dog has a poor approach to the jump. Teach the dog to straighten out his angle when approaching the broad jump. This can be accomplished by using two cones placed just in front of the first two uprights. Next, plant a motivator on the other side of the boards. Practice sending the dog from different angles using the out command when appropriate.

Wings and Electrical Timers on Spread Jumps

Like other jumps, it is possible for spread jumps to have wings. The problem with wings on spread jumps is that sometimes they are placed at the front of the jump, sometimes at the back, and sometimes in the middle. A dog must be taught to judge his takeoff point from the bars and not from the wings. Visually, a spread jump appears very different if the wings are next to the first bar or set even with the last bar.

Many trials now use electric timing. This is a terrific addition to the sport of agility, where placements are often determined by the hundredths of a second. Electric timers can present problems similar to those of wings on spreads. Many dogs misjudge the takeoff point on a triple because of the addition of electric timers. Timers look very much like the standards of jumps, and you must accustom your dog to seeing timers next to jumps. Again, there is no customary placement for timers; sometimes they are placed in front of and sometimes behind jumps and spreads. This makes a visual difference to the dog, and he must learn to judge the takeoff, regardless of where the timers are positioned.

STRIDING AND TIMING

When a dog moves in a cantering gait, each foot will touch down on the ground once; this is called a stride. The distance covered during one stride is referred to as stride length. Stride length depends on the dog's structure and speed and on the surface on which he is running. The distance between jumps can be measured by the number of strides the dog takes between the jumps. It is helpful to know approximately how long your dog's stride is in order to plan and time his commands.

In their book, *Jumping from A to Z*, Christine Zink, DVM, PhD, and Julie Daniels offer a formula for measuring a dog's working stride length. Yet, even they advise that you should "get in the habit of noticing how your dog copes with the different jump spacing he encounters. This is the only way to become an expert about your own dog's work over jumps; no amount of theory can do that for you," (1996, page 75).

Here are a few exercises to improve a dog's jumping form, striding, and timing.

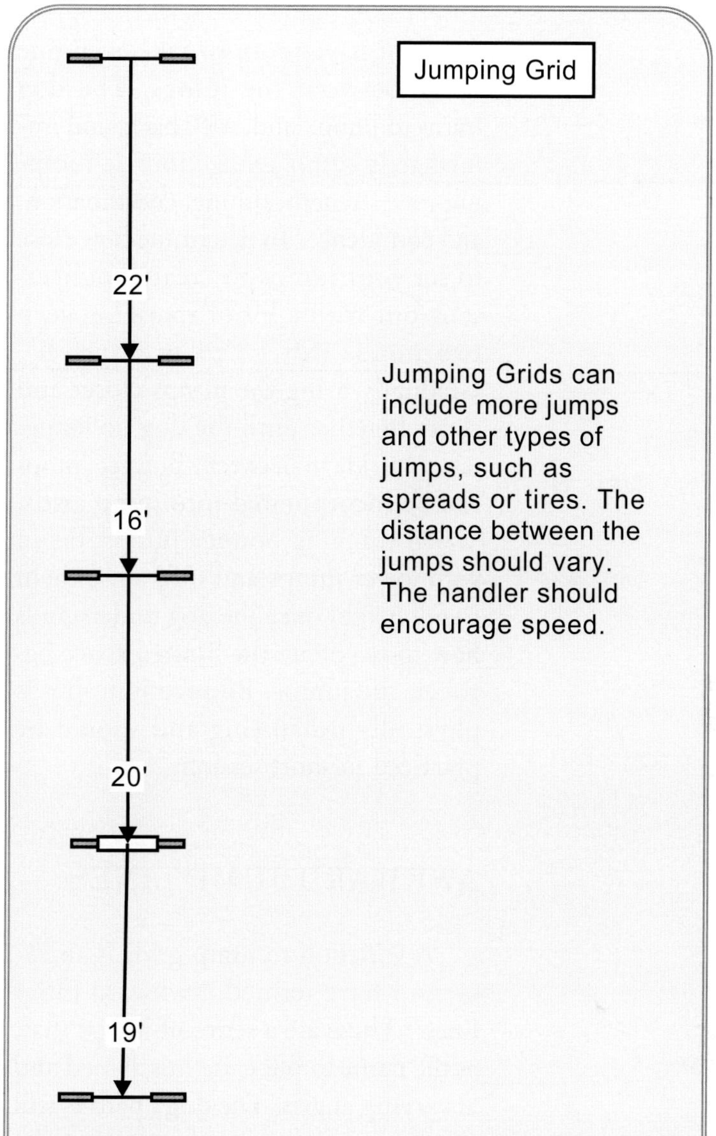

Jumping Grid

22'

16'

20'

19'

Jumping Grids can include more jumps and other types of jumps, such as spreads or tires. The distance between the jumps should vary. The handler should encourage speed.

Fig. 12-1.

JUMPING GRID

A jumping grid, sometimes called a jump chute or gymnastic, is a series of jumps placed in a straight line with varying distances between the jumps. The varying distances help teach a dog to adjust his stride as he jumps down the line.

Jumping a grid is physically demanding and should not be overdone. Two to three repetitions in one session, and not worked every time you train, are reasonable. The important part of teaching your dog to jump a grid is to frequently change the grid by altering the spacing between the jumps. The objective is to teach the dog to extend and collect as necessary and learn to judge the correct take-off points, not to pattern one sequence.

BOUNCE JUMPS

Bounce jumps are a series of jumps spaced so close together that the dog does not have room to take even one stride between the jumps. The dog learns to jump, land, rock back, and immediately jump again. Bounce jumps improve strength, timing, coordination, and confidence. To determine how close to set your jumps to create bounces, start out with a lot of space between two jumps (fifteen to twenty feet). Gradually bring the jumps closer and closer together until the dog no longer takes a stride in between. Bounce jumps can be incorporated into jump grids. When teaching bounce jumps, begin with lower jumps and only raise them to full height once the dog understands how to negotiate the limited space between the jumps. Bounce jumping is physically exhausting and should be practiced in short sessions.

AWKWARD JUMP LINES

A variation to jump grids is an exercise I have termed "awkward jump lines." These are a series of jumps that, as the name implies, are misaligned and at varying angles. The dog's path is still roughly straight, but he must make slight adjustments in order to jump down the line. This is a good exercise to make the dog think about jumping. He must negotiate jumps at angles, while slightly jumping toward and away from you. A tunnel can be placed at the end of the line to encourage speed and forward drive.

Do not try to "handle" the "awkward jump line" sequence. The lines are straight enough so that all you must do is face forward and run parallel to the dog down the line. The goal is to get the dog to make slight adjustments on his own.

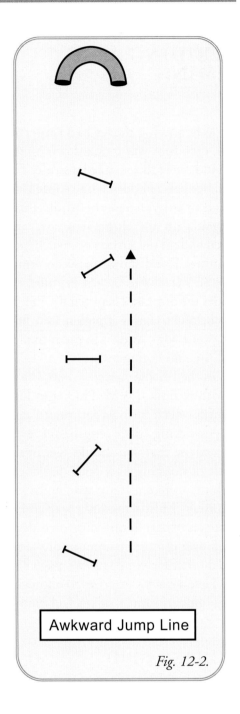

Awkward Jump Line

Fig. 12-2.

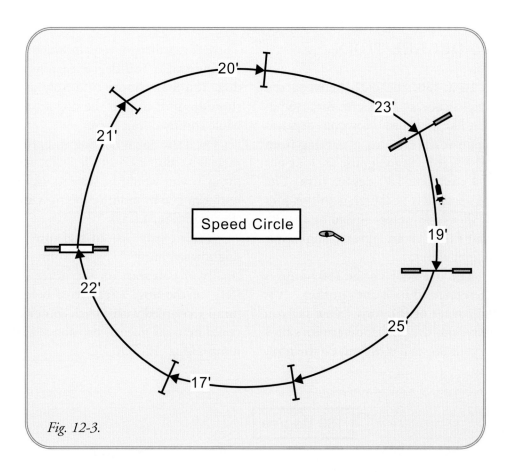

Fig. 12-3.

SPEED CIRCLES

A speed circle is a very large circle of jumps that are spaced and angled irregularly. It is an exercise used to encourage a dog to pick up speed as he jumps so that he can learn to jump on a curve as fast as possible. Because the jumps are placed in a circle, you can run the inside of the circle and be ahead of the dog, who is constantly rushing to keep up. The goal is for the dog to learn to rush without knocking down bars.

JUMP CONFIGURATIONS

Every course in agility is different; the angles and combinations of equipment are limitless. You and your dog never know until the morning of the trial what a course will look like and what agility skills will be required to negotiate it. It is this expectation of new challenges that keeps the sport of agility stimulating and challenging.

While nothing is ever exactly the same, there are patterns and configurations of jumps that appear repeatedly. It would be wise to perfect the more common jump patterns.

Here are a few examples of common jump patterns and how to handle them.

180-DEGREE TURN

In a 180, the path between the jumps makes a 180-degree turn, somewhat like a U-turn. However, depending on where the dog is coming from and where he is going, the arc may not be a complete 180-degree turn. The dog's path may be flatter, requiring him to "slice" the jumps—meaning that he must jump on an extreme angle, not straight ahead.

The area between the 180 jumps is often referred to as the "pocket." It is the corner of the turn. How far you move into the pocket determines how far your dog will move out on the turn.

There are a variety of ways in which you can indicate a 180-degree turn to the dog. You may choose to simply use a shoulder pull to pull the dog around while commanding "here."

Or, if the dog is moving at speed or there is an alluring obstacle in line with jump 1, you would be wise to use the lead-arm cue to indicate the turn after the jump (Fig. 12.5a).

A front cross would also turn the dog toward jump 2 (Fig. 12-5b). And finally, if you start on the other side (left) of the dog, a rear cross behind jump 1 coupled with a back command could be used to turn the dog toward jump 2 (Fig. 12-5c).

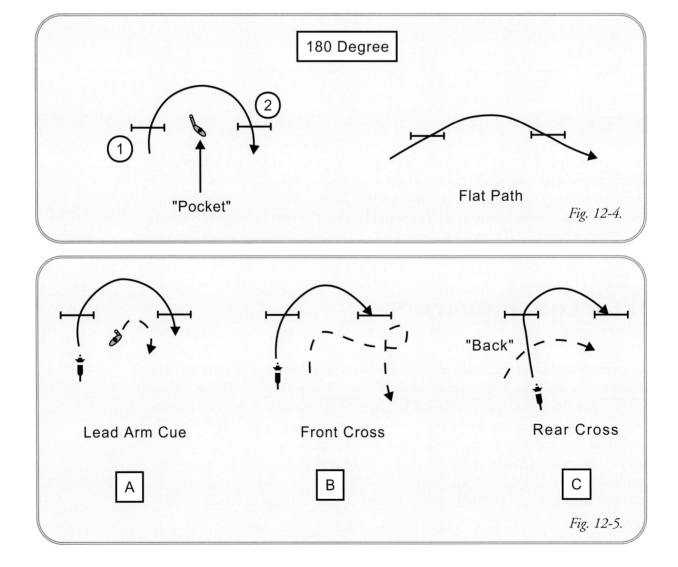

180 Degree

"Pocket"

Flat Path

Fig. 12-4.

Lead Arm Cue

Front Cross

"Back"

Rear Cross

A

B

C

Fig. 12-5.

270-DEGREE TURN

As the name implies, this jump setup involves the dog making a 270-degree arc between two jumps. If you are on the inside of the **270-degree turn**, you must rotate your body toward jump 2 to indicate the jump, and will need an out command to push the dog to the outside of the jump. If the out command is given too late, the dog may cut in and take jump 2 in the wrong direction. It takes some time for a dog to understand and learn to recognize 270s, and you may initially have to step well into the pocket (the area in between the two jumps) to help the dog move to the outside of jump 2. With practice, a dog learns to recognize 270s and you will not need to step as far into the pocket.

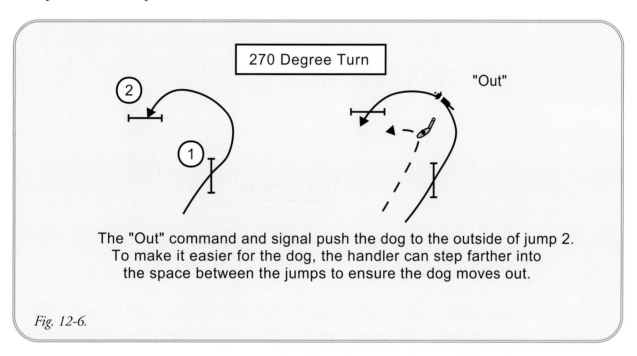

270 Degree Turn

"Out"

The "Out" command and signal push the dog to the outside of jump 2.
To make it easier for the dog, the handler can step farther into
the space between the jumps to ensure the dog moves out.

Fig. 12-6.

PINWHEEL

A **pinwheel** is a set of three or more jumps set in a star shape in which the dog's path is roughly circular. Pinwheels are very common and can be handled in many ways depending on where you want your dog to go afterwards. You can simply pull the dog around the arc, or, if you need to switch sides, you may cross before or after any of the jumps.

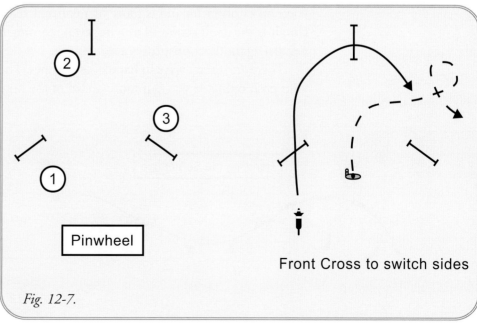

Pinwheel

Front Cross to switch sides

Fig. 12-7.

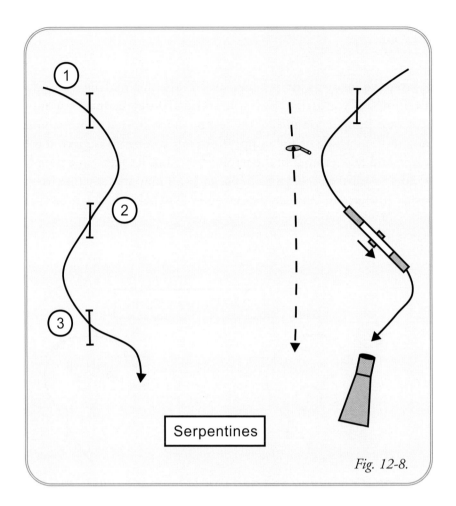

Serpentines

Fig. 12-8.

SERPENTINE

A serpentine most commonly refers to a series of jumps that require the dog to jump back and forth along a line of jumps. The dog jumps away from the handler, then toward the handler, away from the handler, and so forth. A serpentine can involve other obstacles and is more of a concept than simply a configuration of obstacles. It is the dog's action of moving away, coming back, then moving away from the handler again that constitutes a serpentine.

There are several ways to handle serpentines. The commands employed depend on your positioning. If you can move ahead of the dog, use the arm that is closest to the dog and give an out command to move the dog over the jump (Fig. 12-9A) and away from you. To get the dog to come back toward you on the second jump, you must turn toward the dog and signal the jump with the hand that is farthest from the dog. In essence, you are executing an RFP.

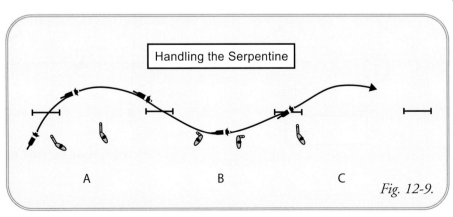

Handling the Serpentine

A   B   C

Fig. 12-9.

This asks for a change of lead. (Fig. 12-9B.) Once the dog is committed to going over the jump, you again turn in the direction in which you were going, and the dog runs at your side as you both continue moving to the next jump. (Fig. 12-9C.)

It is important that you give the dog room to jump and that you do not perform the RFP too soon. If you turn toward the dog too soon, you might pull him toward you before the jump. You must reach the far side of the jump before you can perform the RFP.

Serpentines can also be handled with crosses and side switches. You could, theoretically, perform a front cross in between each jump (Fig. 12-11.) While this works, it requires you to be very mobile and may not be necessary. The decision to cross depends on where you want to end up at the end of the serpentine.

Regardless of the style of handling used, be aware that if you can get your dog to go over the first jump of the serpentine on a flat angle (also called "slicing" a jump), it sets the dog on an efficient line over the next two jumps. If the dog jumps straight over the first jump, he will land farther away from the jump and will be pointed in the wrong direction. He will have no choice but to make a wide loop back to the next jump. See Fig. 12-12.

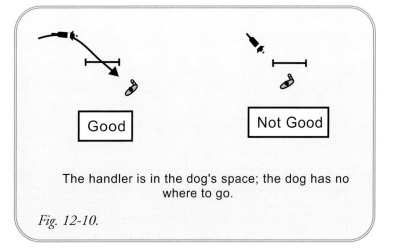

Good   Not Good

The handler is in the dog's space; the dog has no where to go.

Fig. 12-10.

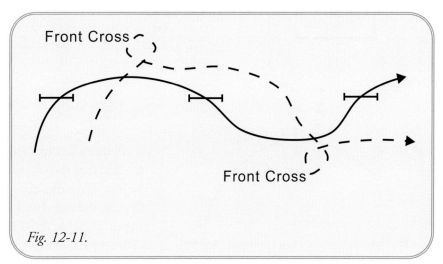

Front Cross

Front Cross

Fig. 12-11.

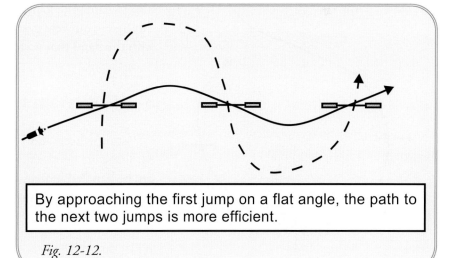

By approaching the first jump on a flat angle, the path to the next two jumps is more efficient.

Fig. 12-12.

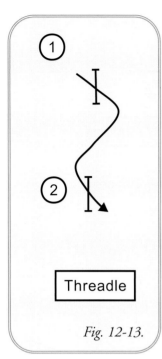

Fig. 12-13.

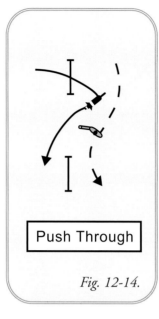

Push Through

Fig. 12-14.

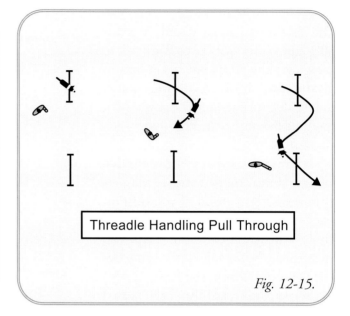

Threadle Handling Pull Through

Fig. 12-15.

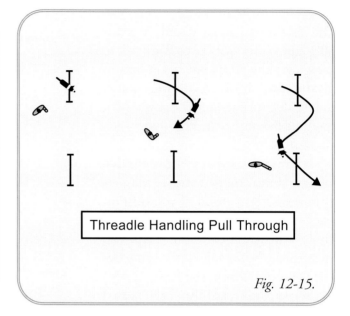

Fig. 12-16.

THREADLE

A threadle involves pulling the dog in between two obstacles so that he takes the second obstacle in the same direction that he took the first. Threadles can be handled either with a push or pull-through. To push the dog through the space between the jumps, you must be slightly ahead of the dog and step into him, commanding "out." Fig 12-14. To pull the dog through the threadle, you must again be slightly ahead of the dog's path. Turn toward the dog with an RFP to pull him toward you. Once you are through the space, turn back in the direction you were going and direct the dog over the second jump with the hand that is closest to the dog. (Fig. 12-15).

S-CURVE AND FIGURE 8

Put pinwheels and 180s together and you get S-curves and figure 8s. These are good sequences to set up to practice turns and arcs and can be handled in many different ways. Experiment with front crosses and rear crosses at various points along the sequence. (Fig. 12-16).

BOXES

A jump box and extended box is a setup of jumps that forms— you guessed it—a box! Boxes are great, as they incorporate 180s, 270s, threadles, and curves all into one setup. You can use them to practice various exercises and handling maneuvers (e.g., crosses and lead outs). Make sure that you

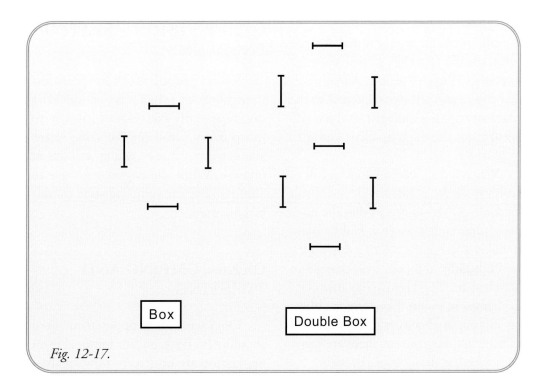

Fig. 12-17.

do not set up the boxes too tightly; give your dog enough room to move and jump. The combinations that can be made from boxes and extended boxes are endless. Get creative and be sure to work with the dog on both sides.

JUMPING PROBLEMS

All dogs will at some point knock a bar; this is not a jumping problem but rather a learning stage. In order to have a jumping problem, you must first have a dog that has been trained to jump. There are usually early warning signs of true jumping problems. These include any change in fluid movement before a jump, strange head ducking, unnecessary angled approaches to a jump, over-jumping, or twisting of the dog's rear legs in the air.

STUTTER-STEPPING

Stutter-stepping refers to short, choppy, foot movement in front of a jump that delays a dog's takeoff. It is extra movement that indicates a hesitation to jump. This jumping problem may be structural, a vision difficulty, or fear of jumping.

If a vision problem is to blame, the dog's view of the jump may become blurred as he approaches the obstacle. With age, the lens of the eye tends to harden, making it difficult for it to change shape and focus on closer objects. As a result, many people older than forty require reading glasses or bifocals to correct the blurry vision they experience when trying to read up close. I believe that this lack of accommodation (called prespiopia) happens to dogs as well.

The jump appears unclear to the dog as he draws near, causing him to hesitate and stutter-step. This has not been scientifically proven, as we cannot ask a dog to read an eye chart, yet it makes sense based on the fact that canine eyes age similarly to those of people. Anatomically, a dog's eyes can appear normal to the veterinary ophthalmologist, and it is still possible for the dog's up-close vision to be blurry.

When a dog receives a clean bill of health from the eye doctor, it is difficult for some owners to accept that the dog's poor jumping is a result of faulty vision. It makes sense to me that if a dog is otherwise healthy and pain free, changes in jumping as a dog ages can be attributed to changes in vision. Knowing the number of people who wear glasses, it is not difficult to imagine that there are many dogs with less-than-perfect eyesight.

Stutter-stepping can be present in young dogs as well. You need to determine if the dog is dealing with a physical or emotional jumping issue. A sensitive dog who has hit a jump may become tense and show hesitation upon takeoff. Lowering jumps and retraining often fix this problem. This is also a good time to go back to working with a jump grid to help the dog regain confidence.

If this does not help, consider that the problem could be visual, even in a dog with anatomically normal eyes. While grid work may appear to initially fix stutter-stepping in a visually impaired dog, this is only because dogs can memorize the number of strides between the jumps. When the dog is faced with a new and unpredictable course, the stutter-stepping returns.

Dogs are very good at compensating for physical disabilities. Time and patience usually will allow a determined dog to figure out how to jump even with distorted vision. These dogs may never do well in bright sunlight and will not be smooth and easy jumpers, but they can still get around a course.

OTHER VISION-RELATED PROBLEMS

Vision problems can manifest themselves in other ways as well. If a dog repeatedly goes out of his way to jump every jump on the same sharp angle, he may not be seeing well out of one eye. While the dog may be able to compensate, the jumping style cannot be corrected.

OVER-JUMPING AND TWISTING

Dogs with short upper arms, poor shoulder lay back, and/or minimal front angulation are limited to how far their front legs will reach. When a dog cannot raise his front legs up very high, he must compensate by pushing off very strongly from the rear and lifting his entire body higher to get over the jump. In this situation, the dog appears to be clearing the bar by a large margin. This is not indicative of a good, efficient jumper. The dog is spending too much time in the air and is working very hard to get there.

Many squarely built dogs, including terriers, standard poodles, afghan hounds, and other square breeds, or any dog lacking reach (due to a short upper arm), may over-jump in this way. Because the problem is rooted in structure, not much can be done to change the dog's jumping style. While it may not be ideal, it is the only way in which these particular dogs can jump. Some dogs learn to compensate by pulling their front legs up close to their chest instead of trying to extend them. To date, I have not figured out a way to teach a dog to do this unless he discovers it on his own. I do believe that giving the dog experience running in fields with very high weeds or grass (as high as the dog is) encourages pulling up the front legs and can be useful in getting the dog to think about the pull-up action. I have seen it transfer over to jumping, and it doesn't hurt to try.

Another sign of a jumping problem is when a dog's rear end twists as he jumps. This is a compensatory behavior for the dog that does not jump high enough and whose only way to get his rear over the bar is to twist. Twisting should be interpreted as a warning sign that the dog is not capable of jumping this high. The dog might lack conditioning and strength, in which case you should lower the jumps and continue working. As time goes on, test the dog over higher jumps to see if he is getting comfortable. If you are dealing with an older dog that does not seem to improve, his days of jumping full height may be over.

AN EXPERIENCED EYE

I once had a student come to me with a highly driven Belgian Tervuren that was knocking bars all over the ring and in practice. She had been told by different people that the dog had a vision problem, but she wanted another opinion. The woman had worked very hard for more than a year with this adult dog and now felt helpless.

I set up a simple jump sequence and asked her to run the dog as she usually did. The dog knocked down every single jump because he was taking off in all the wrong places. He seemed to really enjoy doing agility and was not upset that the bars had come down. I asked her what she had tried to fix this

problem, to which she replied, "Everything!" She had tried jump grids, ground poles, and even correcting the dog for knocking a bar by making him lie down on the ground. She said that she tried to make him feel bad for "breaking the jump" when he knocked a bar, but nothing had helped much at all. The interesting thing was that the dog showed none of the signs of a dog with a vision problem. There was no stutter-stepping, no preference for angles, and no hesitation.

It did not take me long to discover the source of this dog's jumping problem. He never took his eyes off of his handler and, as a result, never looked at the jumps. This kind of "handler focus" is often caused by handlers carrying food rewards in their hands. They encourage the dog to check in with them by continuously rewarding from their hand after every few obstacles.

I assured the student that her dog could see and that this was fixable. We began by working with a food tube (something she had never done) and lower jumps to teach the dog to send and look ahead toward the food tube. Next we progressed to a run-by with a target to keep the dog's eyes focused forward and on the jumps. By the end of the first lesson, his jumping had improved tremendously. We quickly raised the jumps back up to full height, still targeting forward to keep the dog's focus ahead and toward the jumps, not on the handler. After a few lessons, no one would ever have known that this dog had been a bar knocker. It is extremely important that when you run into a training problem, you seek the help of someone who has a lot of experience and is good at analyzing what a dog is doing, even if it happens very quickly.

Work Hard on Jumping Skills

- Since jumping is such an integral part of agility, it is important for every dog to develop good jumping skills.

- Handlers should encourage dogs to jump over many different kinds of jumps and allow puppies to hop over logs and low jumps and explore uneven ground as a way to develop body awareness.

- Correcting a dog for knocking down a bar does not teach jumping.

- Handlers can help dogs learn to negotiate different jumping situations with the use of ground poles and jump grids.

- Both a dog's structure and attitude play a part in the final outcome of the dog's ability to jump. While structure cannot be changed, good trainers can enhance their dog's jumping attitude, strength, and skill.

References

Zink, Christine, and Daniels, Julie (1996). *Jumping from A to Z.* Canine Sports Productions, Lutherville, MD, p. 75.

Perfect form over the double jump. Only one hind leg is visable because the dog has started the turn before taking off for the jump.

Jumping close to the stanchion.

Photo by M Nicole Fischer.

CHAPTER 13

THE TIRE

The tire is a unique jump obstacle. Teaching a
dog to jump through a tire is a lot like teaching him to jump through a hoop. Dogs
that dislike small spaces may initially find jumping through a tire uncomfortable.

Not all tires look alike. Some are made of wooden frames and others of PVC
pipe. The obstacle can have long support boards sticking out at the base. Some tires
are very big and bulky. Many tires are very colorful, while others are simply striped.
All tires are adjustable in height but can be attached to hang from their frames in
different ways. The opening of the tire itself ranges in size depending on the organization sanctioning the equipment. In AKC, the tire opening has a diameter of
twenty-four inches, while in USDAA, the diameter of the opening ranges from
seventeen to twenty inches. For these reasons, it is important that you train and
accustom your agility dog to many different tires so that he learns to recognize the
obstacle on the course.

The tire always frames the next obstacle. Because it acts like a window opening
or camera lens, it funnels the dog's attention to the obstacle directly in the dog's
line of vision. In advanced-level courses, what the dog sees through the tire is rarely
the next correct obstacle in sequence. You must pay close attention to what the tire
frames when planning your handling strategy.

It is common to find the tire as the first or last obstacle on a course. Because the nature of the obstacle obstructs the dog's view, it is good to practice many call-tos through the tire, especially in situations where you are not directly in view through the opening. When a course ends with the tire and electronic timers are used, the timer stanchions may look strange to a dog that is not used to seeing them placed next to the tire.

Dogs need to learn to approach the tire from all different angles and be able to straighten their takeoff enough to jump through the opening. They must learn to look for the opening of the tire and not run next to it or underneath it.

The best part about the tire is that is it difficult to knock down—not impossible, but this rarely happens. However, due to the tire's "rigid" nature, dogs that do not learn to safely jump through it run the risk of injury. For this reason, some agility organizations have adopted the displaceable tire—one that can be knocked down if it is touched by the dog.

The tire funnels the dog's attention.

TEACHING THE TIRE

Adjust the tire low enough so that the dog would have a difficult time running underneath it. Begin in call-to format and call the dog to you through the tire opening. If your dog does not know a sit-stay, have an assistant hold the dog as you move to the other side of the obstacle. Command "okay, tire" and use an overhanded motion, ending with your hand (which should be holding a motivator) pointing to the middle of the tire. Because the tire is framing you and a dog is usually motivated to get to his handler, the dog should come through the tire. If he is reluctant to jump through the tire, reach your hand with the motivator through the tire and lure the dog to you.

SEND

When the dog will perform a call-to through the tire, progress to working on a send. Position the dog at your side, but make sure that he is also lined up in front of the tire. With a toy or food tube in the hand that is closest to the dog, give a send signal and slowly toss the motivator through the tire. The dog should follow the motivator and jump through the tire. Give the verbal commands "okay, tire" as you throw the motivator.

What If?

• **What if the dog goes around or under the opening?**

Lower the tire so that it is impossible for your dog to go underneath it. Move the dog up very close to the tire opening. Hold on to the dog's collar with the hand that is farthest from the dog. Give a send signal with the hand that is closest to the dog as you toss a motivator through the hoop. As the dog gets up and moves through the tire, release his collar and praise him. If the dog attempts to go around the tire, simply hold onto the collar and do not allow him to go right, left, or backwards. He will eventually make the choice to go forward and through the tire (power of time!).

As soon as the dog is comfortably passing through the tire, start to raise the tire to full height so that your dog is now jumping through it, not stepping through it.

Run-By

Teaching your dog to do the tire as a run-by is truly a test of the dog's understanding of the obstacle. If a dog has not learned to look for the opening of the tire, he will go around it as you attempt a run-by.

To start teaching a run-by, place a motivator as a target on the landing side of the tire. Make sure that the dog is close enough to see it through the opening. Begin with the dog on a stay, and position yourself parallel to the dog but far enough away so that you can run in a straight line.

With a run-by signal, command "okay, tire" and run forward. The dog should get up and run through the tire. If he does not, start him closer and stand next to the tire as you give the command.

ANGLES

Once the dog can perform the tire in all four ways, it is time to teach him to jump through the tire from different angles. Start teaching angles in the call-to format. Gradually increase the difficulty of the angle as you ask the dog to jump.

SEQUENCING

When the dog can jump the tire from any angle, begin to build sequences using the tire. Some of the

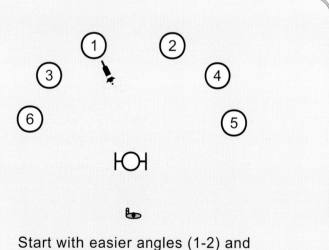

Start with easier angles (1-2) and progressively work to more extreme angles. Always use the hand closest to the dog to give the Call-To signal.

Fig. 13-1.

Looking through the tire, the twelve weave poles appear as one pole.

more difficult sequences are: the tire to the weave poles, the chute to the tire, and the tire followed by a sharp turn to another jump. When the tire is placed directly in front of the poles, the entrance to the weave poles is more difficult for a dog to find, because he must jump straight through the tire and can only see one pole. As a dog exits a chute, he is momentarily disoriented. The dog must work harder to negotiate his body through a tire as compared to clearing a bar jump; therefore, the sequencing of these obstacles requires practice. Finally, because the dog must jump straight through the tire, it is more difficult to make a sharp turn immediately after the obstacle. Practice sharp turns off of the tire in both the run-by and call-to formats.

Always pay attention to where the judge has placed the tire in a course. Usually a lot of thought goes into where the judge wants to use a tire. See if you can tell what challenge the judge is attempting to create.

Practice tires are easy to build. Purchase a piece of flexible drain pipe and form it into a circle. Then find a way to hang it in a doorway or position it in a PVC frame. This will get your dog familiar with jumping through a circle.

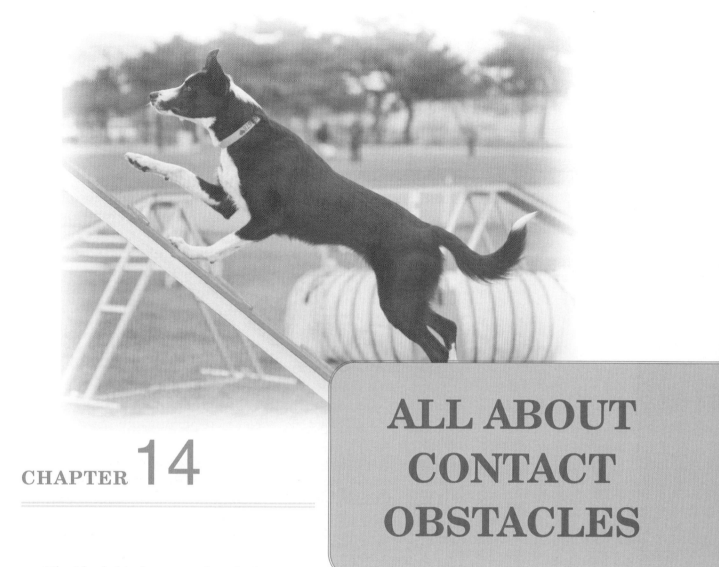

CHAPTER 14

ALL ABOUT CONTACT OBSTACLES

The idea behind contact obstacles is to simulate a dog climbing a rock, running up and down a steep hill, and walking across a log or other natural obstacle. In agility, the term contact obstacle is used to refer to the seesaw, the A-frame, and the dog walk. These are all obstacles that the dog should run across while making contact with a specific part of the equipment. This area, located at the end of a ramp, is called the "contact zone," the "safety zone," or just "contact" for short. It is painted in a contrasting color, usually yellow. Contact zones are located on both the ascent ramp ("up" contacts) and the descent ramp ("down" contacts). The size of the contact zone, the obstacle specifications, and the performance criteria vary depending on the organization sanctioning the equipment and event. For example, at this writing, the dog walk down contact in AKC events is forty-two inches long, while in USDAA they are thirty-two inches long. NADAC has no slats on any of its equipment while other organizations do, and the height of the A-frame varies from venue to venue. As the sport grows, rules change, and it becomes important for you to stay abreast of current rules. The equipment specifications of a certain venue can also play a part in your decision on how to train your dog to perform contact obstacles.

WHY CONTACTS?

Supposedly, the purpose of contact zones is "safety"—requiring the dog to touch the lower part of the boards prevents them from leaping off of the elevated planks. The reality, however, is that large dogs (and smaller ones, too) traveling at top speeds have the impulse to pull up (i.e., jump) off of the ramps before they reach the contact zone to avoid the feeling of plowing straight into the ground. This is more pronounced on the A-frame than on the dog walk or seesaw. In my opinion, it is actually unnatural for a dog to want to run that far down the ramp toward the ground. Think of it this way: Imagine an airplane diving at a sharp angle toward the ground. If the pilot waits too long before pulling up, the airplane will impact the ground. A dog's heavy body, moving at high speed down the angle of the A-frame, is affected by the same law of physics. The dog's natural tendency is to pull up, often earlier or at the very top of the contact zone, to keep from feeling like he is crashing into the ground.

A small dog, with a lower center of gravity, develops less momentum and therefore can pull up later, well into the contact zone, without feeling as though he is going to crash into the ground. This is not to say that small dogs will not miss contacts; they are just more likely to hit them because of their smaller size and stride.

Nevertheless, the rules require that every dog touch the contact zone, and it is your job to train a behavior that will allow your dog to meet this performance criterion.

THE OBSTACLE AND THE CONTACT BEHAVIOR

To ensure that a dog hits the contact zone, he will need to be taught a "contact behavior." This is a specific behavior that you teach and require your dog to do on contact obstacles. Its purpose is to guarantee that the dog will hit the yellow zone with at least one paw.

For the dog walk and A-frame, teaching the contact behavior and teaching the actual contact obstacle are not the same things. While the contact behavior is a major part of the obstacle's complete performance, the dog must still learn to negotiate the rest of the obstacle. Just because a dog has been taught to stop at the end of a dog-walk descent ramp (one contact behavior method), he must still be taught to run the length of the planks at top speed until he reaches the end.

Contact-obstacle training includes teaching the "contact behavior" and teaching the dog to "run" the obstacle—what I like calling the "discovery phase." Several components are involved in teaching contact behaviors, but first and foremost, you must decide which behavior and method you are going to use.

Once you have decided this, you can initially teach the contact behavior away from the equipment, then later introduce it on the contact obstacles themselves. The discovery phase involves letting the dog learn and become comfortable with the concept of "run up and over the board as fast as you can." Even if the dog is going to be taught a stopped contact behavior, you want to encourage your dog to run before you ask him to stop or make stride adjustments.

Where a dog touches the contact depends on size and structure.

You can always slow a dog down, but it is very difficult to speed him back up once he has learned to slow down. Teaching the contact behavior and the "discovery phase" should occur at the same time; the dog can start learning the contact behavior while he learns to run the equipment. Once the dog is proficient with the contact behavior and is confidently running the lengths of the dog walk or climbing the A-frame, the two parts are combined.

This approach not only encourages speed on the obstacle but also gives you the time to study and evaluate what your dog is capable of doing. This information will help you decide what contact behavior to teach your dog. Because most dogs find touching contacts an unnatural task, they are easily stressed when learning contacts. Add to this pressure handlers tend to place on contacts, and it is easy to see why some dogs slow down and want to avoid them in general.

Learning is stressful, but to minimize the stress of contacts in the beginning, I recommend training the contact behavior of choice away from the equipment. For example, if your goal is to have the dog touch a certain spot on the contact zone with his feet while moving, teach him to touch a target away from the equipment before ever moving the target onto the equipment.

If you decide to have the dog stop in a "two-on, two-off" position at the end of the dog walk, teach him how to assume and hold the position separately from teaching him to run the full dog walk. These methods and exercises are explained in the pages to come but are mentioned here to explain why the contact behavior is first taught separate from the obstacle.

One of the biggest mistakes made while training your dog on contacts is putting too much pressure on him. A dog cannot learn it all at once. Separat-

NOTE:

The seesaw is taught differently from the dog walk and the A-frame. While it is true that the seesaw has contact zones and will necessitate a contact behavior, the fact that the dog must wait for the board to pivot and hit the ground before he can continue makes a difference in training. The dog cannot simply "run" the length of the board, as he is likely to fly right off of the end. Seesaw training is not separated into two parts; the dog will learn the contact behavior at the same time he learns to negotiate the obstacle.

ing the two parts alleviates pressure by allowing the dog to run and become comfortable on the equipment, while the contact behavior is perfected away from the obstacle.

TOUCHING THE CONTACT

The rules only require that the dog touch the contact with at least one foot. In fact, one toenail would suffice, assuming the judge can see it. The goal, however, is to not make the judge work very hard but to train the dog to clearly, reliably, and efficiently touch the contact zone. There are no bonus points for how close to the end of the equipment the dog touches the contact, nor does it matter if the contact is touched with the front or the back feet; it just has to be touched.

The reality is that each dog should be taught to touch the contact zone in a manner that is physically comfortable and as natural as possible for him. The only way to find this out is to allow your dog the opportunity to run and become comfortable on the contact obstacles without stressing him about stopping or touching a specific spot. Observe your dog's natural movement, then determine a realistic spot on the contact that you will later *teach* the dog to touch.

If you insist that a dog touch a spot that is physically very difficult for him to reach, he will become frustrated and stressed, and he will slow down, bail off, or maybe even stop above the contact and refuse to come down! These are warning signs for you to re-evaluate where the dog is being asked to touch.

Even touching with one foot counts! I mean one toenail!

You may like to see your dog touch contacts well into the yellow zone. This is understandable, because it is easier for you to judge if the dog is correct and makes you feel safer and less nervous. The problem is that the "first slat from the bottom" may not be the best choice for your dog.

If you watch a large dog with a big stride perform a "two-on, two-off" (a popular contact-behavior method), often the only part of his body that will be in the contact are the back feet, and those feet are high up in the zone. No one worries about this because if the dog has stopped at the bottom of the contact, there is no doubt that the dog has hit the contact. Yet a dog with a running contact that may hit the same point with his two back feet often causes concern.

Suppose he gets too high the next time and misses it? Experience has shown that if a dog is comfortable performing a running contact and consistently hits the contact the same way—six inches or so below the beginning of the yellow—chances are very good that the performance will not vary enough to incur a missed contact. If the dog comfortably hits the contact only two inches below the beginning of the yellow, you may want to teach him to touch lower, rather than risk a judge not seeing the touch. The important thing is to assess your own dog and figure out what is most feasible and efficient for him when it comes to contact performance.

TYPES OF CONTACTS

Teaching your dog to touch a contact can be accomplished in a variety of ways. All contact methods attempt to teach the dog to touch the zone either with his feet, his nose, or his body. The assumption is that if he touches the zone with his nose or body, one or more of his feet will also be touching the contact. There are three basic types of contact performances: the running contact, the moving contact, and the stopped contact.

A **running contact** is when a dog runs (canters or gallops) over the entire obstacle and continues through the contact zone without ever breaking stride.

A **moving contact** is when a dog runs over the obstacle until he reaches the contact zone, where he adjusts his stride to deliberately touch the contact with his paws as he continues moving past the obstacle.

A **stopped contact** is when the dog runs the obstacle all the way to the end and comes to a complete stop, waiting for a release command. Some dogs are taught to lie down or sit at the bottom of the contact, while others are required to stand with their front feet on the ground and their hind feed on the board. This is commonly referred to as **"two-on, two-off" (2o2o)** position.

WHICH TYPE OF CONTACT TO TEACH?

It is very important that you give serious thought to which contact method you will teach your dog *before* the training begins. It is confusing to a dog to be taught one method and then have you change your mind and teach another method. Many dogs have had to survive the "smorgasbord method" of contact training because their trainer changed methods every time the dog started making errors in the ring.

This is not to say that you must train the same contact technique for each piece of equipment. For example, a stopped contact can be used on the seesaw (in fact, I strongly recommend it) and a moving contact on the A-frame and dog walk. Many factors must be taken into consideration before you decide which type of contact behavior to teach your dog.

SIZE, STRIDE, AND STRUCTURE

Structure affects the amount of reach a dog has in his front legs. This, in turn, influences the length of his stride and how easily he will or will not hit a contact. Short-legged dogs and very small dogs will have an easier time hitting contacts because the contact zone is bigger in relationship to their body. They usually have a shorter stride that is more likely to land them in the contact, therefore making them good candidates for running contacts.

Small and short-legged dogs also have a lower center of gravity, making it easier for them to balance on a descent ramp. When dogs feel balanced coming down a ramp, they are less likely to bail off of it.

In contrast, tall and leggy dogs with straight fronts and angulated rears (such as Dobermans, Belgian Sheepdogs, Tervurens, Afghan Hounds, Standard Poodles, and Irish Setters) have a very long stride and less balance and may do better with a stopped or moving contact. Dogs with good **shoulder lay back** crouch and lie down more easily than dogs with straight shoulders. This makes them good candidates for a training method that uses a down position.

The dog's bone mass should also be a factor in your contact behavior decision. Heavier-boned dogs have a harder time stopping on an incline than lighter-boned dogs.

ACCESS TO EQUIPMENT

While it is true that any dog will benefit from frequent access to agility equipment, certain methods of teaching contacts require more intensive repetition and therefore more regular access to equipment. If you can get to contact equipment only once a week for practice, a stopped contact might be the best option. This is because a stopped contact can be simulated on a staircase, a **contact trainer,** or any slanted board. Asking a dog to stop on a contact is very clear for both you and your dog, making it easier to teach.

Because running and moving contacts depend heavily on timing and repetition, frequent access to equipment is important. Furthermore, running or moving contacts require that you be able to direct your dog off of the contact to the next obstacle without being there and does not allow you time to catch up. To master these skills requires even more training time on equipment.

HANDLER GOALS AND ABILITY

There are advantages and disadvantages to each contact method. A running or moving contact allows the dog to execute the equipment and the distance to the next obstacle faster than a stopped contact. The running and moving contact, however, is variable, and dogs will often miss contacts in initial training. If you are highly competitive and willing to invest the extensive time and effort required, consider teaching a running or moving contact to reach your goals. If you are more concerned with initial accuracy and overall **qualifying** rates, you might opt to teach a stopped contact.

Also take into account your own physical ability when you choose a contact method. If you feel the need to catch up to your dogs on the course, a stopped contact will do the trick.

If you decide to teach a running or moving contact, you will need help from a training partner from time to time. One of the problems with teaching a running contact is that when you are moving, it's difficult—and at times impossible—to be in a position to see if the dog hits the contact. To train consistently, you must know if your dog performed the contact behavior correctly. If you cannot find a second pair of eyes, you might want to consider a stopped contact.

THE DOG'S PERSONALITY

Some very high-drive Border Collies and light-boned Labradors, for example, are so excited when doing agility that they are inclined to run as fast as they can even if they know they have to stop at the end of the board. These dogs are good candidates for a stopped contact. Other, more sensitive, thinking dogs, if taught a stopped contact, will slow down their contact performance immeasurably, because they see no point in running fast if they are going to have to stop at the end. The dog's temperament always plays an important part in determining what kind of contact behavior to teach.

GOALS FOR CONTACTS

Your goal should be to train your dog to have fast, efficient, accurate, and independent contacts. Agility is a game of speed; therefore, the dog should perform contact obstacles as fast as possible. All dogs are capable of running the length of the dog-walk ramp, quickly climbing and descending the A-frame, and tipping the seesaw board. They simply have to do it in a manner that is comfortable for them. If a dog is physically uncomfortable or stressed by the contact behavior he is required to do, he will not do it quickly, often because he physically cannot. Your goal is to find a way for your dog to comfortably perform the obstacle so that he consistently hits the yellow zone.

Independent obstacle performance is extremely important. Contact obstacles provide you with good opportunities on the course to move into strategic handling positions, provided you do not have to accompany your dog all the way to the contact zone. All agility courses are different, and you cannot count on being next to your dog for each contact obstacle. The dog must be taught how to ascend and touch the contact zone of the obstacle on his own and when you are in different positions. Independent performance is achieved through practice and training.

Sometimes you will be behind the dog, sometimes in front of the obstacle, and sometimes off to one side. It is important that you try to simulate all different positions around the contact so that the dog understands how to do the correct contact behavior regardless of where you are positioned. You need to practice while standing still and while moving as the dog reaches the contact point, for your motion will vary depending on the design of the course.

MISTAKES AND CORRECTIONS

Every new dog will make mistakes when transitioning from the training field to the trial ring. It is important that you plan how to deal with these mistakes in the ring and be prepared to respond appropriately. In order to maintain consistent, good contact performance, you must be willing to insist on the same contact criteria in the ring as you do out of the ring. While it is true that you may not correct your dog in the ring, you can let him know that he has made a mistake and respond appropriately.

It is common for dogs to have beautiful contacts in practice but miss them at trials. Dogs that have learned to do contacts make mistakes in the ring for various reasons. Sometimes the dog misses the contact because he is running faster than he ever was in practice. Now, the dog no longer knows how to perform his trained contact behavior with this newly discovered speed.

Some dogs are so excited by the atmosphere of an agility trial that they "forget" about doing contacts, because they are focusing on the next obstacle of the course.

You, too, may cause your dog to miss a contact by being overly cautious, standing too close, making direct eye contact, or giving a loud and panicky command just before the dog is expected to think about touching the contact. If your dog is looking directly at you, he is off balance and not looking at the contact. This tendency to stay close to the dog is called "babysitting" and is usually brought on by handler nerves. Be sure that you do not "babysit" the contacts in practice, as this will certainly lead to problems at the trial. Good contact performance requires a dog to drive down the obstacle with his head down and positioned straight forward.

When your dog misses contacts in the ring, your first thought should be to analyze the reason for the mistake. Try to re-create the mistake in practice and work through the problem with your chosen method, not by changing to another method. Changing approaches just causes more confusion. While dogs recognize the difference between the competition ring and practice, there is no mistake that cannot be recreated—you just have to be inventive.

CAUSE THE MISTAKE

In order to fix a mistake, you must first get the dog to make it. Training with other dogs and handlers will sometimes get dogs as excited as they are in a trial, which makes this a good way to cause the mistake in practice. In this way, you can help your dog understand his error. Another way to simulate the speed of a dog in the ring is to put a strong motivator (toy or food) on the ground about six feet off of the contact. This will tempt the dog to forget about the contact in a rush to get to the motivator, thereby tempting him to miss the contact. It is necessary to get the dog to make the mistake in practice if you are going to be able to change his behavior at a trial.

Once a mistake occurs in practice, be sure that both you and your dog understand the correction for a missed contact. The correction should be incorporated into the teaching of the contact. The dog must understand what will happen if he does not make the effort to meet the contact criteria. Deciding on your correction, whether it be placing the dog back on the contact in the correct position, lying the dog down on the contact, or rerunning the obstacle, is a key element to the training process, as you want to be fair and consistent.

Remember—a dog should only be corrected if his mistake is due to distraction or choice. There is no correction in the teaching phase—only help. If a mistake happens and help is warranted, simply abort and try again. You may need to make the exercise easier (less speed, less distraction) if the dog is having repeated problems. Once the dog has been taught the contact behavior, what you do for correction depends on which contact behavior you are training. These are discussed later in their respective chapters.

MAINTENANCE

All contacts, even after being taught, must be maintained through regular practice and training, regardless of the technique chosen. Like any other obstacles, contacts are performed in all four ways (call-to, send, run-by right, and run-by left). Maintenance takes different forms depending on the type of contact. When you pull your dog sharply off of a contact to the next obstacle, a running or moving contact wears down. You will need to balance sharp pull offs with exercises that will make the dog go straight and farther down the contact. If you prematurely release a dog off of a stopped contact, the stop quickly disintegrates. To preserve a reliable stop, you must consistently enforce it. Regular maintenance and practices should be part of the training program. More complete maintenance techniques for each type of contact are discussed in the appropriate chapters.

BE CONSISTENT AND PERSISTENT

- Teaching contacts can be a little tricky in that you have to decide what method best suits your dog and your goals. Once you have decided on what you are going to teach, stick with it and be consistent.

- Use a method that is clearly understood by you, your dog, and your instructor.

- Know ahead of time how you will react in practice to a missed contact and how you should react in the ring if the dog does not meet the expected contact criteria. Try not to put too much mental pressure on contacts; treat them as you would any other agility mistake, such as missing an obstacle (refusal) or a dropped bar.

- Remember that all contact methods require maintenance, just as jumping skills do!

A dog looking at a contact. Photo by M. Nicole Fischer.

15

UP CONTACTS

Contact safety zones are also located on the up ramp of all three contact obstacles. Whether they are judged depends on the rules of the particular venue. NADAC rules do not require the dogs to touch the up contact. AKC only judges them on the seesaw and dog walk, while USDAA judges all three.

For many dogs, hitting up contacts is not an issue, as their stride does not allow them to miss the up contact. However, some dogs have long strides that carry them right over the up contact. Then there are dogs that jump up onto the boards and end up missing the up contact as well. Up contacts can be a frustrating problem if you have to deal with them.

HITTING UP CONTACTS

Many up contacts are missed because of poor approaches to the obstacle. If the dog ascends the dog walk or seesaw from the side, he is likely to miss the up contact. Teaching the dog how to approach the obstacle straight from all different angles will help this problem. (See Chapter 20, page 174 for how to teach angled approaches.)

If the missed up contact is not due to an angled approach, you will need to teach the dog to adjust his stride (much like adjusting his stride to hit a down contact) before mounting the obstacle.

USING A LIE DOWN

One way to solve this problem is to teach the dog not to jump by teaching him to keep his head and center of gravity low as he approaches the obstacles. Initially, the dog will be required to actually go all the way into a down position before being released and allowed to mount the obstacle. Because stopping and lying down in front of the obstacle is less than efficient—in fact, it constitutes a refusal—the full down position will not be required indefinitely. After a few sessions, you will fade the down away simply by not enforcing it. Because he has been lying down, the dog will likely shorten his stride while thinking about lying down. Maintenance involves asking for a full down if the dog reverts to jumping, or giving the lie-down command as a reminder to the dog to lower his center of gravity.

It is helpful to precede the dog-walk command with a lie-down command to help the dog with obstacle discriminations. If a dog is approaching a dog walk and tunnel discrimination and you command "lie down" before giving the dog-walk command, the dog already knows that he should look for a contact obstacle. Down is an enforceable command. "Lie -down" becomes a suggestion to the dog to lower his center of gravity but not necessarily drop into a prone position.

USING THE WHOA COMMAND

If a dog has difficulty getting into a down position (tall dogs or dogs with little or poor angulation in their front structure), a lie down is not the best approach to teaching up contacts. For this dog, teach the whoa command to break the dog's stride just before he ascends the obstacle. (To teach the whoa command, see Chapter 7, *Commands You Need*, page 37.)

USING A TOUCH BOARD

Up contacts can also be taught with the use of a touch board or target. Place a touch board on the ground before the contact. When the dog touches the board, it will cause him to break stride and hit the up contact. (To understand how to teach a dog to touch a board, see Chapter 17, *The Touch Method*, page 143.)

A perfect approach to an up contact.

CHAPTER 16

THE CONTACT BEHAVIOR

The contact behavior refers to the specific behavior taught to a dog to ensure that he touches the yellow safety contact zone on the dog walk, the A-frame, and the seesaw. I recognize three types of contact behaviors: the running, moving, and stopped. There are several components to teaching each type of contact behavior, and while some of them apply to more than one method, others are very unique.

In this chapter, I have outlined the advantages and disadvantages of each contact behavior. How to teach each contact obstacle and incorporate the specific contact behavior are discussed in the chapter about each specific obstacle.

THE RUNNING CONTACT

A running contact is a contact behavior in which a dog runs the entire length of an obstacle's boards while moving through the contact zone without ever breaking stride. Running contacts are very dependent on the dog's structure. Some dogs are simply not capable of running full speed up and down the A-frame without jumping or breaking stride to hit the yellow zone. Often, a dog's natural and comfortable stride on the dog walk is such that he strides right over the down contact. This dog will never have true running contacts; he can be encouraged not to jump or go farther down the boards through the use of hoops or motivators, but these aids are only artificially creating the running-contact behavior, which usually disappears when the aids are removed.

Whenever you interfere with the dog's stride and what he does naturally on the contact, it is no longer a true running contact. In other words, running contacts either are, or they are not. Teaching the dog to adjust his stride in order to hit the yellow is my definition of a moving contact.

Observation has taught me that, on the A-frame, a dog that jumps the apex is more likely to land such that he strides naturally into the contact. Jumping the top of the obstacle can be encouraged, but there is no guarantee that a dog will continue to jump, nor does jumping guarantee that the dog will touch the contact.

Little dogs are much more inclined to have running contacts on the A-frame. Their size and short stride allow them to come down the ramp farther so that even if they leap off, they have touched the yellow zone. I advise handlers of small dogs to let their dogs simply run the A-frame and not interfere. Only if the small dog consistently misses the contact should you consider adding a deliberate contact behavior.

It is during the "letting the dog run the equipment" stage, or "discovery phase" as I call it, that you should be able to tell if your dog will be capable of doing a running contact or if adjustments will be required.

HOOPS

Hoops are free standing, U-shaped devices that can be positioned at the end of a dog walk or an A-frame ramp. The idea is to have the dog descend the ramp and pass under the hoop. This encourages the dog to keep his head low and helps prevent him from jumping up and off of the boards. The dog is first taught to go under the hoop away from the equipment before the hoop is placed at the end of the board.

Hoops are props that artificially create the desired behavior, but they *do not teach contacts*. Shortly after the hoops are removed, the dog will most likely raise his head and jump off the end of the board. While the hoops help the dog to figure out how to physically achieve the desired behavior (run down the board with his head low), they do not instill the behavior. The idea that the presence of a hoop and muscle memory will condition the dog to always keep his head low is inaccurate. This is proven by the fact that when you remove a bar from between a jump's standards, the dog does not jump. Dogs jump over bars between standards countless times, but this does not condition a dog to jump when there is no bar. The instant the bar is removed, the dog sees no reason to jump. The same is true for the hoop. While it is a useful tool to help a dog discover how to move his body and run with his head low, it does not teach him to offer this behavior in the absence of the hoop.

Advantages

A true running contact is the fastest way a dog can perform a contact obstacle. It also puts the least amount of stress on a dog's body, as it does not include an abrupt stop or require a dog to assume any unnatural position. This is most pronounced on the A-frame.

Disadvantages

The running contact is very dependent on the dog's size and structure. Not every dog can do it. It is also difficult to judge in and out of the ring. Dogs are moving so fast that judges sometimes do not see the dog touch the contact. In training, it can be difficult for you to see as well. Training partners or video cameras may be necessary.

Running contacts are variable; in other words, the dog does not hit the contact in exactly the same way each time. Because no exact, specific behavior has been taught, the dog's stride, the approach to the obstacle, his speed, his focus, and his direction at that particular moment will determine if and where he hits the contact.

THE MOVING CONTACT

In the moving contact, the dog runs the length of the obstacle and then adjusts his stride to deliberately touch a spot on the contact zone. Moving contacts do not involve a stop; the dog should simply "touch and go." The goal of the moving contact is to be as close to a running contact as possible.

It is up to you to decide the place on the obstacle that your dog will touch, along with the part of his body your dog uses to touch the contact. Be sure when making these decisions to consider the points discussed earlier.

There are two basic ways of teaching moving contacts. One is to teach the dog to consciously touch a specific area of the contact, and the other is to teach him to move through the contact without jumping.

THE TOUCH METHOD

A reliable and efficient moving contact behavior can be achieved by teaching the dog to touch a specific part of the contact. This is accomplished with the use of a "target" and/or a "touch board." The dog is taught to touch the target, which is then placed on the obstacle to show him where on the obstacle he should touch. The dog is first taught the complete touching behavior with the target on the ground, then the process is repeated with the target placed on the obstacle. The target is eventually faded so that the dog runs to the end of the obstacle, consciously adjusts his stride to touch the place where the target used to be, and continues off of the obstacle. While there is a break in stride, the total performance involves minimal slowing and no stopping; the dog learns to "touch and go."

The touch method lends itself well to breeds of dogs that like to paw at things with their front feet. Spaniels and Afghan Hounds seem to be especially "foot conscious" and master the touch game quickly. While any dog can be taught to touch and many love the game, my experience has been that achieving moving contacts via the touch method is easier for dogs with some natural inclination.

Some dogs will develop a way of doing the obstacle that allows them to touch the spot in which they hardly have to break stride at all (resembling a running contact). Great! Others will always have to adjust their footing slightly. I have outlined the process for teaching the touch in Chapter 17, *The Touch Method*, page 143. This foundation work must be taught before the touch can be introduced to the actual contact obstacle.

GETTING THE DOG NOT TO JUMP

If the dog does not jump off of the end of the contact board, he will likely hit the contact zone. However, this very simple concept can be extremely difficult to teach. A method that attempts to teach the dog not to jump involves teaching him to lower his head and body in anticipation of lying down on the board. The reasoning is that a dog in the process of lying down cannot jump up; he lowers his head, and the body follows. In order to teach a moving dog how to lie down, the dog must first be taught a moving drop and then a drop on recall in reverse.

TEACHING THE MOVING DROP

The dog must first be able to lie down on a verbal command without your needing to point to the ground or bend over. (Refer to Chapter 7, *Commands You Need*, page 37, to teach the down.) Because the dog will be running over the contact obstacle, he will need to be able to down on command from a run or gallop. To teach this "moving drop," start by walking slowly with the dog on a leash at your side, and command "lie down" while you and the dog are still moving. The dog should drop to the ground while you *keep moving*.

As soon as the dog lies down, return to him and reward him with a piece of food on the ground in front of him. If the dog does not go down, repeat the command as you continue walking away slowly. If the dog shows no inclination to lower his head and begin to lie down, step slowly into the leash stirrup to gently pull the dog's head down. Take a few steps away from him before returning to praise and reward him. Remember—do not feed the dog from your hand; place or toss the food onto the floor in front of the dog. You do not want the dog to think that he must be next to you to be rewarded.

Once your dog will lie down on a verbal command at your side as you continue to walk, it is time to try it in a call-to format. From just a few feet away, with your dog off leash, casually call your dog to you. When the dog is moving in your direction, command "lie down." Again, the dog should respond by immediately dropping to the ground. If the dog responds, throw him a reward as you continue to move backward. If the dog does not respond, continue walking backward slowly, and softly repeat the lie-down command occasionally. Be patient; it may take some time. I once had student take a few laps around the training building before her dog decided to lie down. If the dog absolutely will not go down, go back to working with the dog at your side, and step into the leash stirrup if necessary.

This training for the lie-down is very similar to the training of the drop-on-recall exercise in obedience. (See my obedience book, *Beyond Basic Dog Training*, Howell 2003, third revision, "Drop on Recall," page 136.)

Drop-on-recall in reverse. Dog is looking at the motivator.

THE DROP-ON-RECALL IN REVERSE

Once your dog will do a lie down while moving at your side and coming toward you, it is time to teach him to do it going away from you. This skill looks a lot like the obedience exercise of the drop-on-recall, in which the dog is coming toward you and is asked to lie down. In the drop-on-recall in reverse, the dog is moving away from you as he is commanded to lie down. The dog drops immediately in the direction he is running and waits for further instructions. In agility, this is necessary, because you are often behind as your dog approaches a contact. The dog must know how to lie down without turning around to look back at you.

To teach this, put the dog on a leash and throw a motivator ahead of him. Release the dog with an "okay, get it" command. A few feet before the dog gets to the motivator, calmly command "lie down." The dog should respond by lying down while he is still facing the motivator. Once the dog drops, allow him to get the motivator by giving another "okay, get it" command. If the dog does not drop, restrain him with the leash and repeat the command until he does. The dog will soon learn that he cannot have the motivator if he does not respect the command (**delayed gratification**). Work until the dog is reliable at fifty feet and off leash. When working off leash, use either a food tube or arrange for a "toy protector" so that the dog cannot self-reward if he cheats.

USING THE LIE-DOWN TO PREVENT JUMPING

When you are first combining the concept of a moving drop as a way to discourage your dog from jumping off of the contact, first ask your dog to come to a complete stop and lie down at the end of the obstacle or on the ground right off of the board. Eventually, the behavior is faded so that the dog is no longer required to come to a

Thinking of lying down prevents the dog from jumping up.

The dog is first asked to come to a complete stop and lie down at the end of the board.

complete stop. Rather, he will lower his body and center of gravity in anticipation of lying down.

While this technique is effective, it is not always reliable. Dogs are not stupid, and over time they will stop thinking about lying down when they are not required to do so. This method requires a lot of maintenance (going back to requiring a stopped lie-down), and dogs are often confused about *where* on the board they are being asked to anticipate a lie-down.

Advantages

The moving contact is an effective method *for all dogs*. Although it is rarely as fast as a running contact (yet it can be), it is often faster than a stopped-contact performance. It is easy on the dog's body and maintains drive in less-driven dogs.

Disadvantages

The moving contact, taught via either method ("touch" or "don't jump"), is labor-intensive and takes a long time to master. It requires frequent access to equipment and an assistant to watch for foot placement. Because the performance criterion is less specific, it takes longer for dogs to understand the concept. Early in training, the success rate is low; therefore a dog that is taught moving contacts is not ready for standard courses in competition as quickly as a dog that is taught stopped contacts might be. Moving contacts can be difficult to judge, although judgment of moving and running contacts is improving as moving contacts become more popular.

THE STOPPED CONTACT

The last type of contact behavior that can be taught is a stopped contact. In a stopped contact, the dog is taught to run the length of the obstacle and

2-on, 2-off.

come to a complete stop in a specific position at the end of the board, then wait to be released.

The position in which you decide to teach the dog to stop should be considered carefully. The most popular position is referred to as a "two-on, two-off" (2o2o). In the 2o2o, the dog is taught to place his front feet off of the contact obstacle and keep his rear feet on the board. A dog can also be taught to assume a down position at the end of the board or just off of the board.

The position and place in which you choose to teach your dog to stop should depend on the individual dog (his personality, structure, and speed) and the particular obstacle. It is much more difficult for any dog to lie down on the bottom of an A-frame than on a dog walk because of the angle of the frame.

The important concept of stopped contacts is indicated in the name itself: the *stop*! In a stopped contact, the dog

must assume his position and wait for your release command before continuing on to the next obstacle. It is imperative that you be extremely consistent and never release the dog before he has assumed a complete stop in the 2o2o position.

Advantages

The biggest advantages to a stopped contact are that it is a very consistent and clear behavior for you to teach, for the dog to learn, and for the judge to judge. If it is taught properly and is maintained, the success rate is high. Stopped contacts give the handler a chance to catch up to the dog on course.

Disadvantages

While stopped contacts can be fast, not all dogs will perform them quickly. Thinking dogs, dogs with less motivation, or those that are simply not ballistic are less inclined to drive down into a stopped position and tend to slow down early. Why run full speed if you have to stop? It can also be more difficult on a dog's body to come to a jarring stop off of the inclined boards (especially on the A-frame). Stopped contacts require discipline on your part, both in and out of the ring. When the temptation to give an early release, for the sake of a faster time, is appealing, you must resist and uphold the full stopped criteria.

CONTROLLING THE DOG OFF OF A RUNNING OR MOVING CONTACT

If you decide to teach your dog to do a running or moving contact, you will need to teach him how to understand where to go following the contact. While this may seem simple, running and moving contacts can be very fast, and when you fall far behind (a common occurrence), the dog is not going to wait for you!

Your body position and movement are the keys that tell the dog whether he is continuing straight off of the contact, turning toward you, or turning away from you. While it is true that the verbal commands "here," "back," "turn," and "out" are used, it is hard for a dog to process these cues while charging down the ramp and thinking about his contact behavior. By the time you can give the command and the dog actually processes it, it is too late, and the dog has already exited the obstacle in the direction of his choice. Most dogs respond better and faster to visual and

movement cues in general, and this is especially true when they are descending contact obstacles.

To get the dog to turn toward you off of a contact, peel off and away from the obstacle. The lateral distance created prompts the dog to orient in your direction and to anticipate turning toward you after he exits the ramp. The distance and "draw" will automatically cue the dog that there is no reason to run straight following the contact. You should also command "here" as the dog reaches the yellow zone or has performed his moving-contact behavior.

To get the dog to continue straight off of a contact, run forward and parallel to your dog. The forward momentum indicates that you are continuing straight, as if you were running a straight line of jumps. If you are far behind, the command "run" is given to tell the dog to continue forward even though you are an obstacle behind. With a moving contact, wait until the dog has touched or lowered his head in the yellow zone before giving the "run" command. With a running contact, you may want to give the command earlier. Experiment to see what works.

To get a dog to turn away from you off of a contact, you will need to be closer to the down ramp. Give the command "turn" in conjunction with the "turn" hand signal as your dog descends the board. Next, while you are running parallel to the obstacle, decrease your speed. The reduced momentum tells the dog that he is not continuing forward; the verbal command, in addition to the hand signal, tells him to turn away. (See Chapter 9, *Handling Sequences,* page 75, for more information on the turn tunnel.)

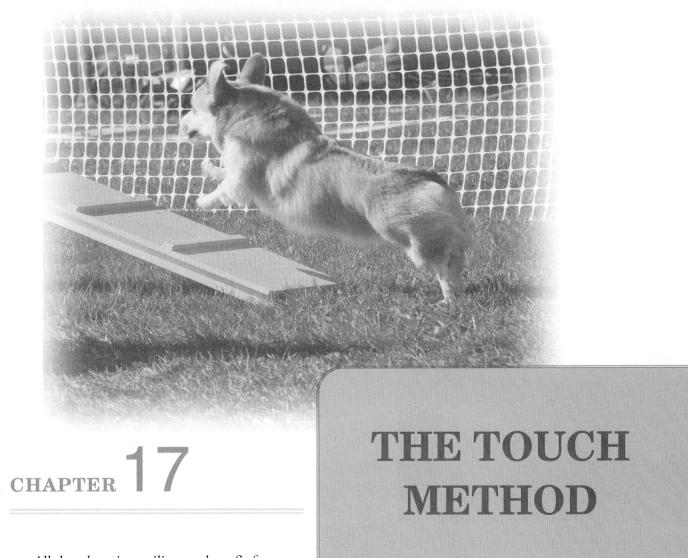

CHAPTER 17

THE TOUCH METHOD

All dogs learning agility can benefit from being taught to touch a *target* or *touch board*. A target is an object that the dog is trained to touch. A touch board refers to a target that is in the shape of a flat board and that can fit nicely onto the contact equipment. This "touching" skill can help teach moving-contact behaviors on the dog walk and A-frame. Targets can also be used to instruct the dog to run ahead of the handler for teaching sends.

The behaviors that will eventually constitute the moving contact performance are first taught to the dog using a board on the ground and are later transferred to the obstacle. The training process for the target and touch board is described below. How to apply it to teach the moving contact behavior on a specific obstacle is described in that obstacle's chapter.

TOUCHING THE BOARD

Targets can be a plastic lid (from coffee cans or yogurt tubs), a circle of paper or cardboard, or a piece of wood that can be cut either long and narrow (like a slat of a dog walk) or larger and rectangular (like the space between the slats of the A-frame or

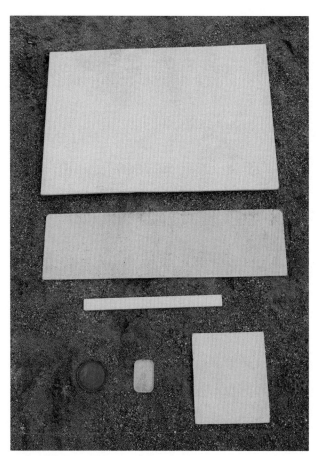

Various targets and touch boards.

dog walk). Whatever you choose, keep in mind that it is easier to teach a dog to touch his paw to a larger target than to a smaller one.

You must first decide with which part of your dog's body you want to touch the target. Dogs can touch boards with their paws, nose, or body. Experience has taught me that dogs demonstrate a preference; for example, if you teach a tall dog a *nose touch*, he will undoubtedly change to a *foot touch* on his own if it is easier and more comfortable for him. Nose touches are better for smaller, short-legged dogs.

THE NOSE TOUCH

In the nose touch, the dog is required to touch the target with his nose. Smooth, round targets (such as lids or cardboard cutouts) are preferable. This concept can be taught to most dogs in a matter of minutes! Hold the collar of your dog in one hand and the target (lid) in the other. Command "touch," and gently touch the lid to the dog's nose. As soon as the nose makes contact with the lid, praise your dog, then pull the lid away and put a piece of food on it for the dog to eat. *Food comes from the target after the dog has touched it, not from your hand.* Begin again, only this time, hold the lid about an inch in front of the dog's nose. Command "touch," and wait. If the dog moves and touches the lid, praise him and then feed him a treat from the lid. If the dog does not move, gently pull the dog toward the lid with his collar. As soon as the dog touches the lid, praise him and offer a treat off of the lid.

After a few attempts, the dog should be nudging the lid with his nose to get you to put a treat on it. Once the dog is taking the initiative to move toward the lid and touch it with his nose, move the lid further and further away from him until the lid is eventually on the ground. Make sure that the dog actually touches the lid with his nose and does not merely bob his head up and down! *Never point to the lid with your hand.* This will draw the dog's attention to your hand and away from the target—the opposite of what you want.

THE FOOT TOUCH

In the foot touch, you ideally want the dog to touch the target with both of his front paws. Touching with one front paw is fine, but incidental touching with the back feet does not count. What is more important is that the dog make a deliberate front-foot movement to touch the board. Larger targets, such as touch boards, work best for foot touches (especially since they can seamlessly fit onto the obstacle for later training).

Some dogs will touch with both front feet, then lie down on the touch board. This is permissible but not required. Just ignore it, and it will go away.

Before you can teach a foot touch, the dog must be aware of his front feet. Some dogs are naturally more conscious of their limbs than others, but it does not hurt to reinforce the awareness. This is done by teaching the dog the common trick of "wave" or "shake" with his front paws.

To teach your dog to wave or shake, have your dog wear a buckle collar, then sit him in front of you. Put a piece of food in your mouth, ready to offer as a treat. (You need to keep the treat in your mouth, because both of your hands will be busy doing something else.) When you try to get the dog to raise his left front paw, hold his collar with your left hand. Pull the dog to your left, thereby taking his weight off of his front left foot. Gently tap the dog's front left leg with your right hand as you command "shake." The foot will eventually come off of the ground, at which time you take hold of it in your right hand, let go of the dog's collar, and reach for the food in your mouth with your left hand. Be sure to reward the dog with the treat while you are *still holding onto his paw.* Now see if you can reverse this process and get the dog to shake with his front right paw.

Deliberate foot touch.

After only a few sessions, your dog should be willing to raise either paw on the shake command. Now it is time to introduce the touch board. Hold a small touch board and command "shake." As the dog raises his paw, put the touch board under it. Touching the board to the paw, command "touch." Praise your dog when his paw makes contact with the board.

Be sure to work with both front paws. After only a few repetitions, drop the shake command and only command "touch" as you present the touch board. Most dogs quickly get the idea to put a paw on the board to get a treat.

Once your dog will consistently put his paw on the board, reward him by putting the treat on the board after he has touched it. When the dog knows how to get you to put a treat *on the board* (by touching it with his paw), start lowering the board to the ground. Continue to move the board further and further from the dog. Always reward him with the treat on the board, and *never* point to the touch board. Remember—you do not want to do anything to encourage the dog to look at your hands.

TOUCHING ALL FOUR WAYS

The touch board is treated as an obstacle. Accordingly, the dog should execute it in all four ways. After all, the touch board will be used to represent the bottom of an A-frame or dog walk. With the lid or the board on the ground, start working to encourage a touch as you do a call-to, a send, a run-by right, and a run-by left.

In the call-to, the dog may be inclined to step over and miss the board as he picks up speed and looks at you in front of him. When this happens, simply abort and try again. Try standing closer or starting the dog closer to the board. Praise your dog as he touches the board, then reward him on the board (i.e., place the food on the board, not in the dog's mouth). Always make sure that the dog is touching the board—a head duck or half an attempt is not acceptable. The front foot must make contact with the target.

You also must be able to "send" your dog to the target. On the command "touch," the dog should leave your side, move out to the board, and touch it. While you would normally give a send signal to the obstacle, you do not want to do this in the case of the touch board. The goal is to get the dog to look for the board completely on his own without your assistance. If the dog is having trouble leaving your side and going to the board, back up in your training and start closer to the board. You can also show the board to the dog, then move away from it and send him to it.

The run-bys will be the most difficult to accomplish, because the dog will be torn between looking at you and the target. Work until the dog will focus on the target even as you run next to him. Remember not to let the dog cheat; he must fully touch the target with his front paw or nose to get the reward.

To reward the dog, either throw a motivator on the ground past the target, or reward him back on the target by placing a piece of food on the board. Throwing a motivator on the ground past the target keeps the dog's focus forward and away from you. On the agility course, as the dog gets to the yellow part of the board, you want the dog to be focused on the contact and thinking ahead to the next obstacle. If he turns to look at you—a behavior conditioned by always receiving the reward from your hand—he will be off balance and more likely to jump off.

What If?

• What if the dog runs at the target but misses it with his feet or nose?

Do not reward your dog. Give the dog another chance to hit the target. If he seems distracted, kick the target with your foot but do not point to it. (If you point, you draw the dog's attention to your hand.) If he tries but misses again, hold the target in your hand just above the ground. Sometimes a dog has a hard time acknowledging the board; by raising it, you are making it more obvious and him more aware of it. Ask him to "touch," and let him slam it out of your hand to the ground. Reward him on the target.

• What if, when you send the dog to touch the target, he first turns to face you?

The dog should touch the target in the direction in which he is moving; curling back toward you is discouraged. To accomplish this with a dog that wants to turn around and face you, place a food tube beyond the target. When the dog touches the target, go out and reward from the food tube. This will give the dog a reason to continue to face the direction in which he was moving.

TOUCH AND GO

To achieve a moving contact, the dog needs to adjust his stride to touch the board but should not plan on stopping on the board. The goal behavior is thus to have the dog "touch and go."

Sometimes dogs become "sticky" on the touch boards, meaning that they go to touch the target and stay on it. Do not be too

Helper raising the board to assist in sending the dog.

concerned about this. As the dog develops more speed and desire to move forward, such as to continue to the next obstacle in sequence, he will be less inclined to stop and stay on the board, especially as he realizes that you are not requiring the stay.

To instill the idea of "touch and go," set up situations that will entice and encourage the dog to want to move forward after the board. You can do this by throwing a toy or food tube ahead of the dog or sending him ahead to a planted motivator after he has touched the target. This exercise is difficult, as dogs will often forget to touch due to their focus on the motivator beyond the touch board. Teaching the dog that he must first touch before he can get what he wants is the key in moving contact training. To prepare for teaching full contacts, you must teach your dog that if there is a touch board/lid on the ground, and something he wants beyond the target, he must first touch the target before he can have what he wants. I call this concept "delayed gratification."

DELAYED GRATIFICATION

Dogs that usually hit contacts will often start to miss them in early training as the behavior becomes incorporated into a sequence and course. This happens because the dog is anticipating what the next obstacle after the contact will be. This causes him to look up to find the obstacle or look to you for information, instead of looking down for the target.

Place your dog on a leash (at least six feet long) and buckle collar, and have him stand or sit four feet in front of the target. Place (do not throw) a motivator beyond the target. Command "touch," and let the dog move forward. If he tries to bypass the board, prevent him by using the leash and softly repeating "touch." As soon as the dog touches the board, release the leash and tell him "okay, get it." Go out and give him his reward away from the board.

When the dog starts to understand the game, try throwing the food tube or toy beyond the touch board. If the dog is still successful, remove the leash. He will undoubtedly make some mistakes. This is a good thing, because by working through his errors, he will learn that the touch takes priority over whatever else he desires. Do not make a big deal out of the mistakes—simply do not reward them. Bring the dog back, and try again. As the dog becomes more and more proficient, start lengthening the distances so that the dog has to run further from you to touch before getting the reward. Use a toy or foods that the dog really likes, and see if he will continue to hit the touch board before going to the reward.

"LIVE" VERSUS "DEAD" REWARD

Dogs find moving objects much more exciting than stationary ones. When you first start to teach "delayed gratification," *place* the reward beyond the touch board. Later, as the dog's training progresses, the motivator can be *thrown* to make it more desirable. By now, you have hopefully noticed this pattern in training. I sometimes refer to the stationary reward as a "dead reward" and the moving reward as a "live reward."

NOTE:

If you have an assistant who can act as a "toy protector" and step on the toy in the event the dog tries to get it before touching the target, you can use a toy as a motivator. Otherwise, use a food tube or place the toy in a Tupperware container (that the dog will not view as a toy) so that the dog cannot self-reward if he cheats!

SEQUENCING

Because the touch board represents a contact obstacle, the next step is to incorporate it into sequences. Place a jump before and after the target on the ground. Allow adequate spacing so that your dog has room to learn to adjust his stride to hit the board after landing from the first jump before continuing over the second jump. Sometimes reward the dog after the second jump by taking him back and feeding him on the board. Alternate this with rewarding him at the end of the exercise, after the second jump.

It may take the dog a few tries to figure out how to hit the target while also thinking about the obstacles and the increased speed brought on by the jumps. When a dog lands off of a jump, he lands in a canter stride. Most dogs cannot be sure to touch a board unless they change to a trotting pace. This is why dogs must learn to adjust their strides to hit a contact. Think of the baseball player who is running from home to first base. He, too, must learn to adjust his stride in order to touch at least one foot on the base.

If at any time the dog fails to touch the board, freeze! Your sudden stop will alert the dog that something has gone wrong, and he will learn that if he wants to continue running the sequence, he must first touch the board.

HANDLING MANEUVERS

Teaching the target is also a good time to start introducing a dog to handling maneuvers that will eventually involve contact obstacles.

PEELING-OFF

There will be times on course when you will need to peel off and move diagonally away from the contact obstacle to prepare for the next part of the course. Peeling off can initially be taught with the use of the touch target on the ground away from the contacts.

Begin with your dog on a sit. Place the touch board fifteen feet in front of him, and put the reward six feet beyond the board. Stand next to your dog as you command "okay, touch." As the dog gets up, run as if you were doing a run-by, but instead of running parallel to the dog, move diagonally away from him to one side (i.e., peel off). When the dog gets to the board, praise him and command "okay, get it." If the dog comes with you instead of going to the board, shorten the distance and try again. If the dog has repeated difficulty acknowledging the touch board, try having a helper elevate the board slightly so that it is more visible and the dog must push it to the ground as he touches.

Be sure to practice this on both sides of the dog. When you throw the tube to the dog, throw it *straight in front of him*, not to the side you are on. The dog's tendency is to curl toward you. To combat this, the dog must have a reason to stay focused straight ahead, not to the side.

CROSSES

Once your dog is comfortable with you peeling off to both sides, start crossing in front of and behind the dog. Practice front crosses and rear crosses with the touch board on the ground. If you cannot see that the dog is actually touching the board, enlist the help of a friend to watch the dog's paws as you perform the handling maneuvers.

ASSUMED CONTACTS

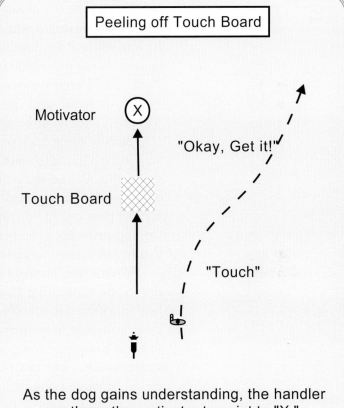

Fig. 17-1.

In the final step of teaching the touch board/lid, you want the dog to assume responsibility for touching the board even if you do not give the command to touch. This will prepare him for what will eventually become an "assumed contact." There are many advantages to teaching an assumed contact. Not having to tell your dog to "touch" on course frees you to prepare for the next obstacle.

Many handlers give very "emotional" touch commands that distract the dog from doing his job. Some dogs actually look up at their handler upon hearing these hysterical commands, causing the dog to take his eyes off of the contact and pop up and off the end of the board. The handler becomes a distraction at a critical moment when the dog should be thinking about keeping his head down and touching the contact.

It is the nature of the dog to anticipate things. As soon as you teach a dog anything, he will anticipate what is going to happen next. This allows him to chain behaviors together. For example, in obedience, the dog is taught to retrieve a dumbbell over a high jump. In the initial teaching, the dog is given the command to jump, to retrieve, to jump again, and finally to sit in front of the handler. After a few repetitions, the handler removes the retrieve command, and the dog assumes (anticipates) that he is to retrieve the dumbbell that was thrown to the other side of the jump. Next, the handler removes the second jump command, and the dog anticipates that after he picks up the dumbbell, he is to jump back over the jump with it. Finally, the handler removes the sit command, and the sit front is also anticipated. The end result is that the handler gives one jump command, and the dog performs a chain of behaviors that he has learned to anticipate.

When a handler stops reminding a dog to do something that he knows how to do, the dog actually has to think about it harder. Why then do handlers feel it is necessary to repeatedly command "touch?" The fact is, it isn't necessary! Anytime a dog performs a moving contact, he is going to be expected to "touch"; it is part of the obstacle, not a separate behavior. You can train your dog to assume responsibility for touching the contact; it just takes time, consistency, and the belief that your dog is capable of doing it!

If you continue telling your dog to touch, you are not allowing him to put the act of touching the contact into his "automatic memory" (something that is so practiced it has become automatic).

You are doing your dog a disservice, for as you tell the dog to do what he already knows, he will stop to think about it when he should just be responding automatically.

To teach the "assumed touch," begin with a target four feet in front of the dog. With the dog on leash, throw a toy or food tube a few feet beyond the board or lid. Command "okay, get it" (the "touch" is assumed), and if the dog does not first touch the target, hold the leash to prevent him from getting the reward. Repeat this until the dog remembers to touch the target. As soon as the dog touches the target, drop the leash and allow him to get the reward. If the dog has repeated difficulty acknowledging the target, have a helper elevate the board slightly so that it is more visible and so that the dog must push it to the ground as he touches. It doesn't take long before a dog realizes that to get the reward, he must first touch the target, even if no one tells him to.

As a dog gains more speed in agility, he will start to miss contacts. This is because he must relearn how to use his body correctly at the newly developed speed. In a sense, a dog learns how to perform contacts many times—each time he increases his speed. Eventually, a dog is moving as fast as he possibly can. Only now can the dog learn how to execute the contact behavior for the final time.

At this point, the dog should be extremely comfortable with the target. He should be moving toward and deliberately and enthusiastically touching any touch board he sees. You may now transfer the target to the A-frame or dog walk and repeat the touching process with the target on the ramp.

CHAPTER 18

THE TWO-ON, TWO-OFF

The term two-on, two-off (2o2o) refers to a dog's position with two hind feet on a contact obstacle and two front feet off of the obstacle, touching the ground. It is a position at the end of a ramp that the dog must learn to assume. The 2o2o is a practical technique to teach stopped contacts on all three contact obstacles. The dog is taught to run the length of the ramps as fast as he can to get to the 2o2o position, which he must maintain until he is released. This provides a definitive contact behavior for the dog to learn and for the handler to reinforce and ensures that the dog touches the yellow zone.

ABOUT THE 2O2O

The key to teaching the 2o2o is to understand the 2o2o as a specific position in a particular location. The dog's job is to get to that position in that location as quickly as possible, then stay there until he is released. The thinking should be "run to the position" rather than "slow down to stop."

> There are three components to the 2o2o: the body position, the location, and the stay and release.

2-on, 2-off. M. Nicole Fischer Photography.

BODY POSITION

The body position of the 2o2o is simple: stand with the front feet touching the ground and the back feet touching the board. That is it. The simpler the task, the more easily the dog will master it. Experience has taught me that complicating the contact behavior—such as requiring nose touches, sits, downs, or perfectly straight body positions—only adds stress and unnecessary precision that does nothing to enhance the contact performance. Running to the very bottom of a pitched ramp is unnatural enough; you want to keep the pressure of contact performance to a minimum.

The dog must learn to assume and maintain the 2o2o position. Some dogs initially choose to sit or down on the board in the 2o2o position; that is fine. It can even be helpful in the initial teaching stages to have the dog assume a sit or down to help keep him balanced. However, this is not a requirement of the 2o2o behavior, and you should not correct a dog for failing to sit or lie down as long as two hind feet are on the obstacle and two front feet are on the ground.

Nose Touch?

Some dogs are taught a nose touch to the ground in addition to standing in a 2o2o position. The thinking is to keep the dog's head lowered so that he will not jump up. While the concept is correct, I do not believe that the nose touch is necessary. Some dogs have bodies such that touching their noses to the ground is physically challenging. Do not be concerned about a dog leaping off of a contact because the dog that learns *where* 2o2o is will keep his focus down on that spot (i.e., on the end of the board on the ground) and as a result will keep his head lowered. Once he has assumed the 2o2o position, he no longer needs to be staring at the ground. In fact, it is more logical for the dog's head to be up, looking for the handler and for the place where he will be going next.

LOCATION

While a sit or down only requires the dog to assume a specific body position, the 2o2o requires a body position *in a specific location*. The particular "spot" for 2o2o is at the end of a contact ramp, because that is where the dog can place his rear feet on the board and his front feet on the ground. You cannot ask a dog to assume a 2o2o in the middle of an empty room (the trained dog should look for a ramp on which to place his rear feet).

A dog that understands that 2o2o happens where the board meets the ground will be able to position himself correctly from anywhere.

Target?

I do not use a target to teach the 2o2o for several reasons. The target does not teach the dog the concept of putting his front feet on the ground and his rear feet on the obstacle. If the dog has been taught a foot touch, the presence of a target only gets the dog to think about his front feet. If the dog has been taught a nose touch, the dog is not thinking about the placement of his feet at all.

Nor does the target teach the dog the location of the 2o2o. While it might get the dog to move down the board and stand in the correct place, he is not learning *where* the 2o2o is supposed to occur. The dog only goes to the end of the board and the ground because that is where the target is placed. You want your dog to understand that the 2o2o position is where the board meets the ground, not where the target is placed.

Finally, the target is an extra prop that will have to be faded. Because the ground and the board are always there, why not use them from the beginning? The 2o2o position asks the dog for awareness of his rear feet. The "touch" of a target touch board asks the dog for awareness of his front feet. It is simpler for the dog to keep these two concepts separate.

STAY AND RELEASE

As with all stays, the key is in the release. Because the 2o2o involves the dog staying in position until he is released to achieve a stopped contact, the consistency of the release is extremely important. A dog should never be allowed out of a 2o2o and off of the contact unless he is released. The rule of release applies: you need to be motionless when giving the command so that the dog learns to rely on the verbal cue for the release and on your body only for direction.

Holding the Contact

You must require your dog to achieve the complete 2o2o position before releasing him to the next obstacle. How long you hold the dog in position depends on the situation and the dog. In the early parts of training, and especially at the beginning of a dog's trial career, require your dog to stay in position for a solid few seconds before you release him. Although it costs time, holding contacts reinforces and instills the behavior and is an essential investment in the dog's ultimate contact performance.

Very driven, ballistic, or "pushy" dogs may need to be held on contacts longer than slower or less-motivated dogs, as they may take more convincing to learn to maintain their position under all circumstances. Slower or less-motivated dogs may have less course time to spare and might be inclined to slow down drastically if they are stopped for too long. These dogs should be released as soon as they have placed both front feet on the ground.

TEACHING THE 2o2o

The 2o2o can be used for all contact obstacles, and the foundation for the behavior is the same. A verbal command is used to designate the behavior. Common choices include "touch," "target," "bottom," "spot," or "place." The word used is your choice, but it must be unique from other commands. For example, if you have taught your dog to touch a target or touch board on the command "touch," this word cannot also mean "assume the 2o2o position." For the purpose of this chapter, I will use the command "place" as the 2o2o command.

INTRODUCING THE CONCEPT

The first part of 2o2o training is getting the dog accustomed to the body position. The dog must learn that he can stand on the end of a board with his back feet on and front feet off. It takes some time for a dog to understand that the placement of both his front and back paws is important. In the beginning, his back feet seem to constantly fall off of the board; do not worry. Dogs start off "wobbly" but soon settle and start to think about the placement of all of their feet.

Note:

Large, heavy dogs can be helped up onto the side of the A-frame or dog walk by having them first jump up onto a table placed next to the side of the contact.

The introduction to the 2o2o does not necessarily have to be on the actual contact equipment. **Contact trainers,** mini A-frames, or any elevated ramp with one end resting on the ground will work. You can even practice "place" at the bottom of a flight of stairs (where the stairs meet the floor) once your dog has been introduced to the concept on a ramp.

Start with your dog on a buckle collar. Have him climb onto the end of the board from the side. Never ask the dog to jump up onto the board and turn around. The dog must get onto the board facing the direction in which he will stop.

Command "place" as you guide him into the 2o2o position and gently hold him there by his collar. Reward him with a treat while he is on the board with both front feet on the ground and his back feet on the board. Release him with an "okay" to allow him to exit the board. Repeat the exercise a few times while varying the side onto which the dog climbs.

To initially help a dog that is having some problems staying at the end of the board or keeping his rear feet on the board, hold onto the dog's collar in order to steady him, and keep him from moving around. If the dog's rear feet slip off, you can reposition him by gently lifting his rear end back into place. Gently stroke his body as he stands in the 2o2o to steady him and keep him from moving. Another option to help your dog with balance is to get him to sit with his rear end on the board and his front feet just off the end. Do not give the sit command, but rather entice him into the sit by raising his head with a treat once his front feet are touching the ground.

STOP HELPING

As training progresses and the dog gains experience, your goal is to get the dog to take the initiative to properly position himself. After guiding the dog onto the board from the side, let go of his collar, command "place," and move to the end of the board to face him (as in a call-to). Stand still and wait for the dog to make a move. The dog will either jump off of the board, move forward, move into a 2o2o position (which would be awesome), or just stand there. Be patient and let him think. If the dog gets off of the board, put him back on it and give the place command again. If he stands there, wait for him to try taking a step forward. Praise his effort and reward him as soon as a front foot touches the ground. If the dog is very stuck, you can softly say his name or "place" to entice him to move forward. Do not continue to lure the dog into position with food. He needs to decide to move on his own.

Be sure to vary your positioning around the end of the board. Practice by placing yourself ahead of the dog, facing the dog, behind the dog, and off to either side of him. The dog should be able to move into a 2o2o position regardless of where you are standing. At this point, you should not be moving or pointing once you have given the place command. You do not want the dog to be dependent on your forward movement or hand gestures to find the 2o2o position.

WORKING THE STAY

The dog needs to learn that 2o2o implies holding the position until he is released. Initially, the dog was being held in position, but with more freedom, he will be less inclined to stay. While it can be helpful in the very beginning to give a soft stay command to let the dog know that he should hold the position, quickly stop giving the command and progress to the "assumed stay."

Whenever the dog breaks or moves out of a 2o2o position before being released, simply place him back in the 2o2o position without saying a word. The dog will make mistakes, but remember—dogs learn through trial and error and will only understand how to do it right, by doing it wrong!

Start by simply taking a few steps away from the dog in the 2o2o, then returning to him to reward and release him. Progressively increase the amount of time and distance. You may also vary your speed; will the dog stay in position as you run by him? In the beginning, always return to the dog to reward him with a treat or petting. I do not advise using toys in the early parts of 2o2o training, as they tend to get the dog excited and moving. You want your dog to stay. Toys can be used later in training when the dog already has a clear understanding of "stay in position" and can play with the toy (mouthing a ball or tugging) while remaining stationary.

As you gradually increase the distance and duration, alternate between returning to the dog to reward him and releasing him to a motivator or another obstacle. Rewarding the dog on the board teaches him that the 2o2o is a good place to be. However, a dog also needs to understand that continuing on to the next obstacle is a reward as well. Remember—even when you release your dog to a motivator or obstacle, he must first come to a complete stop in the 2o2o position with his front feet on the ground and his back feet on the board. If you say "okay" before he has assumed the 2o2o position, you will confuse the dog and ruin the behavior.

QUICK AND EARLY RELEASING

As mentioned earlier, it is your decision how long your dog will be required to hold the 2o2o position. Obviously, the longer a dog is held, the more those precious seconds go by. Agility is a game of speed, with top placements frequently being decided by tenths and hundredths of a second; no one wants to waste time. It is often tempting to release a dog early or quickly off of the contact in an effort to save time.

Quick releasing is when you release a dog from the contact as the dog's front feet hit the ground. The dog is only in the 2o2o position for a heartbeat (if that) and is not being asked to hold the position at all. An early release is when you say "okay" before the dog has definitively placed his front feet on the ground. The dog may be at the very bottom of the board, about to stop in position, but has not clearly assumed the 2o2o position. Quick releasing is dangerous; early releasing is deadly.

A handler who frequently quick-releases his dog will soon find that the dog is no longer committed to stopping in the 2o2o position. While he still might touch the yellow zone, the dog will start to jump off of the end of the board earlier and earlier in anticipation of the release. This jumping will eventually result in a missed contact, and when the handler tries to reinstate the stop, the dog will resist. To avoid this problem, regularly intersperse longer-held contacts in practice and especially at trials.

Early releases are deadly because they encourage inconsistency and confuse the dog. If a dog is no longer required to move to the end of the board and stop in the 2o2o position, he will take advantage of this leeway and start jumping. When he is corrected for jumping, he will start to slow down and creep down the contact because he does not know when he will be released. Early releasing creates gray in what should be a black-and-white situation. Always wait until the dog has touched his front feet to the ground before giving the release command.

There are occasions when a very quick release can and should be used: International Standard Class (ISC) classes, runoffs, the final round at nationals, the standard runs for the final few MACH points, or any other run in which time is critical. Save your quick releases for these important and special occasions and invest the rest. An early fault in a standard agility class (like a knocked bar) may result in a non-qualifying score but provides a perfect opportunity to hold contacts and reinforce the 2o2o position.

Some dogs will perform the 2o2o contact behavior faster then others; it depends on the nature, structure, and disposition of the dog. Slower, less-motivated dogs do not need to be held as often or long as pushy dogs. Be mindful of your dog and your criteria. The more clear-cut the behavior, the easier and more willingly your dog will master it.

CHAPTER 19

THE A-FRAME

The A-frame is the most difficult obstacle to teach a dog because of the steep angle that dogs must learn to negotiate with speed and accuracy.
Because the A-frame requires balance, coordination, and substantial strength in the dog's rear end, do not begin teaching it at full height until the dog is nine months to one year of age. It is the last obstacle I introduce to the dog. I use the command "frame" to indicate the A-frame. Other popular choices include "climb," "scramble," or "walk it."

TEACHING THE OBSTACLE

Small dogs seem to have more trouble getting up the frame, while large dogs experience more trouble coming down it. For safety's sake, the A-frame should always be lowered to about four feet at the apex when training begins. This way you can easily steady the dog if necessary, and if the dog does fall or awkwardly jump off, he will not get hurt.

The first goal is to get the dog running confidently over the A-frame. As with the dog walk, do not worry about formal contact behavior at this point. I call this the "discovery phase" because both you and your dog are discovering how he can physically negotiate the A-frame as fast as possible. To ensure that the dog does not bail off of the A-frame in an unsafe manner, put a toy or food tube on the ground about a foot from the bottom of the board (closer for smaller dogs.) This encourages the dog to move forward over the frame and helps to keep his head down. A dog whose head is down is less likely to jump up. Using the motivator works better than using a hoop, because it gives the dog more freedom to discover what to do with his body. Passing under a hoop off of a steep slope is not easy for a large dog!

INTRODUCING THE OBSTACLE

Before you ask the dog to climb blindly up the frame, show him how to get down. Place the dog, off leash, halfway down the descent ramp, and simply let go and let him come down. This helps the dog to learn where the motivator is and get comfortable exiting the obstacle. Large, heavy dogs can jump up onto the side of the A-frame from a table that you position next to the contact.

Note:

"Full height" is a relative term. The height of the A-frame varies depending on the organization sanctioning the equipment. If your dog will be required to execute frames of different heights, be sure to practice both, as the height of the frame affects the dog's timing and stride.

To teach the dog to climb the lowered A-frame, take hold of his collar with your hand that is closest to the dog. With your other hand, hold a motivator and encourage him forward. Some dogs will have no problem climbing up and over the ramp; others will be less enthusiastic. Try putting something that the dog would really like at the top of the A-frame. Give the dog a small running start, and encourage him to get the prize at the top.

After a few repetitions, let go of the dog's collar and give a hand signal up to the top of the A-frame. Command "frame" and then "get it" as the dog reaches the apex to tell him to get the motivator. Work the A-frame on both sides, and do not position yourself right next to the dog; stay either ahead of him or behind him. To avoid "babysitting" the dog, stay a few feet away from the frame. This allows the dog to feel that he is capable of performing the frame on his own.

RAISING THE FRAME

As soon as the dog is confidently climbing over the obstacle, it is time to start raising the frame. There is no point in leaving the frame low for very long, as the physical demands of negotiating a low A-frame are very different from those for a full-height A-frame. The dog needs to figure out a comfortable way of performing the obstacle with the proper incline. Raise the A-frame over a period of two training sessions. You do not need to move in inches, because you have waited for the dog to mature before starting to teach this obstacle.

Your dog may initially slow down with the incline changes. This is normal, but you want your dog to stride down the frame, not come down one slat at a time. Continue to encourage speed and do nothing to inhibit the dog's forward drive.

OPERATION OBSERVATION

Once the dog has been working at full height for a few sessions, he should start to develop a more or less consistent "system" of negotiating the frame. Make note of the dog's striding. How many strides is he taking? Where does he first hit the descent ramp? Does he jump the apex? Does he do it consistently? The goal is to consider the dog's physical and mental disposition and his natural A-frame performance tendencies, in order to devise a way for him to properly execute the obstacle.

Personally, I have had more dogs injured performing an A-frame than any other piece of equipment. Strained shoulders and backs seem to be the most common injuries. In an effort to keep physical stress to a minimum, I search for the most natural, comfortable way for each individual dog to execute the A-frame and still manage to touch the contact zone; there is no "one-method-fits-all process."

The "discovery phase" is the time to experiment with the A-frame. Moving the planted motivator farther or closer to the base of the frame might change from where, or if, the dog jumps off of the board. Striding can be altered by attaching soft foam "noodles" (such as those that kids play with in swimming pools) to the frame. Simply rest them on the ramp itself, or attach them with bungee cords. The noodles, acting as stride regulators, will encourage the dog to open up his stride and discourage him from sliding down the frame slat

by slat. Introduce the noodles on the ground first by having the dog run over them so that he is not surprised by them on the A-frame.

JUMPING THE TOP

Some dogs naturally jump the top of the A-frame once they are confident. A foam noodle can be used to encourage a dog to jump the top of the frame. It is my experience that dogs that jump the apex are more likely to land in the contact zone. This is because the jump usually puts them farther down the descent ramp, and one more stride puts them into the contact zone. Dogs whose structure includes a short upper arm and/or a straight front (a front lacking angulation) are more likely to jump the top when moving at high speed.

After many years of trying to *teach* all dogs to jump the top of the A-frame, I have concluded that it is not possible. Some will and some will not, and there does not seem to be much you can do about it other than to encourage the dog to do it. Try placing a foam noodle at the top of the descent ramp just past the apex. The dog must have good propulsion and speed in order to jump over and clear the apex of the frame and the noodle. Whether the dog continues to jump the top once the prop is removed is uncertain, but it can be a useful tool to show the dog that it is physically possible and that he could choose to do it. Some dogs think that it is fun, and maybe you will get lucky!

Keep in mind that this is the "discovery phase." It is a time to observe what the dog can physically do, what he is inclined to do, and what he wants to do. You are not *teaching* contacts yet. Do not be afraid that the dog is learning

Foam noodle on an A-frame.

Jumping the top of the A-frame.

how to jump off, miss contacts, or other undesirable behaviors. He needs to learn how to run across the equipment before he learns the contact behavior. The dog should be running enthusiastically at full speed before you add a contact behavior.

After you have observed the dog confidently climb up and down the A-frame for some time, you should have a good idea about which contact behavior you should teach this dog. Unlike some trainers, I am not concerned with how far down the contact a dog goes. Yellow is yellow; no extra points are awarded for touching the very bottom of the contact zone. The goal is a fast, fluid, and stress-free performance in which the dog clearly touches the contact with his front or back feet. Yes, that is correct—back feet are acceptable. The stride of some dogs is so long that to require the dog's front feet to hit the contact might cause him to jam his shoulders or toes upon descent. The A-frame is the one piece of equipment where I feel that you must work with the dog to determine the criteria for performance.

INCORPORATING THE CONTACT BEHAVIOR ONTO THE A-FRAME

The next step of A-frame training is teaching the dog a contact behavior to solidify his A-frame performance. A running, moving, or stopped contact can be taught on the A-frame.

THE RUNNING CONTACT

I believe that many more dogs are capable of doing a true running contact on the A-frame than on the dog walk. Small dogs with short strides are more likely to run naturally into the contact. Even if they jump, their strides often carry them down into the yellow. This is not to say that small dogs cannot miss A-frame contacts—simply that they have an easier time running, uninterrupted, down the frame and still hit the yellow zone. There is no reason to stop or alter the stride of a small dog that would naturally touch the contact if left alone.

Testing the Tendency

It should become apparent whether the dog is regularly hitting the contact during the discovery phase. It is now time to remove the planted motivator and see what happens. Give only the A-frame command, and run the dog over the obstacle as usual. Reward him by throwing a motivator low and straight ahead of the dog as he exits the board.

The key to the running contact is to not interfere. The less interference and the more speed the dog has, the better. When you are running the frame, do not slow down or turn to see if your dog has hit the contact because this will change his performance as he lifts his eyes to see what you are doing. Enlist the help of a training partner, or set up a video camera, to watch the dog's feet. Running contact performances on the A-frame can be so fast that it is often hard to tell if the dog makes the contact or not. A partner with a keen eye is critical. There are also training devices on the market that make a noise or light up when touched. These can take the place of a "contact watcher." At this writing, the size of these training devices makes them more suitable for use on the dog walk than on the A-frame.

Practice different sequences and handling maneuvers to discover how each affects the dog's A-frame performance. If the dog starts drastically changing his stride—such as picking up his

head to look at you during a front cross—target the bottom of the frame as you execute the maneuver to encourage him to keep his head down.

The running contact is not a fixed behavior. Dogs do not touch exactly the same spot on the board every time. In my experience, a dog running straight and fast is more likely to hit the contact. With a running contact, it is quite possible that the dog will sometimes miss an A-frame contact if he is being pulled sharply off of the frame or being turned back into an adjacent tunnel. If this happens, do not become upset. Practice the situation in which the missed contact occurred, and plant a motivator at the bottom of the frame to encourage the dog to go straight down before turning.

I think of a missed running contact in much the same way as a knocked bar: it will happen, but it is no big deal. Fast dogs will occasionally knock a bar, and fast-running dogs will occasionally miss a contact. As trainers, we work to perfect all of our dog's skills. Why should we put more importance on a missed contact than a dropped bar in this situation?

THE MOVING CONTACT

The moving contact is an option if the dog does not naturally or consistently stride into the yellow zone. It is also a good choice if you do not feel comfortable stopping the dog on the A-frame. The "touch method" or "teaching a dog not to jump" can both be used to achieve a moving contact on the A-frame. The touch method is preferable, because asking a dog to lie down on a steep slope is very difficult to achieve and enforce. A dog will often slow down excessively if he is

Head down; thinking of down.

Head up; causes jumping.

required to stop and lie down on an A-frame ramp. Because it is so difficult to lie down on a steep slope, this dog is inclined to jump directly to the ground (and miss the contact) when a down position is required.

Touch Method

Before the dog learns the "touch" on the A-frame he must first have been taught the entire touch board and target process on the ground. (See Chapter 17, *The Touch Method*, page 143, for the complete process.)

To successfully transfer the touch behavior onto the A-frame, I recommend using a larger touch board that fits seamlessly onto the ramp between the slats. The more the touch board resembles and feels like the contact obstacle, the easier it will be to remove. The touching behavior is more difficult on the A-frame than on the dog walk because of the steep incline and resulting momentum that the dog gains. Giving the dog a bigger board to touch makes the task easier. It reduces the strain and pressure (both physical and mental) on the dog while still providing a clear target for the dog to touch. Be aware that some A-frames have large slats that can hurt toes and interfere with a dog's touching performance; removing the two bottom slats of the frame helps deal with this problem.

Board on Obstacle

Begin by placing the touch board on a lowered A-frame, midway in the contact zone (you may change the placement of the board later in training, but this is a good place to start). Lowering the frame allows for less physical strain on the dog and makes the initial process of learning to touch the board on the way down the ramp easier. Show the dog that you have put it there, then plant a motivator on the ground beyond the frame. Run the dog over the obstacle and softly command "touch" as he reaches the apex.

Do not yell the command just before the dog reaches the target, as this may draw his head and focus up to you instead of down at the board. You go back to saying the verbal command even though the dog does an assumed contact on the ground, because you have changed the picture. Once the dog has had *considerable* experience with the board on the A-frame, at regular height, you may return to assumed contacts.

The dog must make a deliberate move to touch the board. As soon as he touches, encourage him to get the toy or food tube with a "get-it" command. Because the touch board is large, the task should be easy for the dog to accomplish. If the dog misses the touch board, **back chain** the behavior on the lowered A-frame to draw more attention to the board.

Remember to use a motivator from which the dog cannot self-reward. Either a food tube or an assistant acting as a "toy protector" will prevent the dog from getting the reward if he fails to touch the board. You may also reward your dog by feeding him from the board. After the dog has touched the board, praise him and put the treat *on the board* for the dog to eat. It does not matter if the dog is off the frame or is no longer touching the board when he is eating; he already touched and is simply being rewarded from the board.

How Deliberate is "Deliberate?"

As mentioned earlier, consistently touching a particular spot is more difficult on the A-frame than on the dog

Dog hits the touch board on the A-frame. As the dog gains experience the touch board should be painted yellow.

walk because of the steep incline and the dog's resulting momentum. While you want your dog to consciously touch the board, his touching action may not be as deliberate as it is on the ground. Do not stress over this. As long as a front paw makes contact with the board, the performance is acceptable. If you insist that the dog slow down or stop when touching the board, the result will be a slow A-frame performance. Look for deliberate, but err on the side of giving the dog the benefit of the doubt. If you doubt very strongly that the dog is consciously touching, you may always repeat the touch command and have the dog go back to the frame after a miss and then touch very deliberately.

"Mileage": Full Height, Board Placement, and Practice

Work with the board on the lowered A-frame in all four ways for several weeks. As the dog's muscles, coordination, and confidence develop, progressively raise the frame. With each new incline, the dog may slow down or miss the target, but keep working and allow him the freedom to learn how to maneuver his body and perform the task.

This is also the point where you can, and may need to, experiment with the placement of the touch board. If the dog is continuously struggling to touch the board, try placing it higher or lower in the contact zone. Does this help the dog execute the obstacle more fluidly?

Once the obstacle is at full height, the mileage begins. It takes time for the dog to learn to touch the board under all circumstances and situations. Practice sequences, peeling off, front crosses, rear crosses, blind crosses, and sends. Alternate with planting a motivator on the ground beyond the next obstacle and going back and rewarding your dog with a piece of food placed on the touch board. As the dog's speed increases, it is normal for him to have trouble hitting the touch board. If you encounter problems due to a dog's increased speed, make the sequence to the A-frame easier (for example, table to the A-frame instead of a series of jumps to the A-frame).

It is important that you train contacts by placing yourself in every possible position around the A-frame. You never know if the dog will be ahead of you, behind you, or next to you on either side. Do not be afraid to make the dog wrong! If he tends to miss the touch board when you are far behind him, great; practice sends until he figures it out. If a tunnel placed directly after the A-frame is so alluring that he jumps over the board to dive into the tunnel, practice the sequence. Remember to vary your position and do not pace yourself to the dog; move to the position you need to be in to handle the sequence.

What If the Dog Misses the Target?

If the dog misses the target at any time, freeze and wait for him to make a move. A dog that has a firm understanding of the touch-board concept will go back and touch the board on his own. When he does, you should praise him and try again. If the dog does nothing but stand there, walk one step at a time back toward the bottom of the frame and softly command "touch." After the dog touches the board, praise him and repeat the A-frame. Do not point to the touch board, as this draws the dog's attention to your hand. You want the dog to think about the mistake and try to figure out what went wrong.

Removing the Touch Board

Removing the touch board is a simple process for some dogs, others find it more upsetting. The best approach to removing the board is to intermittently take it away and then put it back. When first removing the board, back chain the end of the frame as you did when first putting the target on the obstacle. Since the picture has changed slightly, go back to commanding "touch" to remind the dog what he is supposed to do. The dog should make an effort to touch the area where the board was.

Keep saying "touch" until the dog has been successfully working the full-height A-frame with the touch board intermittently present for some time; now you can return to assumed contacts. The goal is to get the dog not to care whether the board is there or not. In other words, the dog should not alter his A-frame performance just because the touch board is no longer present.

This fading process is much easier and less drastic when the touch board resembles and cleanly fits on the obstacle. If you are having trouble removing the target, first try switching to a yellow touch board that feels and looks like the surface of the contact and then work at removing that board.

Assumed Contacts

After the dog has been successfully negotiating the A-frame for many months (yes, A-frame training takes a while), it is time to return to the assumed contact. This transition is not usually difficult, for by now, the dog should be anticipating the touch. By no longer giving the touch command, you are placing more responsibility on the dog and asking him to think about what he is doing and remember how to do it. The dog already *knows* that he is supposed to touch the board, so stop nagging him!

Whenever the dog misses the contact, you know the drill—freeze and do not continue. Wait for the dog to go back and touch the board or walk back slowly as needed.

THE STOPPED CONTACT

Stopped contacts are difficult on the A-frame due to the obstacle's sharp incline. Dogs moving at speed up and over the A-frame must either slow down or come to a jarring halt at the bottom of the frame in order to stop. Jammed shoulders and hurt backs are not pleasant, and dogs will often slow down to avoid this physical stress. The decision to teach a stopped contact on the A-frame should be made only after careful evaluation of your dog's temperament and structure, as well as your goals and access to equipment. (See Chapter 14, *All About Contact Obstacles*, page 123.)

I prefer the 2o2o for stopped contacts on the A-frame because balance and stability are easier if dogs can brace themselves on the ground. The dog should be introduced to the 2o2o concept on a ramp, stairs, or the bottom of the frame before being asked to perform the entire obstacle. (See Chapter 18, *Two-On, Two-Off*, page 151, for the entire process.) Work the 2o2o on the bottom of the A-frame until the dog can reliably find the "place" and hold the position until he is released. Again, when you are first teaching this, the dog is not ascending and descending the frame into the 2o2o, he is just climbing from the side onto the very bottom of the board and getting into the 2o2o position.

Mini Frames and Back-Chaining

Now that the dog has a firm understanding of the position he should be in, it is time to start teaching him how to get there. The goal is to have a dog climb up the frame as fast as possible, clear the apex without stopping, and drive down the descent ramp into the 2o2o position. It will take the dog some time to figure out the physical maneuvers. Having let him "run" the frame during the discovery phase has already let him develop some idea of how to negotiate the frame quickly, but now he must figure out how to move fluidly into the 2o2o position. Most dogs will initially slow down in the effort to stop in the correct position. Be patient—this is all part of the learning process. Anytime the dog does not stop in a proper 2o2o, simply and silently place him back into position, praise him, and release him. Speed returns with experience and confidence.

A useful tool to help teach your dog to drive into the 2o2o position is a mini A-frame. This is exactly what the name implies: a frame that is about two to three feet high with boards that are about three to four feet long. With such a small frame, the dog is not fighting too much inertia and gravity on the descent and therefore will have an easier time stopping and controlling his body. He also will be up and over the apex before he knows it and subsequently will be moving more quickly. This promotes speed and the idea of "diving" or "driving" down without stopping. You can also get more repetitions with the smaller frame because it is less physically taxing.

Start working call-to's over the mini frame while you stand about two feet from the bottom. This gives the dog enough room to place his feet on the ground but blocks him from being able to jump off. As always, the call-to format creates forward drive (because the dog wants to get to you) but forces the dog to stop. Once the dog is comfortable with call-to's, work the run-bys and sends. The dog should already be famil-iar with moving into the 2o2o position regardless of where you are standing (if he is not, go back and read the two-on, two-off chapter) and is now just learning how to reach that position after climbing up and down the frame. (If you do not have a mini frame or **contact trainer**, simply move on to the next step with the lowered frame.)

The next step is to move to a full-size but lowered frame. Back-chain the 2o2o position by placing the dog midway down the descent ramp and then commanding "place" (or whatever word you are using). The dog should move down the ramp and into the 2o2o position. If he does not move into position, you need to move and face the dog at the bottom of the board (as in a call-to), encourage him forward, and ensure that he stops. After back-chaining a few repetitions, start working the entire frame. Practice call-to's, run-bys, and sends. When working sends, plant a motivator on the ground beyond the end of the board (to keep the dog's focus and drive forward), then release him to the reward.

Full Height

Work with the lowered frame until the dog is confidently, comfortably, and reliably climbing up, over, and down into the 2o2o position. Remember to alternate between rewarding the dog while he is still holding the 2o2o and after he has been released. As long as the dog is physically fit, mature, and developed enough to handle the physical demands of the frame, start working toward a full-height frame. Progressively raise the frame to full height over a few sessions. Once a dog has grasped the concept of "climb up, drive down, 2o2o," he just needs to figure out how to physically negotiate the sharper incline.

Begin sequencing the frame and incorporating handling maneuvers, such as crosses and peel-offs. Does the dog hold his 2o2o under all circumstances? Anytime he breaks or fails to fully assume the 2o2o, physically put him back on the obstacle in position, return to where you were standing, then release him and try again. If your movement causes the dog to look at you or forget about the 2o2o and stop early on the board, simply freeze and wait for him to come all the way into position. Do not release him until both of his front feet are on the ground. If the dog is very frozen, softly repeat the place command to remind him what you are waiting for him to do.

Speed

Initially, a dog may be slow to come down into the 2o2o. You may see him break into a shuffle, slide, or trot or even creep down the board. This is usually the result of a dog carefully thinking about what he should do. Thinking dogs are good! Do not encourage speed on a dog that is processing the situation; it will come with practice and familiarity.

The slowness may also be the result of the physical difficulty of assuming the position. A dog's structure, drive, and attitude play a large part in the speed of the 2o2o on the A-frame. Not all dogs will be able to flawlessly dive into position; this is dependent on structure. Not all dogs will be willing to race down a ramp full speed knowing that they are required to stop; this is dependent on attitude. Allow the dog time to figure out his stride. If speed never increases or the dog is demonstrating avoidance, great stress, or discomfort, the 2o2o may not be the best option for this dog.

There is always a relationship between how fast a dog can negotiate an A-frame and his ability to stop in a 2o2o position. You should understand and accept this reality or opt to teach a moving contact. Stay attentive to your dog and recognize when he has reached his maximum 2o2o A-frame performance potential.

Maintenance

Once again, maintaining a behavior is all about consistency. If you allow your dog to self-release, it will not be long before the 2o2o disappears. The same will happen if you quick-release your dog or release him early too often. Refer back to Chapter 18, *Two-On, Two-Off,* page 151, for a more in-depth instruction on maintaining 2o2o contact performance.

TRAIN THE MOST SUITABLE CONTACT BEHAVIOR

Most dogs love running over an A-frame. If it were not for contact requirements, it would be a simple obstacle. For dogs that do not naturally stride into the contact zone, performing the frame becomes a very physically demanding task. Wait until your dog is physically mature, then take the time to train the most suitable contact behavior for your dog.

Photo by M Nicole Fischer.

CHAPTER 20

THE SEESAW

The seesaw can be unnerving to some dogs because it is the only obstacle that moves when the dog gets on it. The board moves and makes a noise when it hits the ground. It is important to teach the dog that he can control the obstacle and is not the victim of a moving plank! Remember also that the seesaw moves at different rates, depending on the composition of the board.

I always use a stopped contact on the seesaw with a down or stand position at the end of the board. The stand is for a dog that cannot lie down quickly. The dog should run to the end of board (as this makes the board fall faster) but should stop and wait for the board to hit the ground before exiting the obstacle. With the weight of the dog, the seesaw board has a tendency to bounce up a few inches after it hits the ground. The dog must learn to ride the bounce and not be thrown off balance by the rebound. The down position helps the dog maintain his balance and control the board on the way down.

Dogs that have not been taught to "ride the bounce" start to leap off early to avoid getting touched or thrown by the rebounding board. I prefer to have a dog in the down or stand position with all four feet on the end of the board. The 2o2o position on the seesaw does not give a lightweight dog good control over the board. Unless the dog is large and heavy, the plank is likely to bounce back up after pivoting. This causes the dog's rear end to be lifted, throwing him off balance—sometimes completely off of the board. The 2o2o position is a possibility only if you are working with a dog that is strong enough and capable of "riding the bounce on two feet."

The ideal execution of the seesaw occurs when a dog squarely approaches the board and hits the up contact with at least one front paw. He then runs up the ramp, past the pivot point, and all the way to the end of the board. Assuming a down or stand position, the dog rides the board to the ground and remains in his position until he is released. The goal is for the dog to get across to the very end of the board without any hesitation at the pivot point.

TEACHING THE SEESAW

In order to teach the seesaw, you will need an adjustable seesaw and a chair with arms. The chair is used to block the dog's path so that he will stop at the end of the seesaw.

Adjustable seesaw into chair. The chair is used while teaching all four ways and angle approaches, and how to control the board.

PREREQUISITES

Before beginning seesaw training, the dog must be able to lie down on a verbal command, without you luring him, bending over, or pointing to the ground. The dog must also be comfortable walking across a board or plank on the ground. He does not need to be running straight across it, but he must be willing to move and lie down on a wooden board. With this in mind, it makes sense to teach the table before beginning the seesaw. This ensures that the dog has had some experience walking on wooden surfaces.

A dog that is preparing to learn the seesaw should also have had some prior experience on surfaces that move, bounce, or wobble. This experience can be gained by using a **wobble board**, also called a **Buja board**. A wobble board is a board that is big enough for the dog to stand on and that has a ball attached to its underside. The ball prevents the board from resting flat, and when the dog touches it, the board "wobbles." Letting a dog play on a wobble board gets him used to walking on moving surfaces.

Wobble/Buja boards are available for purchase from agility equipment companies, or you can make one yourself! If you do not have a board, you can even make a "wobble table." Place a bar under the leg of your table so that the table is uneven. Now it will move as the dog jumps up onto it. Be sure to use a very low table when teaching this.

Some parks have sway bridges as part of their jungle gym equipment for children to play on. These bridges would also be useful to get a dog used to movement under his feet. Be sure that the bridge is not too high and that the dog cannot fall off of it.

INTRODUCING THE SEESAW

I like to introduce dogs to the seesaw by teaching them that they are in control of the obstacle. A great introductory and confidence-building exercise is to teach the dog to pull the plank of the seesaw down with his front feet while his hind feet are on the ground. It is a little like teaching counter-surfing!

Teaching the Dog to Control the Board

Begin with a lowered seesaw and put a treat on the board just past the pivot point. Bring the dog to the side of the seesaw and show him where you are putting the treat. Next, encourage the dog to get up on his hind legs, put his front feet on the board, and pull down the board to get the treat. If the dog is able to reach the treat without putting his feet up, simply move the treat further up the board.

Gradually move the treat higher and higher up the board so that the dog must work harder to get the board to lower. You must help the dog at first by

Wobble board.

ensuring that the board does not bounce back up and hit him under the muzzle. Ideally, you want the dog to pull the board down and stand on it to get the treat.

Dogs feel safe learning this game because they are standing on solid ground as they learn to control the moving seesaw with their front feet. They get used to the sound of the board landing and start to understand how

Teaching the dog to control the board. Initially use the chair so the board does not fall very far.

they can make the board bang. Once his confidence level rises, the dog will be much more willing to walk across the board and push it to the ground.

First Steps Across the Board

Now that the dog has experience moving the seesaw, it is time to start teaching the proper execution. Lower the seesaw far enough so that the end of the board rests in the seat of the chair and does not move. Encourage the dog to walk up the plank and lie down (or stand) at the end. To get the dog to walk across the board, you may gently guide (*not pull*) the dog by the collar, drop little pieces of food along the board, or simply lure the dog with food in your hand.

Once the dog has reached the end of the board, you command "down/stand," and wait for the dog to respond. At this point, and only if necessary, use food to lower the dog's head into a down position. Reward your dog when he is in a down/stand position by putting the food on the edge of the board, not in the dog's mouth. You are not a food-delivery service! By putting the food on the plank, you keep the dog focused on the obstacle and not on your hands.

Because you want the dog to lie down/stand at the *end* of the board, do not tell him to down/stand when he is in the middle of the board! Give the appropriate command when the dog reaches the end of the board; he *will* stop, as there is a chair in front of him.

Once the dog has been rewarded, release him with an "okay," and either pick him up off the board or simply allow him to jump off. Allowing the dog to jump off of this seesaw in this manner does not teach him to bail off

of the seesaw! It actually tends to relax the dog, for when he learns that he can get off of the obstacle, he feels less trapped and is more willing to get on it.

What If?

- **What if the dog gets on the seesaw and jumps off before he reaches the end?**

This is the dog's normal trial-and-error process of learning. Do not reward the dog for jumping off; do not try to prevent him from jumping off. Begin again as if nothing happened. I once had a Papillon that, in early seesaw training, jumped off of the seesaw twenty-one times in a row. On the twenty-second attempt across the seesaw, she thought about jumping off, realized that she could if she wanted to, and decided to scc what would happen if she went to the end of the board. After lying down and receiving her reward, she still jumped off of the obstacle on the next attempt, but only twice before deciding to go all the way across. This is a normal learning process, and you succeed by allowing your dog *the right to be wrong*. (See Chapter 2, *A New Approach to Training Philosophy*, page 3.)

- **What if the dog reaches the end of the board but will not lie down and just stands there or jumps off?**

If the dog is standing at the end of the board and a down is required, you may repeat the down command (this assumes that the dog will do a down on a verbal command on the ground; see "Prerequisites," page 170, in this chapter). If the dog jumps off of the end of the obstacle before lying down, ignore it and start over. Sometimes, doing the seesaw as a call-to rather than as a run-by, or turning to face your dog at the end of the board, will help. When you face the dog, he feels more balanced and is less likely to fall off of the board, because he is focused straight ahead.

• **What if the dog is afraid of getting on the board at all?**

First, make sure that the dog is comfortable walking over a board flat on the ground. If that is no problem, gently hold the dog's buckle collar (with your hand that is closest to the dog), and position him with all four feet on the beginning of the seesaw plank. Put a motivator in your other hand in front of the dog. *Do not pull the dog forward.* Prevent the dog from going left, right, or backwards. Now relax, and *wait*. The dog is not going to remain stationary on the board forever. If he cannot go backwards, left, or right, he *will* eventually move forward, at which time you can reward him. I have never had a dog stand longer than ten minutes before

deciding to move forward. Do not fight the dog; moving must be his decision. By preventing other options, you can manipulate your dog into making the correct choice. Remember—you have the power of time on your side.

Another option is to reteach the dog to control the board, discussed at the beginning of this chapter (see page 171).

All Four Ways and Angles

As you work the obstacle, be sure to do the seesaw in all four ways (yes, even a send). Next, progress to the call-to as soon as the dog is comfortably climbing on the board. Remember to reward your dog after he has assumed a down/stand position by putting the food on the board itself. Begin the send by targeting the end of the board with a piece of food to get the dog to focus and drive ahead of you. You can keep

Run-by with the handler facing the dog at end to ask for a down. Initially this is done with the seesaw landing into a chair. As the dog gains confidence, the chair is removed and the seesaw falls further onto the ground.

Using food under a bungee cord to teach the send. Initially, the board lands into the seat of the chair.

signal, command "okay, seesaw." The cones help the dog visualize a straight approach and encourage him to mount the board head-on. Repeat this process from different angles but always in a call-to format. This way, the dog learns an independent approach to the contact.

This is the foundation training for the seesaw obstacle and should not be rushed. Work at this step until the dog is confidently running to the end of the board and anticipating the down/stand command.

the motivator on the board by putting it under a bungee cord strapped around the plank.

Now is also the time to start teaching angled approaches. Place a traffic cone on each side of the beginning of the board. Leave the dog on an angled approach but facing the seesaw and stand behind the chair. Using the hand that is closest to the dog and a call-to

ADDING MOVEMENT

When the dog is confidently running to the end of the board, assuming the down/stand position, and comfortably negotiating the obstacle in all four ways, it is time to add the element of movement. Raise the height of the seesaw so that the end of the board is approximately four to six inches above the chair. The board will now drop as the

Teaching an angled approach to the seesaw. This concept is initially taught when the seesaw board is landing into a chair. As the dog gains confidence, the chair is removed. Continue to teach angled approaches to the seesaw as in this picture.

dog crosses it. Continue to put the dog on the seesaw all four ways. Ideally, the dog will not slow down upon feeling the movement of the board but will continue running to the end and lie down.

What If ?

- **What if, upon feeling the movement of the board, the dog bails?**

This is a common reaction. The dog needs to be comfortable with the idea of the board moving out from under him; this comes with repetition and familiarity. Repeat the exercise, letting the dog jump if he feels the need to, but do not reward him. Most dogs quickly ignore the slight movement of the board. Either the dog will eventually ignore the movement of the board, go to the end, and lie down/stand for his reward, or this situation will get worse and he will refuse to get on the board.

- **What if the dog refuses to attempt the seesaw anymore?**

Gently take hold of the buckle collar and escort the dog to the beginning of the obstacle. Hold him there and *wait*. Do not allow him to move backwards, left, or right, but do not drag or pull him onto the board. Put a motivator in the hand not holding the collar and suggest to the dog that he could move forward. No dog is going to stand there forever. You need patience to teach the dog to find courage from within. Do not become frustrated. Remember that you, as the trainer, control time; you decide when the session begins and ends, not the dog. If the dog decides that he cannot cross the board, fine—but he is not going to do anything else until he does. This kind of thinking puts mental pressure on the dog as opposed to physical pressure. Feeling that he has a choice, the dog is less likely to fight you than he would if you were to physically force him across the board.

When the dog makes the correct decision to move forward, praise and reward him, but do not release him off of the obstacle. Expect the dog to complete the down/stand at the end of the board. Work with the board at this height until the dog is running across without hesitation and shows no reaction to the movement of the board. Continue working all four ways and angled approaches. You may start combining angled approaches with run-bys.

Another option for the fearful dog is to reteach the dog to control the end of the board (see page 171 in this chapter).

MORE HEIGHT AND HANDLING MANEUVERS

Continue to gradually raise the height of the board, four to six inches at time, until the seesaw is at full height. At this point, the seesaw is still dropping into the chair.

If the dog begins to slow down at the pivot point, it is an indication that he is losing confidence, and you should work this height until he no longer slows down. Remember—the ideal seesaw performance is for the dog to drive all the way across the board without hesitation. Do not be afraid to lower the seesaw to rebuild confidence. Whenever possible, work your dog on different seesaws, but always into a chair.

Noise

As the board gets higher and the drop becomes more pronounced, the seesaw will make more noise as it hits the chair. If your dog seems upset by the noise, try placing a cushion on the chair to muffle the sound. With experience and confidence, you can gradually wean him off of the cushion.

Work on rear crosses, front crosses, and peeling off as you progress to full height.

Getting to the Ground

When the dog is comfortably executing the seesaw behavior at full height into the chair while you are moving and crossing, it is time to continue. You are now going to teach the dog that sometimes the seesaw lands on the ground and not in a chair. As usual, have the dog climb the seesaw and do a down or stand at the end of the board in the chair. Then, instead of letting the dog jump off, encourage him to turn around so that he is facing and moving down the seesaw in the opposite direction. Now when the board tips, there is no chair,

Handler is right there, facing the dog to reward him.

and the dog will lie down on the end of the board that will be on the ground. Do this for only one session until the dog is comfortable lying down on the board as it hits the ground; you do not want the dog to learn to spin on the seesaw. Start this step on a soft surface such as grass or dirt.

Removing the Chair

The dog is now ready to do a full-height seesaw without a chair. Begin the obstacle as a call-to. Stand facing the dog and hold the end of the seesaw. Command "okay, seesaw," and as the dog runs across the board, let it drop but prevent it from crashing down (help the board down). As the weight of the dog lowers the seesaw and the dog reaches the end, command the dog to lie down or stand. You will be right there, facing the dog to reward him once he has assumed the proper position. Remember that the food goes on the board—not in the dog's mouth.

Release the dog off of the seesaw with an "okay." As the dog gains confidence, start to let go of the board sooner and sooner. Continue working in call-to format until the dog is happily slamming the board down in front of you.

It's time to progress to working the obstacle in all four ways. Add angle approaches, rear crosses, front crosses, peeling off, and obstacles before the seesaw. Take the dog to different equipment. In this way, he learns that seesaws might have different weights, sounds, and balance points.

NORMAL CONFUSION

I prefer to teach the seesaw before teaching the dog walk. It is common when teaching the seesaw and dog walk in this order that at some point in training the dog is going to go up a dog walk and stop suddenly as if waiting for the board to move. This is normal, and given time and encouragement, the dog will realize that there are two obstacles that are similar yet different. If you teach the dog walk first, most dogs become very unnerved when the seesaw moves, and it's a more difficult situation to resolve.

What If?

- **What if your dog starts stopping at the pivot point?**

  If you are training a small dog, this is normal. As soon as the small dog feels the board move, he wants to stop. This stalling, however, does not afford you the best performance. To insist that the dog come to the end of the seesaw, go back to working on a call-to and hold the board up until the dog gets to the end of the board and lies down. Then lower the board.

  If you are training a large dog, this problem can still develop. Place a bungee cord around the end of seesaw and slide a piece of food or toy underneath it. This should motivate the dog to come all the way to the end of the board. Be sure to work on sends to the motivator. If the dog is still hesitant, lower the height of the seesaw.

- **What if the dog suddenly becomes fearful of the seesaw?**

  This can happen following an unexpected fly-off or when a dog gets on a new piece of equipment and is not expecting the board to tip so early. Some seesaws make very loud, banging noises when they tip, while others land more softly. If a dog is not used to hearing a loud seesaw, he may develop a new fear of the equipment. Back up to the earlier steps of teaching the obstacle and rebuild the dog's confidence. Usually a few sessions back with the board landing on a chair helps.

Holding the board up until the small dog is all the way to the end and lying down.

MAINTENANCE

When a dog is in a high-drive state of mind, he will want to leave the seesaw before completely lying down, standing, and/or being released. Never allow this to happen. Always insist on a full down or stand and that the dog hold the position until he is released by an "okay"—however short it may be. Allowing the dog to self-release will quickly lead to a dog that flies off of the seesaw.

Calling a dog sharply off of a seesaw will also cause the seesaw contact behavior to break down. If a course requires you to turn a dog sharply off of a seesaw, you will

Cones on either side of the board help the dog balance when lying down.

HAVING PATIENCE, TEACHING CONFIDENCE

As you can tell from reading this chapter, mastering the seesaw has a lot to do with confidence. Even the most wild and seemingly fearless dogs can develop seesaw phobias and should not be rushed through seesaw training. Take the time to help your dog truly understand the seesaw obstacle.

need to go back and target the end of the board in practice to maintain the concept of "run to the end of the board." This is normal maintenance training.

SPECIAL CASES

With tall dogs (for example, Afghan Hounds, setters, and Dobermans), or dogs that do not lie down easily and quickly, the down position can be replaced with a "bow" in addition to the stand. For these dogs, it is only necessary that their front legs be down on the board to achieve maximum performance.

For square dogs with straight shoulders (for example, many terriers, Keeshonden, Elkhounds, and Icelandic Sheepdogs), teaching a stand at the end of the board is probably the most efficient, as it is very difficult for them to bow or lie down quickly.

For very small dogs who barely weigh enough to tip the seesaw, make sure that the board comes down when the dog gets to the end of the board. Artificially weight the seesaw so that the dog cannot tip it in practice. Ask the dog to come to the very end of the board, then you push the board down to the ground yourself. This teaches the dog to always go to the end of the board, even if it is not moving. Small dogs often panic in a ring when a heavy seesaw does not start to move when they expect it to move. This practice will help them overcome this fear.

If a dog falls or slides off of the board when he tries to lie down on it, put a traffic cone on either side of the bottom of the plank. This will help the dog get his balance.

Photo by M. Nicole Fischer.

CHAPTER 21

THE DOG WALK

Once your dog is comfortably negotiating the seesaw, you can begin dog walk training. The dog does not need to be perfectly performing the full-height seesaw, but he should be comfortably climbing, moving, and lying down on the board. You must select a command for the dog walk; common choices include "walk-on," "walk-it," "climb," or "dog walk." As mentioned earlier in Chapter 7, *Commands You Need*, I believe that there should be a separate command for each contact obstacle, as the performances for each obstacle are very different. To indicate the up contact, I precede my obstacle command with "lie down," making my full dogwalk command "lie down, walk on."

TEACHING THE OBSTACLE

Initial training for the dog walk involves getting the dog comfortable running across the narrow planks. To prevent accidents and major fly-offs, target the bottom of the dog walk with a toy or food tube, encouraging the dog to keep his head down but not requiring a formal contact behavior. Remember—you are first teaching the obstacle and later will incorporate the contact behavior. At this point, no command is given as the dog reaches the contact. The goal is to get the dog to run confidently and quickly up, across, and down the ramps to reach the planted motivator.

A hoop may be used to encourage the dog to lower his head and not leap off of the dog walk. Make sure that the hoop is large enough so that the dog can easily pass underneath it but cannot jump up. You might need to experiment with its placement to figure out what works for your dog. Remember—*the hoop is not being used to teach the contact behavior.* It is simply a useful tool to encourage the dog to lower his head as he races down the ramp. (See Chapter 14, *All About Contact Obstacles,* page 123.)

Hoop at the end of the dog walk.

INTRODUCING THE DOG WALK

Begin with a low (two-foot-high) dog walk to avoid injury in case the dog loses his balance or decides to bail. Place the dog midway down the descent ramp, and coax him to the end of the board by placing food drops in front of him as he walks down the board. (I call this the Hansel-and-Gretel approach!) The dog should learn how to exit the obstacle before getting on it.

If the dog panics and jumps off of the board, ignore it and try again. The freedom to jump off eventually gives him the confidence to stay on the board. Non-food-motivated dogs can be similarly lured with a toy.

Remain quiet and calm; too much talking will draw the dog's attention to you instead of to the board. Do not be concerned if the dog happens to jump up onto the dog walk from the side or turn around on the plank. Encourage any and all interaction with the plank. At this stage of training, any experimentation that the dog offers is good because it helps the dog become comfortable with the obstacle.

Have a motivator placed at the end of the descent ramp, on the ground, and allow the dog to get it as he reaches the ground. Do not worry if he comes off of the board while getting his reward; the concern is not the contact behavior but becoming comfortable moving and running across the boards. If you are using a hoop, you can place the motivator off of the ramp just past or underneath the hoop.

As you progress, start the dog closer and closer to the beginning of the up ramp of the dog walk. Eventually, let the dog start at the very beginning and run across the entire obstacle. This entire process can usually be accomplished in one training session.

When your dog can run confidently and in a balanced manner across the entire lower dog walk, progress to the full-height obstacle. Work until the dog is galloping across the full-height dog walk to reach his reward.

Position yourself so that you are either running behind the dog or in front of the dog, but never next to the dog. Running next to a dog encourages him to pace himself to and look at you. Both are undesirable behaviors on a dog walk. Dogs that run while looking at their handlers easily lose their balance and can fall off of the narrow plank.

If a dog falls off of a dog walk and becomes so frightened that he does not want to get back on, do not push the issue in the same session. Work on other things and return to the dog walk a few days later when the dog has had time to relax and forget about the fall. When you return to work on the dog walk, begin by back-chaining and rebuild the exercise. (See Incorporating the Contact Behavior in this chapter, page 182.) The old adage, "If you fall off a horse, get right back on," does not apply when working with dogs. Trainers often make a dog's fear worse by trying to deal with the fear when a dog is too stressed to learn.

Practice running the dog walk in all four ways: call-to, send, run-by-right, and run-by-left. Introduce handling maneuvers such as crossing and peeling off. This will accustom the dog to keeping his focus down (toward the planted motivator, and later toward the contact), even when you are moving in front of or behind him. Remember—you are teaching the dog to run the equipment; no contact behavior is expected, but a motivator is always planted at the end of the descent ramp.

What If?

• **What if the dog has trouble getting his hind legs onto the dogwalk board?**

This is a fairly common problem with many large dogs. It represents a lack of rear-end awareness. I have seen it frequently in Rough Collies, Belgian Tervurens, and Belgian Sheepdogs. To help make the dog more aware of his rear end, place a traffic cone or similar support on either side of the beginning of the dog walk plank to offer a guide and support. If the dog is still having trouble, place a baby gate on either side of the plank to make a channel for the dog to initially walk through.

Take your dog to a set of bleachers at a nearby park or school, and have him practice walking across the low-level bleacher seats. This will help him become more aware of his rear legs and of his balance on a narrow plank.

ANGLED APPROACHES

The approach to the dog walk might not always be straight on, and the dog needs to learn how to adjust his path to ascend the ramp head on in order to ensure that he hits the up contact. To teach the dog how to negotiate angled approaches, place traffic cones or baby gates on the sides of the up ramp. The cones discourage the dog from climbing on the ramp from the side and encourage him out and around, thus placing him on a straight approach to the obstacle. Your command is "out, walk-on," and a signal to the line of approach of the obstacle is given.

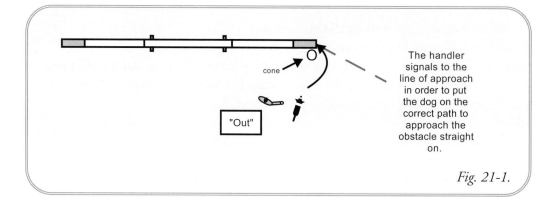

The handler signals to the line of approach in order to put the dog on the correct path to approach the obstacle straight on.

Fig. 21-1.

OPERATION OBSERVATION

As the dog becomes accustomed to the obstacle, he will develop some tendencies, or a specific "way" of negotiating the obstacle. During this "discovery phase," pay close attention to what the dog is physically doing on the dog walk. Where does his stride tend to carry him? Does he naturally land on the contact, or is he inclined to jump? How motivated is he? Pay close attention to how your positioning and movement affect the dog's behavior. Does the dog stride down to the end of the board toward the motivator when you peel off? Does the dog pick up his head to look at you? This information will give you an idea of which contact behavior is best suited to your dog.

INCORPORATING THE CONTACT BEHAVIOR ONTO THE DOG WALK

Regardless of the type of contact you are teaching, all contact behaviors will be introduced through back-chaining. Back-chaining is the process of working from the end to the beginning. The dog starts at the end of the obstacle and is only asked to perform the contact behavior. Gradually, the dog is placed farther and farther back along the ramp and is asked to complete more of the obstacle, including the contact behavior at the very end. This continues until the dog is starting at the beginning of the obstacle.

In the learning stages, anytime the dog does not offer the correct contact behavior, simply abort the process and begin again. There is no penalty; there is no reward. Because you hold the power of time, and because life as the dog knows it does not continue until the correct contact behavior is offered, the dog is subtly compelled to perform correctly.

This approach—repeating until the dog does it correctly—is only appropriate for the learning stages and is not used in the ring. A dog in the competition ring should be well past the learning stages, and the correction that you employ, to let your dog know that he has made a mistake depends on the chosen contact behavior.

THE RUNNING CONTACT

Being blessed with a true running contact on the dog walk is rare and wonderful. For most dogs, it is more natural to leap off of the end of the dog walk than it is to run through it. You should be able to tell whether your dog is consistently running the length of the board and hitting the yellow zone during the discovery phase.

TESTING THE TENDENCY

It is now time to remove the planted motivator and/or hoops. Run the dog over the obstacle as if the aids were still there. Your only command should be for the dog walk; nothing should be said for the contact. Reward your dog by throwing a motivator low and straight ahead of him. The movement of the motivator should coincide with the dog moving off of the board. Throwing the toy while he is still on the board is an unfair distraction that might cause him to jump.

If the dog is successful, add a jump before and after the dog walk to make a little sequence. If the dog is still consistently striding into the contact zone, try placing a table straight beyond the dog walk. Because tables often cause dogs to look up, this is a test to see if your dog is still inclined to hit the contact.

If the behavior is holding up, make longer sequences and work to increase the dog's speed. Be sure that your dog is not stopping or slowing as he runs down the descent ramp. Test angled approaches and exits on the dog walk. Will a sharp approach to the dog walk, which slows the dog's speed, change his ability to stride into the contact?

No dog is perfect, but if you are getting a high percentage of correct behaviors, then it is probably worth your while to continue using a running con-

tact. If you are not comfortable with your accuracy rate—because it can vary—consider teaching a moving or stopped contact.

THE MOVING CONTACT

As discussed earlier, there are two different methods that can be used to achieve a moving-contact behavior. On the dog walk, the touch method works quite well, because the incline of the descent ramp is not as steep as the A-frame and dogs can easily adjust their stride to touch a specific spot of the contact. The "do not jump" method is effective on the dog walk as well. It all depends on the individual dog and handler team (See Chapter 16, The Contact Behavior, page 135.)

THE TOUCH METHOD

If you are using the touch system with a target or touch board to achieve moving contacts, the dog must first have gone through the entire process of learning the touch board/target on the ground (See Chapter17, The Touch Method, page 143.)

BACK-CHAINING THE TOUCH BOARD

Start by placing the touch board between the last two slats of the dog walk. Put a food tube on the ground beyond the end of the board. Now position the dog on the descent ramp just above the contact zone. Release the dog with the

Helping the dog remember to touch.

command touch. (Yes, you are going back to saying "touch" even though you have assumed contacts on the touch board away from the equipment.) The dog should move forward on the ramp and touch the board with one or both front feet. As soon as the dog touches the board, tell him to "get it!" and encourage him to move forward to the food tube. Meet him there and give him the reward.

If the dog is successful, continue by starting the dog higher on the descent ramp. If the dog is unsuccessful, repeat the exercise and draw attention to the touch board by slightly lifting it with your hand that is furthest from the dog. Command "touch," and when the dog steps on the board and pushes it out of your hand, respond with a "get it!"

Gradually back-chain the behavior until the dog is able to do the entire obstacle. You do not need to move in inches; this can be accomplished in one training session. As the dog picks up speed and starts farther and farther back, he will miss or try to jump over the target. This is normal, because his stride is changing and he must learn to adjust, just as he did when the touch board was on the ground. To let the dog know that he has made an error, simply do not allow him to get his reward. Never yell "no!" at the dog. Call him back and try again. You can always go back to helping the dog by lifting the board slightly (leave him in a stay so that you can get into position) or starting him closer to the touch board. Remember that you must never point to the touch board as the dog performs the obstacle, for this will cause the dog to look at *you* instead of at the target.

As you are back-chaining, be mindful of your positioning. Either run ahead of the dog or behind the dog, but never right next to him. Most importantly, be sure that you are not adjusting your movement to the touch behavior. Do not slow down or stop next to the target to try to get the dog to touch. He must do it on his own. While the dog may slow down or stop to touch deliberately, your movement should be unchanged. Simply say "get it!" once the dog has hit the board and encourage him forward to his reward. Be sure to practice sends as much as run-bys.

"MILEAGE": APPROACHES, MANEUVERS, AND SEQUENCES

It takes time for the dog to learn how to touch a target on the ramp under all different circumstances. The dog's stride and speed over the obstacle will vary depending on the approach, your position, and the dog's focus. Only with practice will dogs figure out how to maneuver their bodies and feet in order to touch the target every time. The dog may initially slow down to hit the board; do not worry! He is learning, and with experience, his speed and comfort will increase.

Work with the touch board/target on the contact for many months. Incorporate handling maneuvers such as peeling off and crosses at both ends of the dog walk. You can also start sequencing the dog walk. Plant the motivator after the next obstacle. Once the dog has touched the target on the dog walk, give the command for that next obstacle, followed by the "get it" command. Keep in mind that your position will draw the dog's attention away from the contact. When you peel off or cross in front, the dog will want to look at you. This may cause him to lift his head and will increase the chance of him jumping. Make sure that you work

through these more difficult situations and consistently enforce the deliberate touch.

During this training time, it is normal for the dog to make mistakes. Stay calm and consistent, and do not become upset. Never accept anything other than a deliberate touch. Always get the dog to touch correctly in every training session. You can always back up in your training steps if the dog is having a bad day.

Behaviors that the dog appears to have mastered often deteriorate before they improve again. Remember that behavior precedes learning, and the dog will touch the target long before he actually understands that he is supposed to touch the board every time, all the time, and as fast as possible.

There will be days when you are very frustrated and may consider changing your contact method. Do not do it! Give the dog time to learn the behavior at his maximum speed. While some dogs grasp the concept in a matter of months, I have worked with dogs that took two years to understand a moving contact.

ASSUMED CONTACTS

When the dog has been performing the dog walk for a few months, stop saying "touch" and return to assumed contacts. The dog has already experienced this on the ground so it should transfer easily to the obstacle. If the dog misses the contact, do not praise him or reward him. Simply repeat the dog walk. If the dog continually fails to hit the touch board, you can once again lift the board and/or return to back-chaining the obstacle, but do not revert to saying "touch."

REMOVING THE BOARD

Touch boards and targets are only training tools and will not be present on the obstacles in competition. Dogs need to learn how to perform the touching behavior without the aid of a board or target. When your dog is deliberately and repeatedly hitting the touch board, it is time to consider removing the board. For some dogs, this is a simple process; for others, it is very upsetting. I like using touch boards and targets that are painted yellow and look very much like actual contacts because this makes the transition easier.

To fade the touch board off of the contact, remove the touch board and back-chain the behavior like you did initially when introducing the board on the ramp. Command "touch," and ask the dog to make a deliberate move to touch the spot where the target used to be. Because the picture has slightly changed, the dog is reminded to touch with the "touch" command. Once the dog is deliberately touching the spot where the board used to be, return to the assumed contact.

Even if the dog is successful, replace the touch board intermittently until the dog does not appear to care if the board is there or not. The idea is to get the dog to think about the location of where to touch and not about the touch board itself. If the dog loses the concept of touch when you remove the touch board, do not panic. Stand the dog near the bottom of the contact and command "touch." Wait for the dog to make some attempt. He should move to the board and touch the spot in the contact zone where the target used to be. If necessary, go back to occasionally working with the touch board on the ramp to remind the dog of the required

behavior. Think of the target as a leash. When you need more control, you put it back on!

What If?

• **What if the dog comes off the side of the dog walk as the handler attempts to peel away?**

For small dogs, place a baby gate flat on the ground next to the plank of the dog walk so that if the dog jumps off of the side, he will land on the gate. Dogs do not like to land on uneven surfaces. Therefore, most dogs, upon seeing the gate lying on the ground, opt to run to the end of the board before dismounting.

For large dogs and dogs that are not convinced by the gate on the ground, plant a motivator ahead of the plank. After a few sessions in which the dog goes to the motivator as you peel off, try throwing the motivator ahead of the dog instead of planting it. This way, the dog goes to the bottom of the board, regardless of whether you peel off, because even if he does not see a motivator, there may soon be one flying through the air ahead of him!

CORRECTIONS IN THE RING

When a dog fails to perform the contact behavior in practice, you correct the dog by freezing, waiting for him to offer the correct behavior, then repeating the obstacle. In practice, the exercise is then repeated, but in a trial, you do not have this luxury. In the competition ring, if a dog jumps the contact, you need to freeze and wait to see if the dog fixes the mistake (goes to a 2o2o position or returns to touch the contact). If you are using a lie down to discourage the dog from jumping the contact, immediately get your dog to completely lie down. At this point, you will undoubtedly hear the judge's whistle, indicating that you are being excused for training in the ring. Thank the judge, go to the dog, praise the dog for lying down or fixing his mistake some other way, and gently escort him out of the ring. This should be enough to educate the dog that a mistake has been made and therefore the game does not continue. This system will only work if you are consistent in practice and in the ring.

Both the "do not jump" and "touch" methods can create fast, reliable, moving-contact performances. It is your choice, based on your dog's personality, physical structure, drive, and preference, as to which method you teach in training.

STOPPED CONTACT

To achieve a stopped contact on the dog walk, you must first decide on the position in which the dog should stop. I will describe the process using a 2o2o position. For other positions, be sure to have a clear picture of the behavior in mind, and do not accept a crouch when a down is desired.

Before the 2o2o behavior can be incorporated into the entire dog walk performance, the dog must first have learned how to assume and stay in the position on the end the ramp. (See Chapter 18, *The Two-On, Two-Off*, page 151.)

Back-chaining the two-on-two-off. Start with the dog above the contact zone.

Command "place." The dog should move forward as the handler stands still.

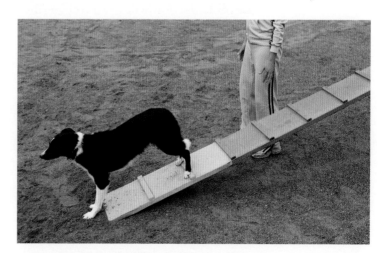

Back-chaining, the final position.

DRIVING INTO THE 2O2O

The dog will already have some experience moving into a 2o2o position on a board, ramp, or stairs. Bring the dog to the bottom of the dog walk ramp and give your place command. The dog should assume the 2o2o position and wait for the release. The next time, start the dog higher up the ramp, and he should still run to the 2o2o position and wait to be released. Finally, place the dog on the top ramp and command "place." The dog should drive forward and into the 2o2o position. Continue to back-chain the dog walk. See photos page 187.

You do not need to move in inches and should be able to work your way back to the beginning of the obstacle in a few training sessions. Vary the amount of time you require the dog to stay on the board, and change your position as he stays—sometimes be ahead of him, sometimes be behind him, and sometimes be moving. If at any time the dog breaks, calmly and silently put him back into the 2o2o position and leave again. Go back to him and reward him, then release him with an "okay." Once you have worked back to the beginning of the obstacle, you will need to give the dog walk command to indicate the obstacle, then give the place command as the dog reaches the descent ramp.

The goal is for the dog to be confident driving into the 2o2o position. It may take some time for him to figure out his footing and learn to rock his weight backward in order to stop on the ramp with his back feet on and his front feet off, but be patient—he will work out a system. If the dog looks hesitant or is moving step by step while looking to you between each step forward as if saying "is this it?" he does not understand where "place" is or is not yet physically comfortable moving into the position.

A dog that truly understands the 2o2o will keep his focus on the bottom of the board (where he is going) and will not look to you until he has reached that spot. If your dog is creeping down the dog walk slowly, slat by slat, simply wait, stay still and silent until he has reached the bottom and the 2o2o position, then immediately release him. If the dog is very stuck, you may softly say his name or repeat "place." Go back to the early training, and back-chain the behavior to the end of the board again.

If the dog knows the position but is just moving slowly, encourage him as he is on the obstacle. You can try planting a toy at the end of the dog walk and not holding the contact position as long. The less stopping and more moving forward the dog does, the more speed he will generate.

SOME MILEAGE

Since the 2o2o is a much more consistent and clear-cut behavior than a running or moving contact behavior, not as much "mileage" will be required. Nevertheless, the dog must learn how to perform the dog walk from all angles, in all four-ways, with you crossing and peeling off, and in sequence with other obstacles.

ASSUMED CONTACTS

After the dog has been working the dog walk for many months, it is time to progress to assumed contacts. By this point, and especially with a behavior as consistent as your 2o2o has been, the dog knows what to do at the end of the board and does not need you to tell him to do it. In fact, if you repeatedly tell him to do something that he already plans to do, you are detracting from his inclination to think about it.

MAINTAINING THE DOGWALK PERFORMANCE

Throughout the dog's agility career, you will need to work on maintaining dog walk contacts. Courses that require sharp pulls off of the contact weaken the moving and running contact performance, because the dog begins to anticipate being called off early. This leads to missed contacts. Two-on, two-offs can also deteriorate as the dog may start to shift his position off the side of the board instead of straight off the end. To counteract these tendencies, practice peeling off of the dog walk. When the dog gets to the contact, throw a motivator to the side away from where you peeled off. Or, return to a stopped dog (if you taught the 2o2o) and reward him straight at the end of the board.

These techniques teach the dog that there is no reason to come off the side of the board toward you because the reward might suddenly appear straight ahead of him.

MOTIVATIONAL DOG WALKS

To maintain dog walk performance speed, it is a good idea to occasionally do "motivational dog walks." Show the dog that you are planting a motivator at the end of descent ramp, then run the obstacle, telling the dog to "get it." This is just like the earlier obstacle-training phase when you were teaching the dog to run the equipment. The emphasis is on speed, and since the motivator is planted at the end of the board, the dog (and you) need not worry about the contact zone. If you feel that the dog is getting "sticky" or is slowing down too much on his running or moving contacts, a few motivational dog walks should do the trick. The purpose of the motivational dog walk is to remove the pressure of contact performance.

While motivational dog walks do not interfere with moving and running contact behaviors, they do not work well with stopped contacts once the stopped-contact behavior has been taught on the equipment. The dog has learned that he is to move to and assume his position, and stay there until he is released. Encouraging the dog to

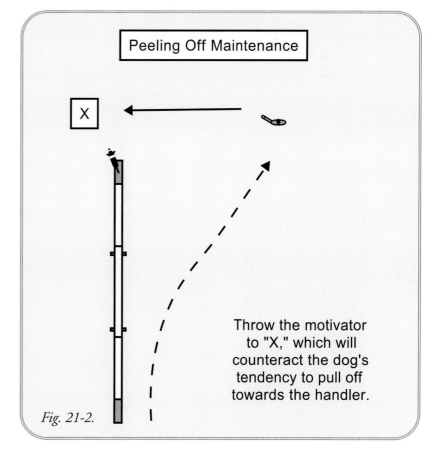

Peeling Off Maintenance

Throw the motivator to "X," which will counteract the dog's tendency to pull off towards the handler.

Fig. 21-2.

run over and off of the ramp without assuming his position would confuse him and ruin the behavior. You may plant a motivator just off the end of the dog walk that the dog can reach. The dog is rewarded while still maintaining his 2o2o position.

PROOFING THE DOG WALK

To the dog, not all dog walks feel the same. Some dog walk planks have more bounce than others. Some boards have more sand for traction. Even the size of the slats varies from one piece of equipment to another. It is important for beginning dogs to gain experience on many different dog walks before you can feel confident that your dog will be comfortable going over a strange dog walk in a ring.

Proof the dog walk further by placing a piece of material over part of it, a branch across the board, and wet the surface to simulate rain. If you own a dog walk, be sure to move it around your training field so that the dog experiences it in different locations. It is very easy to become lazy and leave a large piece of equipment set up in one place so long that the dog associates it only with that location.

CHAPTER 22

WEAVE POLES

When spectators watch agility, weave poles seem to impress them the most. While weaving in and out of a line of poles seems like a very difficult behavior to teach, it is actually quite simple and natural for the dog. Weaves reflect what a dog would do naturally while running through the woods, weaving in and out of trees.

Three components must be addressed in order for a dog to properly execute weave poles. First, a dog must focus and look at the poles. Second, the dog must understand that the obstacle has a specific beginning and ending. Finally, the dog must have efficient footwork to move fluidly and rhythmically through the poles. I developed a training method that addresses these three essential skills.

LOOKING AT THE POLES

The key to teaching good weave poles is training a dog to look at the *poles* and not at you, regardless of where you are positioned. Trained dogs miss and pop out of poles for only one reason—they look at something other than the poles!

Sometimes the dog's attention is drawn to a nearby obstacle. At times it is *your* motion that draws the dog's head—and focus—away from the poles. Noises or sounds may also interfere with a dog's weave-pole performance. In any case, distraction is the root of the problem. To immunize the dog against distractions, proofing will be necessary to teach him to focus on the poles and only on the poles.

The best way to teach the dog to focus solely on the poles is to have him learn how to go through weave poles completely on his own. In order to accomplish this, you must *stay away* from the dog and not make eye contact with him. If you look at the dog, the dog looks back at you, and then no one looks at the poles!

In my training method, the dog first learns the weave poles in the call-to format. This accomplishes two goals. By removing yourself from the picture, the dog does not rely on your position for help and learns to find the entrance and stay in the poles on his own. Additionally, because you are not moving or physically helping the dog, he is not inclined to look at you and can instead focus on the poles in front of him.

The dog is taught how to perform weave poles as a call-to and send before he ever experiences having you move next to him. This ensures that the dog's ability to weave is not reliant on you. He will learn to find the correct entrance and weave through the entire set of poles completely on his own. This technique not only gives beginning handlers confidence to work away from their dogs but also creates dogs that are confident weaving away from their handlers.

You and your dog should always view the weave poles as one obstacle, not a successive set of two poles. If the dog is looking at the weaves, he must learn that, as long as there are poles in front of him, he should continue weaving. Accordingly, if the dog makes an error at any time, you need to start the entire obstacle over from the beginning. Do not attempt to put a dog back into the middle of the line of poles.

When a dog pops out of the weave poles at any point, restarting him from the beginning will teach him that the obstacle starts with pole number one and is not complete until there are no more poles in front of him. This concept takes time for the dog to comprehend, and it requires patience.

In the teaching phase, if a dog skips a pole or two (because of tangled feet or lost rhythm) and goes back in on his own and continues weaving, praise his effort and act as if he is totally correct. While a dog has skipped a pole, the important part is that he is trying to weave and understands that the obstacle was not completed. If, on the other hand, the dog pops out and does not attempt to go back into the poles and continue weaving, simply start over.

When mistakes occur and you choose to bring the dog back to the beginning of the weaves, novice dogs often become confused and start to back-weave (weaving in the opposite direction). Because the dog is offering a behavior that he has just learned, there is no reason to discourage him. While I do not stop the dog from back-weaving, I also do nothing to praise or encourage it. Ignore it, and it will work itself out.

FOOTWORK AND STRIDE

Dogs cannot simply run through the poles—they must develop an effective movement to navigate back and forth. Furthermore, dogs must learn how to switch from a canter or gallop into their weaving stride when they are approaching the poles.

STYLES

Dogs have different styles when performing the weave poles. You can teach five dogs to weave using the same method, and each is likely to develop his own way of weaving. It depends on how tall the dog is, how long he is, and where his shoulders allow him to carry his head. The method used to teach weaving does not necessarily dictate the style the dog will choose to weave. Style is more dependent on the dog's structure. You do not need to be concerned with which style your dog uses to weave, as long as it allows for efficient, consistent, and comfortable movement through the poles.

The dog should maintain a rhythm and not change his form midway through the poles. Small dogs and dogs with short backs usually choose to bounce or hop from side to side, with two front feet landing on the same side at once. Large dogs and dogs with long

Bouncing side to side, or double striding.

Single-striding style.

backs often **single stride**, placing one front foot through the poles at a time as they plow through the weaves. Very small dogs may be seen trotting in and out of the poles, because the spacing between the poles is so large relative to their tiny stride.

When teaching small dogs to weave, it is helpful to use poles with less distance between them. A set of poles that are eighteen inches apart or less works well. When teaching giant breeds to weave, try using poles that are twenty-four inches apart. It is easier for a dog to develop a weaving rhythm if the spacing is proportional to his size. Eventually, after a rhythm is learned, the dog will adjust to regulation spacing.

STRIDE ADJUSTMENTS

A dog must always enter the weave poles with the first pole next to his left shoulder. See Fig. 22-1. After entering the space between pole number one and pole number two, he continues weaving back and forth through the line of poles in an uninterrupted fashion until he has passed through every pole.

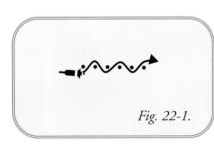

Fig. 22-1.

In order to physically make the correct entrance to the weave poles, the dog must collect his stride, rock his weight back on his haunches, and step into the poles, leading with his left leg. Beginner dogs who find themselves approaching poles faster than they are used to will often refuse or miss the entry because they are unable to properly adjust their stride in time. Some may make the entrance through the first two poles but then pop right out be-

cause they did not collect their stride and/or did not plan to be on the left lead early enough.

When you first teach weave poles, the dog approaches the poles from a stationary position or from a walk or trot. If a dog can weave only when he approaches the poles slowly, he has not learned the proper physical weight and stride adjustments required for weaving. Incorporating angled entrances and adding sequencing to weave-pole training will help a dog learn to enter the weave poles when he is running at top speed.

SPEED

Learning to weave is actually a lot like learning to type. At first, the dog must think about where to put his feet, just like you think about which finger to use to hit a specific letter. With practice, the movements become automatic, and the dog starts to weave without having to think about it—the way people learn to "touch type."

Weave-pole speed is dependent on understanding, confidence, and a learned pattern of foot movement. Do not push the dog for speed in the teaching stage; it would be like someone pushing you to hit the keys of a keyboard faster before you learned to type. The extra pressure creates undue stress and mistakes and actually interferes with speed.

At some point during weave-pole training, a dog transitions from thinking while weaving to weaving automatically. During this transition phase, the dog will make many mistakes as he flip-flops between conscious thought and automatic movement. You can recognize this stage when your dog, who has been weaving well, suddenly seems to fall apart. The more the dog tries to weave, the worse his weaving gets. It is important that you not become distressed. Understand that your dog is merely in a learning stage. This is a time in training where "less is more." If, at this time, the dog is drilled on weave poles, he will worry and think even harder about what he is doing instead of relaxing and letting the weaving movement come automatically. Brief, infrequent training sessions are the best approach during this phase. Encourage the dog's efforts, and do not overdo it!

WEAVES AND PUPPIES

Puppies (dogs that are not yet full-grown) are flexible and bend easily. Teaching the first steps of weaving in which the poles are tilted and open puts no undue stress on a growing puppy. I do not continue puppies past the first steps until they are full-grown in height and length. This is not because it will physically harm them in any way, but because a dog's weaving style is dependent on his size and structure. With a changing body, the puppy will have to relearn poles when he reaches his full size. For more information on training puppies, see Chapter 4, *Puppies in Agility*, page 19.

WEAVE POLE SYSTEMS

Many different options and training methods are available for teaching

GOALS FOR TEACHING POLES

Regardless of the method you use to teach weave poles, you want your dog to be able to do the following:

- Independently execute the obstacle.
- Enter weave poles without your assistance (independent entries).
- Develop a rhythmic weaving style.
- Maintain total focus on the poles and avoid distractions.
- Allow you to execute crosses before and after the poles.
- Be able to perform the weaves poles in all fourways.
- Rock back when approaching the weaves at a high rate of speed.
- Complete the set of poles even if you peel off away from the poles.

weave poles. Before starting to teach, you must decide on the technique best suited for you and your dog. I have experimented with all different ways of teaching weave poles and with many different breeds of dogs. My preference is a system using Weave-A-Matic poles. This is a set of training poles designed to tilt so that the dog views a path through the middle of a V-shaped passageway. Using Weave-A-Matic poles gives the dog the best understanding of entrances to poles, and it teaches footwork.

It is important that you purchase a quality set of Weave-A-Matic poles that will stay on the angle toward which they are tilted. Nothing is more frustrating than poles that fall over when they are

Weave-A-Matic poles.

Channel system.

barely touched. An excellent set of Weave-A-Matic poles has been designed by Max 200 Dog Obedience/Agility Equipment Company.

My second choice is the **channel system**, which I recommend for use only with medium- to large-size dogs. In this system, poles are straight up but are staggered, again creating an obvious path through the middle of the poles. Channel poles do a good job of teaching the weaving motion but are not as useful for training entrances and footwork. They are a superior system when working strong, fast dogs that think nothing of running straight into poles and breaking them! Small dogs have a more difficult time learning a rhythm when using channel poles. Quality

channel poles may also be purchased from Max 200 Dog Obedience/Agility Equipment Company.

Because the Weave-A-Matic system is my preference, the method outlined in this book uses Weave-A-Matics. People have told me that they find it difficult to transition in training from tilted poles (Weave-A-Matic) to straight-up poles. I have not found this to be the case, but you do need to know how to train it—so continue reading!

POSITIONING THE POLES

Because the dog must enter with the first pole against his left shoulder, pole number one should be tilted to the left.

Poles that are open too wide for most dogs.

Pole number two would then be tilted to the right, and so on. When you first introduce the dog to a set of open poles, be sure that the poles are not open so much that the dog is inclined to jump through them. How far you first tilt the poles will depend on your dog's size and on his natural inclination to jump over them. If you see your dog jumping through the poles, raise them a few inches at a time until you reach a height where the dog steps through the poles.

SEEING THE "V"

To help the dog understand what to do with weave poles, you want him to learn that there is a path through them. The open poles of the Weave-A-Matic or separated channel poles make this path clearly visible. It is important that both you and your dog see the path through the poles. When you are teaching with

Dog's view of the "V" through the poles.

the Weave-a-Matic system, focus on the "V" (the straight path through the poles) and do not look at the dog. If you make eye contact with the dog, then the dog will look at you and not at the poles. Remember—a dog that does not stay focused on the poles will pop out.

INTRODUCING THE DOG TO THE WEAVE POLES

The dog must be able to do a sit-stay, or you must have an assistant who can hold the dog in a stationary position before you begin to teach the weave poles. Begin with the dog in a sit-stay about a yard from the first pole. The dog is now facing a set of open poles (preferably twelve). Position yourself behind the second pole (straddling the base of the poles) and face the dog. Give a hand signal and a verbal command to begin the exercise.

THE CUES

The verbal command will be "okay, weave." The "okay" releases the dog from his sit-stay, and "weave" indicates the obstacle.

The hand signal is more difficult for most beginning handlers to master and it will take some practice for you to perfect. Always signal with the hand that is closest to the dog; if the dog is directly in front of you, either hand is acceptable. As you start to work on angled approaches, the choice of which hand to use becomes more critical.

The hand signal is an extended arm pointing to the air space about a foot above the opening of the first two poles. The dog should not see the hand until it

is completely extended. To keep the signal "a secret," slide your hand up close to your body until it passes above your shoulder. At this point, extend your arm, and when it stops moving, give the verbal command. The purpose of this is to draw the dog's eyes up and over to the entrance of the poles. See photos page 199. Once the dog has entered the poles, begin to slowly and steadily lower your hand signal as the dog progresses forward. Reward the dog directly in front, while he is still in the poles, with a piece of food given from the hand that gave the signal. Never lower your hand until the dog makes the entrance! You want the dog to figure out the entrance on his own.

The goal is to get the dog to step into the poles to get a treat from your hand. Because you are behind the second pole, the dog only needs to step into the first pole to reach you and his reward. If the dog does not enter the weave poles correctly, do not reward him, then try again. Reward your dog only when he passes to the right of the first pole—which should be easy because it is bent out of his way—and steps into the poles. Be sure to praise the dog for getting to you before you give him the reward. If you give the dog a treat and *then* praise him, you end up praising him for eating!

As your dog succeeds in coming through the poles, gradually move back so that the dog has to come through more and more poles to get his reward. Continue until the dog can run through all twelve poles. This may happen in one training session, or it may take several sessions. It is important for the dog to be able to come through all twelve poles to you, in different locations and from different directions.

Every time the dog passes a pole, say "good" or "yes." As the dog learns to

Position 1 (signaling to weaves, in a call-to).

Position 2 (keeping the hand a secret).

Position 3.

Position 4. Extend the arm and hand to point towards the airspace above the first and second pole.

Call-to though twelve weave poles. Hand starts to lower as the dog makes the correct entrance into the weaves.

Dog's view though twelve weave poles.

weave, your praise helps set the rhythm for his weaving through the poles. You will be chanting, "Good, good, good, good, good." If you are unable to speak that quickly, a hand clap can later be used to help establish a rhythm.

When you are running a course with a dog that has been taught this way, command, "weave," then once the dog has made the entry, start to chant, "Good, good, good, good," etc. It is important that the "good, good, good" is said in rhythm with the dog's speed and does not accelerate or change tone (higher or lower) as the dog gets closer to the twelfth pole and you get excited.

TEACHING THE ROCK BACK

It was discussed earlier why it is necessary for a dog to shift his weight back onto his haunches before he enters the poles. You begin teaching this skill as soon as the dog can move through twelve poles to you. The easiest way to teach a "rock back" is to have the dog come through the poles *downhill*. Position your poles on a hill and continue working in the call-to format. If the dog now experiences trouble entering the poles correctly, go back to asking him to do fewer poles. If you do not have access to a hill, place a set of poles at the bottom of a flight of stairs or at the bottom of a lowered A-frame. With the poles set three feet from the A-frame or flight of stairs, you can re-create the same feeling a dog would have running down a hill.

TEACHING ANGLED ENTRANCES

Angle entrances are first taught with the weave poles on a level surface and then again with the poles on a hill.

You must be able to envision all of the angles that the dog will have to experience in order for him to learn to do independent angle entrances. Imagine a semicircle with a radius of twelve feet, with the first pole in the center of the circle. You want to be able to put your dog anywhere on this semicircle and have him know how to enter the weave poles correctly.

The easiest entrances will be the ones in front of the poles. Gradually move the dog to the right and left of these points for a new starting position. The dog must learn that the correct entrance to the poles is not necessarily in front of him, nor is it in line with you. The entrance to the poles is always to the right of the first pole.

Begin with the dog in position number two, as marked in Figure 22-2.

QUICK SUMMARY

The handler sees the "V" and looks up above the first two poles (not at the dog).

The signal is given with the hand that is closest to the dog.

The hand signal is kept a "secret" until it is above the handler's shoulder.

The hand signal points to the space above the first two poles and does not lower until the dog makes the entrance.

The hand signal slowly lowers as the handler chants "good, good, good" until the dog has met the hand that is holding the treat.

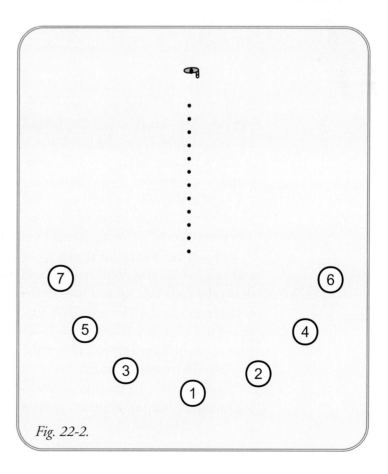

Fig. 22-2.

Angle entrance from the dog's point of view.

Because you are asking for a more complex behavior, go back to standing behind the second pole. Using the hand that is closest to the dog (left in this case), command "okay, weave." Even though the dog is off to the side, the hand signal still points to the air space above the first two poles, and not to the poles themselves. You should be looking up at that space and not at the dog. The raised hand draws the dog's eyes up and over to the correct entrance into the poles. If it does not, at this distance you may slowly lower your hand, holding a treat, and lure the dog into the correct entrance.

Continue placing the dog in all different angled starting positions around the first weave pole. If the dog is suc-

cessful, gradually move back in the poles until the dog can run all twelve poles from that starting point. If the dog is not successful, do fewer poles. *Do not change the dog's starting point.* You can always go back to standing behind one or two poles, where you can ensure that the dog will be successful, then gradually add more poles.

If the dog continually misses one pole, you may tilt that pole a little more open. In general, when things are not going well, change the tilt of the poles, or change your position in the poles— *do not change* the dog's starting point. Work until the dog can perform a call-to to you, through all twelve poles, from any angle.

ADDING EQUIPMENT

Once the dog is moving through all twelve poles and entering from any angle, it is time to start sequencing the poles. Remember—the poles are still open at this point; closing the poles comes later, after all the angles and striding adjustments have been taught.

Put a jump, tire, or table on the semi-circle in one of the easier entrances (positions one through three in Fig. 22-2). Sit the dog either on the table or behind a jump or tire. Now, position yourself behind the third weave pole. To indicate the jump, give a call-to signal. Next, raise your hand up and over to the air space above pole numbers one and two to signal the weaves. It is not necessary to say "okay, weave," because the dog is already up and moving, having taken the jump. The commands would be "okay, jump" and then simply "weave."

When a dog lands off of a jump or table, he lands in a cantering stride.

This makes a big difference to a dog that, so far, has not had to enter the weave poles from a canter. To simplify the exercise, so that the dog learns to get into poles from a canter stride, return to standing behind the third weave pole as you instruct the dog to enter the poles. As the dog learns to make the entry from a canter stride, gradually move farther back in the poles until the dog can enter and do all twelve poles coming toward you, having landed from over a jump or off of a table.

TEACHING THE SEND

A dog that understands the send through weave poles will weave through all twelve poles without you moving at all. If the dog reaches the poles on a course before you get there, he needs to be able to enter and weave without your assistance. A send is also essential for certain handling maneuvers, such as the cross-behind at the poles.

GIVING THE SEND SIGNAL TO THE POLES

I am convinced that most dogs miss weave-pole entrances because their handlers do not know how to give a correct signal. The signal to weave poles is always a send signal, unless you are in front of the poles (as in a call-to). Remember that the send signal is an underhanded motion toward the obstacle. The weave poles, however, are a special case. To send the dog to the poles, you should point to the beginning of the **line of approach** to the obstacle, and *not* to the poles themselves.

CAN YOU CORRECT A DOG IN WEAVE POLES?

So far, there have been no corrections for a dog that misses the poles or pops out. You either give the dog another chance or simplify the exercise by moving closer to the dog or opening the poles wider. Whenever the dog makes a mistake, the dog should begin again from the first pole. You want the dog to view poles as one obstacle—never something that can be started from the middle. Throughout all of the teaching phases of weave poles, there are no corrections. Later, when the dog knows how to weave under all conditions and chooses not to, then you are justified in giving a correction that will be discussed at the end of this chapter.

Before you think you are ready to continue, make sure that your dog can enter poles from any angle off of equipment, and that he can do it going downhill toward you! Depending on the age and breed of your dog, getting to this point may take months of training. All of this practice with open poles is teaching your dog how to find correct entrances, how to navigate through the poles, and what to do with his feet.

The line of approach is an imaginary line extending approximately six feet in front of the first pole. This line marks the angled path the dog will have to follow, in order to correctly enter the poles.

By pointing to the beginning of the line of approach, you put the dog on the correct path to the entrance. The dog needs time to adjust his stride and rock his weight back onto his haunches before entering the weave poles. If you point to the *poles*, the information

Visualizing the line of approach.

tion for the dog to run through the poles. In the send, and later in the run-by, you are no longer drawing the dog forward; therefore, a different motivation will be necessary to keep the dog moving straight ahead. Place a target, toy, food tube, or even another obstacle at the end of the poles to keep the dog focused and wanting to move forward. Some ideas to promote forward drive include:

• Throwing a toy or food tube ahead of the dog as he gets to the last pole.

• Placing a target or motivator (i.e., food tube) at the end of the set of weave poles.

• Putting a jump, tunnel, or any obstacle the dog likes to do at the end of the poles. By sending the dog to the next obstacle, you will keep him motivated to keep moving through the poles.

Whatever you choose to do, it is important that the reward not come from your hand! Why should a dog continue away from you if he gets his reward from your hand?

is too late—the dog will likely miss the first pole and may try to start weaving at pole three or four.

Make sure that you always know where the beginning of the line of approach to the poles is. It never changes regardless of where you stand.

MAINTAINING DRIVE

By teaching weave-pole training in the call-to format, the dog is always running toward you. Because you have the reward, you are actually the motiva-

TEACHING THE SEND

Use a set of six open poles to start to teach the send. Begin with the dog in a sit, slightly ahead of yourself. You will be holding your dog's collar. Both you and your dog should face the poles. Holding the dog's collar helps to create drive and build excitement, encouraging the dog to run forward when the collar is released.

Fig. 22-3.

Plant or throw a food tube to the opposite end of the poles. Standing still, command "weave" as you let go of the dog's collar. The dog, who already knows about running through the line of poles, should willingly drive through the poles to get to the target. If the dog goes through all six poles, run up, open the food tube, and reward the dog. See Fig. 22-3.

If the dog misses poles, simply begin again. When the dog is repeatedly successful, add another set of six poles. You should still be chanting "good, good, good" each time the dog passes a pole. Initially, this praise might pull the dog out of the poles or make him reluctant to move forward away from you. Keep working on it, as it is important that the dog learn to stay aware of you, even as he moves forward independently.

If the dog is repeatedly having trouble moving away from you and through the poles, make the task easier by starting with fewer poles. This way, the dog simply has to move forward a few poles to reach the target. Progressively work back to the beginning of the poles until the dog will go through all six poles.

If the dog is still reluctant to move forward on his own, try setting two sets of six poles about four feet apart. Do a call-to through the first six and then immediately command weave again and send the dog through the second set of six poles.

You can continue working on the send and increase the dog's understanding by placing a table eight feet beyond the poles. Target the table with the food tube. Send the dog through the poles and then, as he exits, command "run, table." (See Chapter 7, *Commands You Need*, "Teaching the Run," page 48.)

TEACHING THE RUN-BY

Once the dog can weave both toward and away from you, it is time to change your position so that you will eventually be able to run next to the weaving dog. For some dogs, this transition takes a few sessions, as they must learn to continue to look at poles and not at their handler, even when the handler is moving next to them.

Sit the dog facing the poles on a gentle angle. Stand on either side of the poles, three poles from the end, about even with pole number nine. Face the way in which you want the dog to be moving (toward pole number twelve), and then, using the hand that is closest to the dog, give a hand signal and verbal command to tell the dog to weave by extending your hand back to the line of approach to the poles. See photo page 206. As soon as the dog enters the poles correctly, run to the end of the poles and face the dog, just as you have been doing all along in a call-to. Keep your arm extended as you move to the end of the poles.

If the dog is successful, gradually stand closer and closer to the beginning of the poles (where the dog is sitting). Continue to run to the end of the poles and face the dog as he finishes weaving. You can even practice crossing in front of the poles as soon as the dog exits the last pole. This should not present a problem to the dog because he is used to you facing him at the end of the poles. After all, this is the way he was first taught. Be sure to practice running with your dog on both sides, and always give a proper send signal to the beginning of the line of approach to the weave poles.

Pointing to the entrance from the ninth pole.

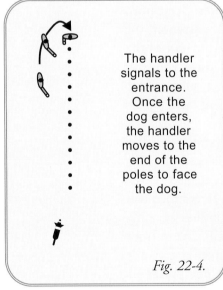

The handler signals to the entrance. Once the dog enters, the handler moves to the end of the poles to face the dog.

Fig. 22-4.

HANDLING MANEUVERS AT THE POLES

FRONT CROSSES AT THE POLE

For complete information on front crosses, please refer to Chapter 8, *Ways of Turning a Dog*, page 57. Front crosses can be performed at either the beginning or end of the obstacle. A front cross before the poles simply allows you to switch sides before the dog enters the poles. When you are performing the front cross, you must make sure to point at the line of approach to the poles; this skill simply requires practice.

When you perform a front cross at the end of the poles, the dog must learn not to pull out of the poles even though you are moving in front of him. To practice a front cross at the end of the poles, place a food tube at the end of a set of open poles. Run slightly ahead of the dog until you reach the end of the poles. Turn to face the dog as in a call-to, and as the dog commits to the last pole, continue rotating until the dog is on your other side.

Because the dog is taught to focus his attention on the poles, it is unfair for you to complete the front cross until the dog's head passes through the last two poles.

QUICK REVIEW OF THE RUN-BY

Even though you are using a send signal to get the dog into the poles, you will run-by next to him once he has entered the obstacle. Do not run too close to the poles or you will act as a distraction and cause the dog to pop out. Give him space (six to ten feet); he was weaving just fine without you next to him, so he does not need your help now. Remember—dogs that take their eyes off of the poles cannot weave! By keeping a target or reward at the end of the poles, you should be able to introduce the dog to having you run next to him without pulling him out of poles. The target helps keep the dog focused forward. The poles are still open, and because they are tilted, the path is clearly visible, making it easy for the dog to move through all twelve poles.

An important point to remember when doing run-bys is to not stay exactly next to the dog. Run slightly ahead of or behind him. Alternate between letting him get his reward from the target or thrown toy on the ground and running to the end of the poles and meeting him. If your dog gets used to you running parallel with him, he will become dependent on your position and later will not be able to execute weave poles without your presence. It is not always possible for you to be next to your dog on a course, so do not rely on it for obstacle performance.

Facing the dog as he weaves does not take the dog's attention off of the poles, especially since he was originally taught weaves in the call-to format. You want the dog to notice your movement, and it is unfair to ask him to register your movement and information when he is not supposed to be looking at anything other than the poles.

Placing a target or toy at the end of the poles will help keep the dog's focus forward. After completing the front cross, you can send the dog from the weave poles to the toy or reward.

CROSS BEHIND AT THE POLES

While a front cross may be executed at either end of the poles, it is much more practical and more commonly done at the exit. In order for you to execute a rear cross at the beginning of the poles, the dog must enter the poles ahead of you. That is, the dog must send ahead, enter the poles, and continue weaving as you switch sides behind him.

As with teaching a send, place a food tube at the end of a set of open poles. Position yourself and the dog directly in front of the poles. Begin by sending the dog into the poles, and as he makes the entrance, cut behind him, thus changing sides. If the dog notices that you changed sides and pulls out, begin again, but remind the dog where the motivator is located at the end of the poles. This second time, wait for the dog to get to the third pole before making the cross.

Note: If your dog is not willing to enter weave poles ahead of you, a cross behind will not be possible. Work more on sending the dog through the poles until he is comfortably weaving the entire set while you stay back behind the entrance.

PROOFING WEAVE POLES

Proofing is a system in which you test the dog's understanding of an exercise before moving on to the next level of training. Weave poles are proofed at two points in training—when the poles are still open, and once again *after* the dog has learned to weave with poles that are straight up.

Each proof is designed to simulate what the dog may find in a ring situation. When a dog first faces a proof, it is normal for him to make an error; after all, you are setting up a situation that he has not yet encountered. It is extremely important that the dog never be corrected for making a mistake on a proof. He should be encouraged to try again. If necessary, you can simplify the task by asking the dog to do fewer poles or by opening the poles more.

Proofing poles will include making sure that the dog can weave any set of poles regardless of how they look, under all different kinds of distracting conditions, and in all different sequences with the other equipment.

Ideas to Proof Poles That Look Different

- Put tin foil at certain points along the base of the poles (sometimes poles are taped with silver tape to the floor).
- Lay bars on the ground, perpendicular to the base of the poles, to simulate weave poles with long legs.
- Use poles with a lot of striping and some with very little color taped to them.
- Use weaves with different spacing between the poles.
- Misalign poles so that two sets of six weave poles are not in a straight line (see Figure 22-5).

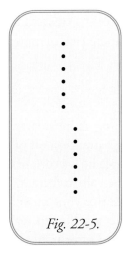

Fig. 22-5.

- Put white baby gates right behind a set of mostly white poles.
- Do odd and even numbers of poles.
- Ask the dog to do a set of six poles, then a space, then another set of six, etc.

- Use more than twelve poles.
- Make a circle of poles.
- Make a square of poles.

Proofing Poles Against Distractions

- Have a person walk near the poles in the opposite direction from the way in which the dog is weaving to simulate a judge.
- Place food smells on the poles (rub hot dogs, cheese, etc., on them).
- Put toys on the ground along the side of the poles.
- Play loud music right near the poles to see if the dog can maintain his rhythm.
- Put tunnel openings, jumps, and tables right next to the poles.
- Roll a ball along the side of the poles in all directions.
- Throw a Frisbee over the dog as he weaves to simulate a bird flying low overhead in an indoor barn arena.
- Peel off away from the poles after the dog gets into them.

Proofing Poles in Difficult Sequences

- Set the weave poles so that the dog is weaving into a wall, fence, or gate.
- Have the dog come out of a chute right into the weave poles. (This is difficult because the dog is disoriented coming out of the chute and does not have a lot of time to gauge the entrance into the weave poles.)
- Practice the A-frame straight into the weave poles. (This is difficult because dog must rock back after coming down the A-frame.)
- Place the tire immediately in front of the weave poles. (This is difficult

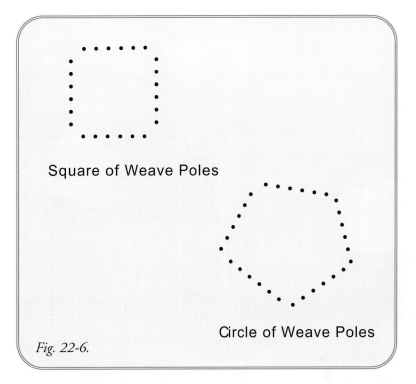

Square of Weave Poles

Circle of Weave Poles

Fig. 22-6.

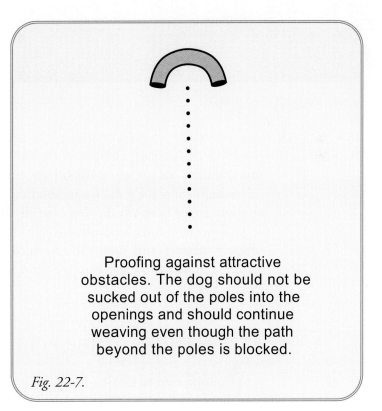

Proofing against attractive obstacles. The dog should not be sucked out of the poles into the openings and should continue weaving even though the path beyond the poles is blocked.

Fig. 22-7.

because the tire frames the first weave pole and the dog cannot see the opening between the first two poles.)

View of weave poles though the tire jump.

- Spread jumps to the poles. (This is difficult because the dog must shorten his stride and rock back onto his haunches.)

Once a dog has learned to weave straight up poles, additional proofing would include tilting the poles slightly opposite to the way in which they were tilted while you were teaching your dog this obstacle. This makes sure that the dog understands how to enter and weave even if the poles are not perfectly straight! All of the proofs done on open poles should be repeated once the poles are closed.

STRAIGHTENING THE POLES

Many handlers try to get their dogs to weave through straight-up poles long before they are ready. Dogs should have learned independent entrances, be able to do poles in all four ways, and should be proofed (see above) before they are asked to negotiate straight poles. If you put the time into training the basics, then when you add this final step of weavepole training, your dog will truly know how to weave.

Straightening the poles is a methodical process. As you progress through the steps, it is important to watch the dog carefully to make sure that he is moving confidently, comfortably, and efficiently through the poles. The goal is for the dog to have an efficient weaving stride and rhythm, which he will need to figure out. The closed poles require him to bend more than for the open poles. Do not rush through the steps to get to closed poles.

STEP 1: EVERY OTHER POLE STRAIGHT

The first step in closing the poles is to set the poles so that every other pole is straight but the rest are tilted. On an even set of twelve poles, this means that one end will start with a straight pole and the other end will have a tilted pole. This creates a "half-V" but still allows for a clearly visible path through the poles.

Placing every other pole straight up teaches the dog to bend more sharply in *one* direction. When the dog is asked to weave, starting from the opposite end, he then learns to bend more sharply in the other direction. Eventually, when all of the poles are straight, the dog will need to bend sharply in both directions, but right now he is learning to make the physical adjustments one side at a time.

Work for a few days with every other pole straight up. Practice the call-to, the send, and the run-by, do front and rear crosses, peel off away from the poles, and work with different sequences. When the dog appears comfortable with the poles set this way, it is time to continue.

STEP 2: OPEN-CLOSED-OPEN

The dog will now meet a series of straight poles for the first time. At this stage, baby gates are used to encourage

Every other pole straight up.

the dog to pass to the correct side of the pole. The poles are set so that the first and last four poles are open and the middle four are closed (straight up). Poles one through four are open, poles five through eight are closed, and poles nine through twelve are open. Four baby gates are placed next to the four straight poles in the middle. The gates go on the side where the pole would have been tilted had the pole been open. The gates should not obscure the correct weaving path.

Open-closed-open poles with gates. Note: The baby gates should only have one set of feet so as not to obstruct the base of the poles.

The gates help guide the dog but are not like wires or baskets (other weave-pole training aids). The gates allow room for the dog to make a mistake if he so chooses. It is my belief that dogs learn by trial and error and therefore must be given the *right to be wrong!* In the event that the dog does pop out at one gate, just begin again. He will figure out the most efficient, and correct, way to navigate through the gated poles.

When you first begin this new setup, stand behind the first gate and call the dog (as in a call-to) into the poles. This assures the dog that he can get around the gate. Gradually, move back one gate at a time until you are calling the dog through all twelve poles. Stay at this step for a few weeks until the dog's speed through the middle section with the straight poles is the *same* as his speed through the open poles.

STEP 3: REMOVING THE GATES

Gates can be removed in one of two ways. With some dogs, you can simply start removing the gates completely, starting with the gate at pole eight. If all goes well, slowly remove the gate at pole seven, six, and five, one gate at a time. If the dog gets confused, you can put a gate back in for a brief period, or you can try another way to remove the gates.

The second way to remove the gates is to gradually slide them away from the poles a few inches at a time. Start by moving one gate four inches away from the pole. If all goes well, try moving another gate a few inches away. While the gates are still present, the dog's opportunity to pass to the incorrect side of the pole increases as the gates slide away and the gap between the pole and gate

Baby gates being pulled away from the poles gradually.

increases. At this point, however, the dog should be grasping the concept of which side of the pole to pass, and although he could try to squeeze through the space, the presence of the gate is a gentle reminder of which way not to pass. When all four gates are four inches away from poles, and the dog understands weaving, gradually pull the gates farther away from the poles.

After a few days of work, your dog should be able to weave four open poles, four straight up poles, then finish with four open poles. Stay at this step until the dog's speed is consistent. You are only asking the dog to bend sharply for four poles. The beginning and the end of the set of poles are easy for the dog to do.

No more gates! Four open poles, four closed poles, four open poles.

STEP 4: STRAIGHTENING THE REMAINING POLES

Poles are straightened one at a time beginning from the inside and moving to the end poles. This means that the poles next to the already straight middle poles—poles four or nine—will be the first poles straightened. The last poles straightened are poles one and twelve. Work for a period of time with only the first and last poles open, since these are the most often-missed poles.

After the dog has been weaving all twelve poles straight up long enough to be confident, go back to the section in this chapter on proofing weave poles (see page 208) and now proof the straight-up poles.

Whenever the dog's speed or confidence suffers, feel free to open the poles and rebuild the exercise. When you are working very difficult entrances, tilting the first pole can help the dog find and make the correct entrance. If the weave-pole performance starts to deteriorate, back up in your training steps for a session before continuing forward.

WEAVE POLE MAINTAINENCE

Like every skill and agility obstacle, weave poles require maintenance if proper performance is to be upheld. Every time you pull a dog sharply out of the poles to the next obstacle, his weave pole performance is worn down as he begins to anticipate the sharp pull. He might react by pulling out of pole eleven or ten, or even earlier. Most attentive dogs learn to anticipate the end of the poles and pop out. To keep a dog driving through the poles, go back from time to time to targeting the end of the poles, working on sends, and throwing a reward ahead of the dog as you peel off away from poles. See Fig. 22-8.

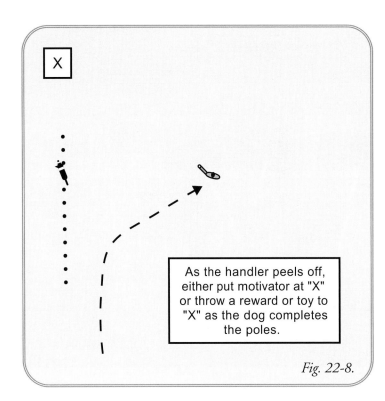

As the handler peels off, either put motivator at "X" or throw a reward or toy to "X" as the dog completes the poles.

Fig. 22-8.

PROBLEM SOLVING

What If?

• **What if my dog pops out of the poles at the tenth pole?**

There are many reasons behind this common problem. The dog may be anticipating a reward, he may be distracted by another obstacle or by your movement, or he may simply be running out of room to maneuver by the time he reaches the tenth pole. Dogs run out of room when they do not rock their weight back enough as they weave. Their speed and lack of balance lengthen their stride, which slowly eats up the space between the poles, and the dog literally runs into the tenth pole.

Popping out at the tenth pole is usually indicative of a "send" problem. To fix this, separate the poles into two

sets of six lined up with about five feet between them. Start by sending the dog through the second set of six poles to a target. When the dog can successfully weave away from you to the target without popping out or turning back, start the dog in front of the first set of poles. Send the dog through the first set, and as he completes them, give a hand signal and command "weave" to send him through the second set. Once the dog can do both sets of six poles reliably, put the poles back together and send him through all twelve poles to a target. Separating the twelve poles into two sets of six accomplishes several goals. It teaches the dog to look for poles, it makes sending him through the poles less overwhelming, and it teaches the dog to rock back and recollect his stride after the first set of six poles.

• **What if my dog pops out at different places along the poles?**

If you tell me that a dog is popping out of weaves, I will tell you that it is most likely related to a "send" problem. Dogs that weave through poles and that are focused forward are not inclined to pop out early. Anytime a dog starts popping out of weave poles, return to working on sends. Sometimes a quick refresher lesson on "sends" through poles is all that is needed to remind the dog to focus ahead of himself and to look at poles, not at anything else. Use the techniques mentioned above, and remember to reward your dog out ahead of the poles to discourage him from focusing on you before he has completed the poles. Rewarding a dog from your hand will inevitably lead to a dog that exits poles prematurely!

• **What if my dog weaves great in practice but not in trial?**

Several factors might be causing a dog that weaves well at home to have problems at a trial.

Speed. It is not uncommon for the excitement of the trial environment to cause a dog to run faster than at home, and when he approaches weave poles with this unfamiliar speed, he is unable to make the entry. It is your responsibility to make sure that the dog has had ample experience entering and performing weaves at top speed before you enter him in a trial. In order to re-create the speed a dog would have on the approach to the poles at a trial, work entries off of long, fast sequences (such as straight tunnels to poles, or a line of four jumps into poles). You can also work weaves downhill to dramatically emphasize the rock-back action on the approach.

Six Versus Twelve. In the AKC Novice level of competition, the dog is required to perform only six weave poles. Because the training method utilizes twelve poles from the outset, it is possible that the dog may not recognize six poles in a ring as the same exercise. To avoid this confusion, simply practice with six poles in preparation for the Novice ring. You can do six poles, another obstacle, and then six poles again in practice.

Stiff Poles. Due to the design of Weave-A-Matic training poles, it is relatively easy for a dog to push the poles out of the way. This is not a problem when you are teaching the obstacle, but if a dog is only used to training poles, the stiff poles that he encounters in the ring will feel very different. Once a dog has learned to do straight-up poles, be sure to use stiff poles that cannot be pushed out of the way. This is especially important for dogs that tend to muscle through the poles, such as stronger Dober-

mans, German Shorthaired Pointers, or Belgium Sheepdogs.

Worrisome Handlers. Sometimes weave pole problems in the ring are caused by the handler. A dog that is accustomed to entering weave poles on his own in practice will be disturbed by an "insecure" handler who tries to babysit or overly manage the dog at the pole entrances in the ring. The dog wonders what is wrong, looks up at the handler, and misses the entry. A good handler runs his or her dog in the ring with the same style and confidence that he or she runs the dog in practice. Do not stay closer, scream louder, or move faster just because you are in the ring. Train as you run, and run as you train!

Pole Phobia. I have known handlers who develop what I call "pole phobia." This happens when a dog begins a pattern of missing weaves in competition but does them easily in practice. Usually, the weaves are the only mistake that the dog is making in the ring, and the handler becomes very stressed in anticipation of the dog's failure to perform. The situation can evolve into a major problem that may last many months if the handler does not change his or her state of mind.

If a dog misses the entry to weave poles in competition, bring the dog back and kindly repeat the command. Usually, the dog is now moving slower and might be more capable of making the entrance. If he misses again, try again. Even if you must repeat the obstacle numerous times, the dog must not be permitted to continue with the course without first completing the weave poles.

If the judge whistles you off the course (because of time or excessive work), the dog will at least learn that he cannot continue to play if he does not weave.

There are trainers who feel that continuing on with the course when a dog has missed poles because of stress is acceptable—even advisable. I do not agree and have never permitted one of my dogs to complete a course if he refuses to perform poles. No corrections are given, and it is not necessary to have a harsh attitude, but in time, the dog understands that in order to continue to play the game, he must complete every obstacle. If you feel that your dog is too stressed to do poles in a ring, then he should not be entered in a trial!

To get out of pole phobia, view the weave poles as equal to any other obstacle. The dog will eventually be able to enter poles in competition. If at any time he needs a second or third try in the ring, be patient and let the dog learn. Be careful when resending the dog to missed poles that you give a good, clear signal and that you also give the dog room to enter the poles. Too often, in a state of panic, handlers spin around, flail their arms, and scream "weave" in a desperate attempt to fix the mistake. No wonder the dog feels anxious!

• **What if my dog was doing great straight up poles but now at trials seems to get a "glazed-over look" as he approaches the poles and runs right past them?**

Assuming that the dog has mastered weave entries, this scenario can be the outcome of a dog that has smacked his shoulder into a pole on an entry and is now leery about entering weave poles. Go back to opening the first pole and practice weaves in as many different locations as you can until the dog once again feels comfortable with fast entries into straight, stiff poles. Be sure that you are practicing on stiff poles. Loose Weave-A-Matics or "stick-in-the-ground" poles are easily pushed and may "give" to the dog's body, making it rather shocking to the dog

when he runs into solid poles at a trial.

Sometimes the "glazed-over look" is a sign of stress or avoidance of distraction. In this case, you need to figure out what is stressing the dog and proof with more distraction training on weave poles.

CORRECTIONS

There will be times when the dog is not in the mood to weave. Perhaps he is tired or has made so many mistakes that he is no longer motivated or willing to weave. When a dog who knows how to weave chooses not to weave, he deserves a correction.

To make a weave-pole correction, take the dog by the collar (in the hand that is closest to the dog) and gently guide him through the poles while chanting "good, good, good." You are physically putting the dog through the poles. Following this correction, give the dog the opportunity to choose to weave on his own, without your assistance. Working with poles of a shorter height makes this task easier.

ALLOWING YOUR DOG TO LEARN HOW TO WEAVE

While it might seem like there are a daunting number of steps to teaching weave poles, the process actually moves along quite quickly. The average dog learns to weave well in a few months. Of course, there are always the phenoms who seem to be born weavers, and those who struggle with the concept. Be patient and *allow* your dog to learn how to weave. Do not become so helpful that the dog learns (or feels) that he cannot weave without you! Weaving is his job; giving the proper signals is yours.

CHAPTER 23

THE PAUSE TABLE

The pause table is a three-foot, square, elevated table. The dog is required to jump up onto the table from any of the three sides considered to be facing the direction from which the dog is coming. A dog that goes behind the table in order to get up on it is considered to have initially refused the obstacle and is scored accordingly. You need to be aware of which side is considered the "dead" side to avoid incurring a refusal. If you are unsure, it is appropriate to ask the judge during the class briefing or walk-through.

In an optimum performance, the dog gets onto the table quickly, faces in the direction of the next obstacle, immediately assumes the correct position, stays in the required position until he is released by the handler, and then dismounts the table on the side of the handler to which he has been called. What should be a relatively simple obstacle to master often costs handlers a lot of time and headaches. Sometimes dogs refuse to get into the correct position, or they slide off as they jump onto the table with speed. Both of these issues are easily remedied with proper training.

In most standard agility courses, a dog is required to pause for a count of five seconds on a pause table before continuing on to the next obstacle. In some venues, the dog may be asked to either sit or lie down on the table; this is determined by the judge before the competition begins. In other organizations, the dog always assumes a down position. It is ideal for a dog to lie down on his haunches, ready to spring into action, as compared to a dog that goes into a down position and gets ready to stay there for awhile. Most dogs will eventually assume a prone down position from which they can easily get up quickly once they understand how to leap off of the table at top speed.

Leaping off of table. Photo by M. Nicole Fischer Photography.

PREREQUISITES

Before a dog can be expected to assume a sit or down position on a table, he must be trained to sit and lie down reliably on the ground with only a verbal command. People who use body language—such as bending over and pointing to the ground to get their dogs to down, or raising their hands to get their dogs to sit—are under the false impression that their dogs understand the down and sit commands. Dogs who will not sit unless someone holds food over their heads have not been taught to respond to the verbal command "sit." To correctly teach the dog to lie down and sit on a verbal command alone and to rectify these problems, see Chapter 7, *Commands You Need*, page 37. There is nothing wrong with using food when you are first teaching a dog to sit or down, but the food must be faded and the dog must reach a point where he understands and responds to the verbal command with no other aids.

Keep in mind that in order for a dog to down, he must lower his head, and in order to sit, he must raise his head. This will become significant as you introduce the positions on the pause table.

GETTING THE DOG ON THE TABLE

The first goal of table training is to get the dog to jump up onto the table on command. The way in which you put your dog on the table will depend on where the next obstacle is located and the direction you want him to face. Like every other obstacle, the table should be taught in all four ways. Be sure to progressively teach the dog to get on the table from the call-to, send, run-by right, and run-by left positions.

To encourage a dog to jump up onto a table, sit on the obstacle yourself as if you are sitting on a couch. Using a treat or toy, command "table," and encourage the dog up. If the dog gets on the table, give him the treat and do not worry about putting him in a sit or down position. If the dog does not get on the table, try a lower table, or gently help the dog up onto the table and then pet him and give him a reward.

Dogs that have not been allowed on furniture or chairs may initially balk at the table, but given encouragement, they will quickly figure out that this is permissible. Do not be surprised if your dog starts jumping onto other tables (picnic tables or coffee tables). This is common, but with a little training, a dog can learn the difference between the tables.

When you release the dog from the table, it is important to give him specific direction to maintain his focus. This is accomplished by following the release command, "okay," with a "here" command. Show the dog the palm of your left hand or right hand at your side, and insist that he come to that side of your body after he dismounts from the obstacle. This keeps a dog's mind from wandering and gives him a clear transition to the next obstacle.

Once your dog is comfortable getting onto a table with you sitting on it, try encouraging him onto the table with a treat and a send signal. Be sure to place the treat in the center of the table to entice the dog to jump up completely and not just put his front feet up to get the treat! Continue to progress until the dog can be directed to the table in all four ways and with you in all different positions. So far, all you have taught

the dog is to get on the table, which should not take very long. It is now time to specify what position he should assume when he gets on it.

With increased speed, a dog is more likely to slide or jump off of the table. He must learn to adjust his stride before jumping up and not just launch at the obstacle. Practice in the call-to format (with your position drawing the dog forward) to allow the dog to figure out how to adjust. If the dog still slides off, simply try again and reward him only when he stops on the table. This problem is usually eliminated once the dog learns how to read the position cues discussed below.

EARLY COMMUNICATION

The sooner a dog knows what position he is to assume on the table, the faster he can get into that position. By planning his position, he is also less likely to slide off of the table when he is running fast. To accomplish this, you will use a non-verbal cue system that tells the dog what position is expected *before* he gets on the table. Dogs read body cues much easier and faster than they process verbal commands, which is why a body-position cue is preferable.

THE TABLE SYSTEM

Remember that in order for a dog to sit, he must lift his head. And in order for him to lie down, he must lower his head. When you want your dog to sit on the table, you walk toward the table and command "sit." As you approach the table, the dog must lift his

Step toward the dog for a sit.

head in order to make eye contact, thus making it very easy for him to sit. Initially, you can hold a treat over the dog's head while stepping toward the dog to help him into the sit.

Conversely, when you want the dog to lie down on the table, you signal to the obstacle. Then, as the dog gets onto the table, you step away from the table and command "down." If the dog does not lie down, you take another step *away* from the table and repeat the command. This is continued until the dog either lies down or jumps off of the table. If the dog jumps off, you simply signal him back onto the table and begin again. If the dog lies down, praise him, walk toward him, and place a treat on the table between the dog's two front feet.

Two things happen as you step away from the table. The dog is able to

Step away from dog for a down.

make eye contact without lifting his head, and the dog feels that you have given him room to put his front feet on or over the edge of the table. Remember that your dog must be able to respond to a verbal down command on the floor before this will work on the table. You may step away from the table in any direction, including walking past the table, if that is the direction you would like the dog to face.

What If?

- **What if the dog is stuck and still will not do a down on the table?**

If the dog is reluctant to do a down on the table, or seems to have "frozen," simply continue taking steps away from the table while softly repeating the down command with each step. This is a situation in which you need to employ the power of time. Physically pushing or forcing a dog into the down causes more resistance and teaches him that, if you do not physically correct him (as in a ring), he does not have to do it. The dog must *decide* to do a down on his own. Convince the dog that it is in his best interest to completely lie down if he would like to get off of the table and continue.

The same concept would apply for a dog that refuses to sit. Step into the dog all the way to the table, and raise your hands over the dog's head to encourage his head to move upward. If the dog will still not sit, keep moving into him and actually kneel on the table if necessary. You will be using your body to push him up. If the dog jumps off of the table, put him back on it, step into him, and command "sit." Life, as this dog knows it, ceases to exist until he decides to sit, but no one is going to force him!

Dogs pick up visual cues for the table very quickly and learn to anticipate what they are going to be required to do. This reduces the stress that many dogs feel when they are approaching the table, not knowing what will be expected of them. Table problems often begin with an anxious dog wondering what to do next. This system of cueing the table position early removes unnecessary stress. Furthermore, when a very fast dog is planning to sit or lie down as he approaches the table, he does not slide off, because he already is preparing his body to get into the required position.

STAYING AND RELEASING

The dog is required to stay in the designated position on the table for a total of five seconds. This affords you time to move into position for the next obstacle. Assuming that the dog has been properly taught the stay command (see Chapter 7, *Commands You Need*, page 37), you simply command "stay" once the dog is in position and walk away. The dog is to stay in position until he is verbally released.

As with all stays, the important part lies in the consistency of the release from the stay. To prevent confusion, which can cause the dog to anticipate a release, give the verbal release command while standing completely still. While you can point or signal toward the next obstacle, or the direction in which you want the dog to go, your arm and body should be completely still when the release command is given. Does your dog release off of the table, or does he wait for *you* to move? If the dog does not release on only the verbal command, you will need to go back and teach this. (See Chapter, *Commands You Need*, "Okay," page 40.)

PROOFING THE TABLE

Proofing is a system in which you test to see if the dog truly understands what he is being asked to do. When you proof, you set the dog up to make a mistake, and when he makes the mistake, you do not correct him. Instead, the dog is helped to understand where he went wrong. Proofing is essential for solid obstacle performance.

One way to proof the stay on the table involves walking circles around the obstacle. Send your dog to the table and command "sit" as you step toward him. Next, give the stay command and proceed to walk a circle around the table. The dog will probably try to follow you with his eyes, which may cause him to get up. If he does, reposition him and begin again. Sometimes you can help the dog understand to stay by resting your hand on his head as you walk around the table. Reward the dog *on* the table, then release him.

Another way to proof stays on the table is to put the dog on the table, tell him stay, and *run* away from him toward the next obstacle. As always, if he makes a mistake, simply tell him to get back on the table, or, if necessary, put him back on the table and try again.

Toys and foods tubes can also be used in the proofing process. With the dog on the table, command "stay" and throw a motivator on the ground away from the table. Work until the dog is not fazed by anything and until he waits

to be released. To proof lead-outs from the table, work long distances. Leave the dog on the table and walk twenty to thirty feet away before you return to praise the dog and then release him.

To proof against sliding off, set up a long call-to toward the table so that the dog picks up speed. Leave the dog behind three jumps straight to the table, and place yourself a good distance behind the table (which allows him room to slide off if he does not adjust).

Table performance can be complicated by external factors. Rain, dew, and frost make the table slippery, and the temperature can make it uncomfortably hot or cold. Sometimes the ground is uneven, making the table wobbly. Be sure to practice shaky tables and slippery tables so that your dog is comfortable facing these extra challenges in the ring.

Proofing should give you confidence to trust your dog on the table. There should be no reason for you to "sneak" away or give repeated and desperate stay commands. Command "stay" once, and walk away with conviction and purpose. What is the worst that will happen? Your dog will jump off of the table, and then you can tell him to get back on it!

SPECIAL CASES

Some dogs seem to have a particularly difficult time lying down on the pause table. If you identify the problem early, it can be dealt with, resulting in minimum stress on the dog.

Sensitive, hairless dogs, like Chinese Cresteds, Italian Greyhounds, Smooth Fox Terriers, and even some Whippets, Vizslas, and Dobermans, have been known to find lying down on a sanded table to be uncomfortable. For breeds with delicate elbows, use a table covered with a soft, cushioned material when you are first teaching the down. Once the dog is confident, use a less-cushioned material, and gradually wean the dog to the table surface. Never force a hairless dog, especially one with straight shoulders, into a down position. It will come back to haunt you!

A dog that strongly resists lying down on a table may be fearful about putting himself in a vulnerable position. To relax his fears, begin by having the dog lie down in your lap, where he will feel safe. If you are dealing with a large

Trusting your dog on the table.

The dog gets on the table, preparing to face his handler.

dog, sit on the floor. Once the dog will relax enough to assume the down position in your lap, move yourself to sitting on the table. As you sit on the table, put the dog in your lap, command "down," and cuddle the dog into the down position. When the dog is comfortable enough to lie down in your lap on the table, try getting him to perform a down right next to you on the table. Feel free to bend over the dog as you slide his elbows into the down position. With you as protection, the dog should begin to relax in the down position on the table. Gradually move further away from the dog until you are no longer in the picture.

A SIMPLE OBSTACLE OR A MAJOR HEADACHE

The table can either be a simple obstacle or a major headache. Eliminate the stress by relying on the positional cues, and teach a sit and a down. Do not plead or beg. The table affords five valuable seconds to strategically position yourself for the remainder of the course. Take advantage of this time by training a reliable stay.

Photo by M. Nicole Fischer.

CHAPTER 24

THE CHUTE

The chute is also referred to as the closed or collapsed tunnel. If you do not own a chute, you can easily make one by attaching a sheet to the end of an open tunnel.

The critical parts of teaching the dog to run through a chute include:

- Teaching the dog to keep his head down as he exits the chute.
- Teaching the dog to find the opening of the chute when it is not obviously visible.
- Getting the dog to run *straight* through the chute regardless of where the handler is running to next.

The length of the chute varies from venue to venue. Some chutes are made of slippery and light material, while others have heavier, canvas-type material. I like to train dogs on a lightweight chute because it discourages them from lifting their heads as they pop up out of the end of the fabric. Always be sure that the chute material is straight before sending a dog into it.

225

TEACHING THE CHUTE

When you are first teaching the chute, always reward your dog by throwing a toy or food tube low and out in front of him as he comes out of the fabric. This encourages him to run straight through the chute and keep his head down. It is easy for a dog to become entangled in the fabric of the chute. To avoid this problem, it is important that the dog keep his head down and run straight. Dogs that jump or "pop up" as they exit the chute not only waste time—they start to anticipate the end of the chute. This causes them to jump earlier and earlier, which increases the risk of their getting caught in the fabric.

I like to allow dogs to discover the chute rather than entice them through it. To begin teaching the chute, take your dog or puppy up to the entrance of the chute, and show him that you are throwing a piece of food into the barrel. Next, hold the dog on the side of the barrel of the chute so that he cannot see the opening, and release him. Watch to see if he knows where to find the food. Most dogs will search and wander into the barrel of the chute to find the food morsel.

Continue playing this game of putting a treat in the barrel and letting the dog figure out how to find the opening of the barrel. Eventually, you should be able to let go of the dog halfway down the outside of the material part of the chute, and he will know how to get into the barrel on his own to get the treat. Be sure that the dog has learned how to enter the barrel from both the left side and the right side. Once he is comfortable finding the opening on his own, it is time to progress.

Plant a piece of food in the barrel, and let go of the dog from the middle of the chute material, commanding "out, chute." The command "out" tells the dog to move slightly away from the obstacle to find the entrance. Now, when the dog's head enters the barrel, run to the end of the material and hold up the material part of the chute so that the tunnel is open and the dog can see you. As the dog eats the food, call him to you through the material part of the chute. Throw a motivator ahead of the dog to encourage him to run straight out of the chute past you to get to the reward. If the dog turns around and exits through the barrel, try again. Eventually, he will take the shorter route and come straight to you through the material part of the chute.

As the dog gains confidence and speed running through a chute that is held open, begin dropping the material on top of the dog just before he exits the fabric. Dropping the material earlier each time teaches him how to gradually push through it.

Most dogs learn to run through a chute with their eyes closed. This is natural, as the fabric slides over their heads. As a result, dogs exit the chute and are momentarily disoriented. It is important to give your dog a second to focus before taking off for the next piece of equipment.

Talking to a dog while he is in the chute usually encourages the dog to arc toward you. If you must alert the dog to a sharp turn at the exit, wait until the dog is almost out of the chute before you call to him. If your dog becomes tangled in a chute, either in practice or in a trial, help him out of the situation before he panics and becomes fearful of being trapped. I usually tell my dog to lie down, and then I untangle the material.

A dog finding the entrance of the chute on his own. Handler commands, "out, chute."

Crossing behind a chute is always risky. If the dog does not know that you have changed sides before he enters the barrel, he will exit and turn the wrong way. Try to cross early, before the dog enters the barrel, so that he notices the change of side. Adding the command "back" indicates a change of lead as you send the dog into the chute and will also alert the dog to notice a change of direction (see Chapter 7, *Commands You Need*, "Teaching the Back Command," page 45).

CHUTE MAINTENANCE

There will be many courses where the dog is asked to turn sharply upon exiting a chute. Dogs learn to anticipate

a sharp turn and may begin the turn while still inside the chute fabric. This is not a good habit to permit, because it will eventually lead to a tangle. When you see your dog starting to arc in a chute, go back to targeting him straight ahead toward a motivator. Do a few fast and straight chutes, encouraging the dog to run straight out of the fabric to a reward. The chute will require constant maintenance, since the courses you run often encourage an early turn.

CHUTE PROOFING

Chutes vary more than most other pieces of agility equipment. Be sure to practice on chutes of different lengths. Chutes can have fabrics of different weights and barrels that may be rectangular and elevated slightly off of the ground. The chute is also subject to weather conditions. Make sure that your dog is comfortable with someone standing on the chute at the end. Sometimes a judge decides that the wind is strong enough to blow the chute out of position and wants a person to anchor it. Practice spraying a chute with a hose to simulate rain, as this changes how the chute feels to a dog that is sliding through it. For dogs that dislike being touched by cold, wet material, try playing a game of "bullfighting" with a wet sheet to accustom them to the feeling.

Because dogs are usually disoriented when exiting a chute, it is wise to practice chute combinations—for example, the chute to weave poles, the chute to spread jumps, the chute to the table, and all other combinations that you can think of. This will help a dog prepare for whatever the course requires.

I do not teach open tunnels to young puppies before they have learned other pieces of equipment. I do introduce the chute early in a puppy's life. I find that teaching the chute before puppies become too inhibited or too tall is a good thing, and most of them love to slip through a light fabric. (See Chapter 4, *Puppies in Agility*, page 19.)

Encourage the dog to run straight out of the fabric. Photo by M. Nicole Fischer.

CHAPTER 25

THE OPEN TUNNEL

Open tunnels, also called pipe tunnels, vary in length, size, and color and can be flexed into many different shapes. Most dogs love the feeling of running through tunnels, and some are prone to picking the tunnel as their favorite obstacle.

While the tunnel is a rather easy obstacle to teach, it is still important to accustom dogs to a variety of tunnel configurations. Depending on the shape into which the tunnel is bent, the exit might not be visible; this makes it harder for the dog to choose to continue through the tunnel. For the novice dog, the more a tunnel is kinked, the more difficult it is to run. Dark-colored tunnels (like black and navy blue) do not allow much light to filter inside and can also be scary to some dogs.

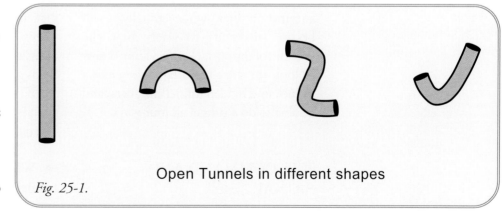

Open Tunnels in different shapes

Fig. 25-1.

In most venues, the diameter of the tunnel opening is approximately twenty-four inches. Small- and medium-size dogs fit easily through the opening, but large and giant dogs must learn to crouch as they maneuver their big bodies through the two-foot-high space. Because of this, there is an advantage to teaching large- and giant-breed puppies the tunnel before they are full-grown. Otherwise, I do not start small- and medium-size dogs on open tunnels until late in the training, when *all* of the other equipment has been introduced. Dogs learn the open tunnel so easily that if they are taught it too young, they quickly develop a preference for tunnels over any other obstacle. Teaching the tunnel later in your dog's training helps prevent what is referred to as "tunnel-sucking" dogs.

TEACHING TUNNELS

I rarely have to teach my dogs how to do the tunnel at all. When tunnels are available, they frequently choose to run through them and explore them. Whenever possible, I prefer to let dogs learn things on their own because what dogs discover, they remember!

While dogs may learn to run though a tunnel on their own, eventually, it will become necessary to teach them the specifics of the obstacle. They must know to look for their handler as they exit a tunnel, find hidden tunnel entrances, and be able to do a tunnel all four ways.

THE COMMAND AND SIGNAL

The tunnel is frequently placed next to contact obstacles and is a large part of obstacle discriminations. To help your dog distinguish which obstacle to go to, the verbal command for the tunnel should sound distinctly different from all other commands. I use the word "tunnel" in a low, baritone voice. This has become such a distinctive trait of mine that people refer to it as the "New Jersey tunnel" command when they hear me or when my students use it in the ring.

The hand signals used for the tunnel are the same signals that are used for all call-to, send, and run-by signals. Because the tunnel is low and on the ground (as opposed to a contact obstacle, which is high and in the air), the signal should point low and toward the bottom of the tunnel's opening.

CROSSES

As with any other obstacle, it can be necessary to cross either behind or in front of the tunnel. Remember that your dog cannot see you when he is inside the tunnel. When you switch sides, you must either perform the cross while the dog can still notice your movement or give a verbal command while the dog is inside the tunnel to let him know where you are. Talking to the dog or making some exciting noise when the dog is in the tunnel helps keep the dog mentally connected to you and also helps alert him to a cross.

What If?

- **What if my dog refuses to enter the tunnel when I try to do a rear cross?**

This problem occurs as the dog senses your movement and anticipates the direction change. To fix this, work on sends through the tunnel. Plant a motivator at the end of the tunnel and send your dog through. As the dog commits to the tunnel, cross behind him and reward him at the other end. Initially, you may have to delay your cross until the dog is actually inside the tunnel, but work until you can send him to the tunnel and can cross behind him before he has passed through the opening.

SHARP TURNS OUT OF THE TUNNEL

The tunnel acts the same as the tire in that it frames and focuses a dog's field of vision. The dog that comes shooting out of a tunnel (especially a straight tunnel) toward the wrong obstacle is likely to earn an off-course. You must inform the dog that you are turning or that the correct obstacle is not right in front of him while the dog is still in the tunnel. To alert the dog of this, cue the dog by softly chanting his name once the dog has entered the tunnel. This verbal cue becomes a warning signal that means "stay alert—you will not be continuing straight out of this tunnel."

When you first begin teaching this concept, it is common for the dog to turn back to you and come back out of the tunnel's entrance. This is a "good mistake" because it means that the dog has noticed that something is different and is paying attention to you. If the dog turns back to you, repeat the tunnel command and signal. The dog will eventually sort this out and will come to understand that hearing his name inside the tunnel does not mean for him to come immediately, but rather to turn sharply toward you upon *exiting* the tunnel.

FINDING THE ENTRANCES

There will be times when the tunnel entrance is not directly visible to the dog (see Figure 25-1). He will need to be taught how to find these "blind" entrances on his own.

To teach the dog to find a hidden entrance, first show him that you are throwing a treat into the opening of the tunnel. Then take the dog away from the opening and send him back to the tunnel. See if the dog can figure out where the opening is and how to get the treat. Here again, you are allowing your dog to discover things on his own. Be sure to throw a motivator beyond the exit of the tunnel to keep the dog driving forward through the tunnel.

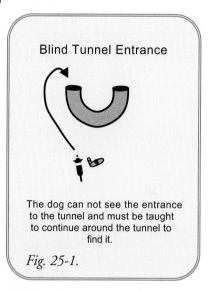

Blind Tunnel Entrance

The dog can not see the entrance to the tunnel and must be taught to continue around the tunnel to find it.

Fig. 25-1.

THE FEARFUL DOG

If you have a dog that is fearful about going into a tunnel, collapse the tunnel so that it is short and straight. Bring the dog to the entrance of the tunnel and have him lie down facing the opening. Place a treat or motivator into the beginning of the tunnel, and encourage the dog to reach in and get it. Gradually throw the motivator farther and farther into the tunnel until the dog appears comfortable stepping inside it.

Next, have someone hold the dog in front of the tunnel while you walk to the opposite end. Bend down, make eye contact with your dog and show him the motivator. Encourage him to come to you through the tunnel (your first call-to.) Gradually lengthen the tunnel until you have a long, straight tunnel. Your helper should not try to force the dog through the tunnel but can help the dog by not letting go of his collar until he chooses to go forward through the tunnel.

Employ the power of time and the dog's motivation to get to you and the reward. If the dog cannot go to the right, left, or backwards, he will eventually come forward through the tunnel. Once the dog is comfortable with the call-to, proceed to sends and run-bys.

When the dog is willing to run through the tunnel all four ways, begin to bend the tunnel into a C-shape. Because the dog can no longer see the exit, he may become reluctant to enter the tunnel, or he may go in, turn around, and come right back out the same entrance. To prevent a dog from coming back out the entrance that he just went into, place a baby gate across the opening of the entrance after the dog enters the tunnel. Now wait. I assure you that I have no dogs that are still in tunnels at my training building. They were all able to solve this problem! Eventually, the dog will figure out that the only way to get out of the tunnel is to continue moving forward, where he will find his reward. Always be sure to throw a motivator ahead as the dog exits the tunnel to increase the dog's drive to get through the tunnel.

SPECIAL CASES

Some dogs try to hide in tunnels to avoid doing something that they do not want to do. You must never let a dog learn that he can hide in a tunnel. If the dog tries to hide from you in a tunnel, either crawl in after him (if you can), or lift one side of the tunnel up until you have removed the tunnel from the dog!

On hot days, tunnels tend to trap and hold the heat. Be careful when you are training in hot weather that you do not discourage your dog's enthusiasm by sending him into a very hot tunnel.

In general, tunnels are easily taught and are a lot of fun for dogs. Be sure to use a good set of tunnel holders made from sandbags to keep your tunnels from moving and changing shape, as fast dogs run through at top speed.

Sandbags are used to keep tunnels from moving.

CHAPTER 26

AGILITY COMPETITION

Agility demonstrations began in England as intermission entertainment for major horse shows. I guess that someone thought it would be cute to see dogs go over small jumps and look like little horses. Since then, agility competitions have become one of the fastest-growing sports and are gaining popularity all over the world. At the present time, there are two annual world agility competitions already in existence, and there is hope that agility may one day become an Olympic sport!

Any physically capable dogs—purebred or mixed breed—can compete in the sport of agility. Different organizations run agility competitions, and each has a slightly unique format. However, most of them use basically the same agility equipment. The American Kennel Club added agility to its list of performance events in 1993, but to date, this registry only accepts purebred dogs. Mixed and purebred dogs are eligible to compete in agility programs of the United States Dog Agility Association (USDAA), the North American Dog Agility Council (NADAC), Canine Performance Events (CPE), the Teacup Dog Agility Association for small dogs only (TDAA), and the United Kennel Club (UKC). New agility organizations are born every year.

Every organization has different levels and types of classes in their agility programs. The names of the levels differ by organization but are structured progressively (from starters/novice to masters/excellent). Theoretically, one level prepares the dog for the next level of competition, but because dogs can progress through the levels rather quickly, I recommend training a dog all the way through the highest level of expertise before you start to compete.

INTRODUCING COMPETITION

I like to introduce dogs to competition without placing a lot of pressure on them. Agility in competition is something to which the dog must become accustomed before he can be expected to perform the same as in practice. I usually start by entering a dog in only one type of class (such as Jumpers) before entering multiple classes in one day. Once a dog understands the trial routine of traveling, warming up, eating on the road, and hanging out at a trial all day, then I will add more classes. Whenever possible, I bring un-entered young dogs with me to trials to teach them how to relax and focus in the trial environment.

I like starting with Jumpers classes, as this provides an opportunity for the dog to learn about agility trials and competition while he is still perfecting contact obstacle training. Jumps do not take as long to teach as contacts, and dogs are often ready to start learning about competition before they have completely mastered contact obstacles. It is important that the pressure of correction be kept to a minimum in early trial experiences. While it would be necessary to correct a dog for breaking the start line, eliminating the possibility of corrections for missed contacts from

these early trials makes for a more positive introduction to competition.

There is no lack of agility trials; in some areas of the country it is possible to compete almost every weekend of the year. If a dog that is trialing regularly develops a major training problem, you would be wise to stop trialing and fix the problem. Just because a dog is entered does not mean that it is always in his best interest to compete.

PREPARATION

Both dogs and handlers should be prepared before entering an agility trial. While the judge will be happy to answer questions during briefings (the judge's chat before the class begins to highlight certain rules or points), you should know the rules of the class in which you are entered. Rule books are available from all of the different agility organizations. A good instructor knows when a dog-and-handler team is ready to compete successfully. When you feel prepared to compete, you are less nervous. There will always be the "fear of the unknown" looming, but it is very reassuring to know that you and your dog have been trained for the skills on which you are about to be tested. If you are a very nervous agility handler, ask yourself if you feel prepared before you decide to enter a competition.

Abraham Lincoln once said, "If I had six hours to chop down a tree, I'd spend the first four sharpening the ax." Nothing feels as good as going into a ring with a dog that you trust to perform because you have thoroughly prepared and trained him. I always train dogs to do much more difficult things in practice than they will be asked to do in a competitive setting. For example, if you need to do twelve weave poles in a ring, be sure that your dog can do twenty-four in practice. Try running without using your voice (body cues only). Occasionally run in practice without first walking the course. Work on hilly grounds and in bad weather. When you feel prepared to meet the challenge of any course that a judge can design, you will be less tense. Thorough preparation, practice, and the magic of time will bring you success!

FAILURE

There is a difference between "nervous excited" and "nervous to the point of feeling ill." If people did not get "butterflies" in their stomach before running agility, they would probably give up the sport for something that would give them a thrill. We enjoy agility because it is exciting; it pushes us to go beyond our normal limits. And after the "rush" and tension of running, we feel calm and relaxed. Feeling excited before you enter an agility ring increases your heart rate and prepares you to perform. This is a good thing! Feeling light-headed and physically ill before running is not. If nerves are making you sick, you need to enter a different state of mind before competing.

For many years, I competed in horse-jumping events. There were many times when I was very nervous about getting injured. A good thing about running agility is that you cannot fall off of a dog! Agility is not a dangerous sport, so why are people so afraid?

Most fear in agility is brought on by fear of the unknown and a fear of failure. If you already know that your dog is going to knock a bar in the ring, you won't be nervous about it, but nor will you be excited. In fact, you might choose not to run and you may go home early to beat the traffic. It is the unknown part of agility that keeps it interesting and challenging, and we certainly do not want to change that. Fear of failure, however, needs to be addressed.

If you feel afraid of failing, ask yourself what your definition of failure is. If you define failure as not earning a Q (Qualifying score), then you are doing yourself and your dog a disservice. Change your definition! Many dogs and handlers have had very enjoyable experiences and have learned a lot on a course where they did not qualify. Was that a failure? I do not consider learning something to be a failure. Thomas Edison was once asked, "How did you keep on going after over 2,000 attempts at creating a light bulb and all of them failed?" He responded, "I did not consider them failures, for I had discovered over 2000 things that did not make a light bulb light up!" Mistakes are not failures but rather great learning experiences. Do not be afraid of them.

For me, the definition of failure is when no effort is made. If I do not attempt to run a course because I might make a mistake, then I have already failed.

THINKING ON COURSE

Agility is a mental sport. Much more time is spent analyzing and studying a course or a training problem than is spent actually running with a dog.

Inexperienced handlers often feel rushed, flustered, and in a state of panic when running a course. The panic filters through the handler's voice and body and is communicated to the dog, who then also panics and loses the ability to think. People sometimes find it difficult to think when they are working at speed. I will never forget the moments before my very first run in Slovenia in 1998 when I was a member of the AKC World Mini Agility Team for the first time. I was very excited, and fear of the unknown was closing in fast. For some reason, I decided to ask seasoned agility competitor Stuart Mah, another member of the team, if he had any last "words of wisdom" for me before I went out into the stadium arena. I have never forgotten what Stuart told me that morning. In a calm, soft, unemotional voice, Stuart explained, "Things are never happening as fast as you think they are." That was probably the best thing anyone could have said to me at that moment. Torville, my Cocker Spaniel, and I had a beautiful, clean run, and I realized that even at world competition, Stuart was right.

No matter how fast things are happening or how fast a dog is running, he still has to jump, climb, weave, and so on. All of this takes time. If you are calm and thoughtful, and if you plan ahead, you usually can negotiate a class smoothly and efficiently. Do not waste motion and energy worrying about things that have not yet happened (such as missed contacts and dropped bars).

If you handle the situation calmly, you can keep your eyes on your dog and hopefully prevent a mistake if you see it start to happen. Being able to avoid mistakes on course is as important as running without making any. From time to time, mistakes will happen.

How you handle them and whether or not you can prevent them depend on your awareness as you run.

I often ask students, "Are you running the dog or are you running the course?" People who run the course are thinking about where they need to be and what they need to do and say, with no allowance for where the dog is and what he may be looking at. People who run the dog pay attention to the dog while still holding the course and handling skills in their mind. If you believe that you may have lapsed into running the course and not the dog, try running someone else's dog. You will automatically pay more attention to the unknown partner, and this will remind you of what it feels like to focus on the dog and not on the obstacles.

People participating in agility and other competitive events often talk about "getting in the zone." The "zone" refers to a mental state where things are quiet, calm, and smooth; the dog and handler are synchronized and movement is automatic. The handler is not thinking about what he is doing—he is just doing it. It takes time and practice to find this mental state. Once you have been there however, you will probably be hooked for life.

STRESS AND NERVES

Stress occurs when your mind resists reality. For example, you are at an agility trial and the carpet on which the dogs are running is slick. Or it is raining, or maybe it is very hot. You become stressed because you do not want this reality to exist. You begin to worry and lose focus on the task of planning and running the course. It would be much more productive to plan how you are going to run given the conditions.

I was once running a course on a very rainy, muddy day. Coming off of the table, there was a jump to a ninety-degree turn to the weave poles. I chose to handle it very differently than most other people. We were successful and people later commented on what an unusual handling strategy I had used. When asked why I had chosen this strategy, I responded, "I didn't want to slip, and the other side was too muddy!" Instead of worrying about trying to make the mud go away, I devised a plan to avoid it.

Doubt and indecision lead to stress as well. As soon as you say you will "try" to do something, you doubt your ability to do it. The little word "try" immediately adds stress. Do not "try" to make the front cross—just run!

I have become very comfortable running agility on my practice field at home. This feeling of comfort is useful, as I can carry it with me to other locations. When I find myself walking out to the start line of a very important class and I can tell I am nervous, I pretend I am back on my practice training field at home and the comfortable feeling returns. Being able to mentally transport yourself to a different, calmer location is a good tool to have available.

BEFORE YOU RUN

Once you feel that you and your dog are mentally and physically prepared for competition, there are a few things to consider before you actually run.

WALKING THE COURSE

Every time you attend an agility trial, there are new courses set to challenge you. It is helpful to watch a course being built and, when available, read the course map beforehand so that you have an idea of the course's path before you get to walk it. I always look at the course from the outside of the ring and from all different angles. Things can look very different, depending on which side of the ring you are standing. While course maps provide a general idea of the flow, do not rely on them alone to plan your strategy. The course on the map and the course in the ring are rarely identical.

Handlers are permitted a limited amount of time to walk around the ring, memorize the course, and plan a handling strategy. Judges generally allow eight to ten minutes for **walk-throughs** that can be divided by class and/or jump height. Sometimes there are "general walk-throughs" (also referred to as obsessive walk-throughs) early in the morning before the scheduled start in which the course is available to everyone. At times, walk-throughs can be very crowded, and it may be difficult to see the equipment and spacing. This is all the more reason why early planning as the course is being set is useful.

If, while you are first walking the course, you have difficulty finding the next obstacle in the sequence, make a mental note; this as a warning signal. If the path does not seem logical to you, it will undoubtedly cause concern for the dog as well. You will need to be especially careful to give your dog the correct information early and clearly at this point in the course.

There will be times when you will need to walk more than one course, and you will have to remember multiple courses before you run the first one. This is best accomplished with early planning and practice.

Remembering the Course

Beginning handlers are inevitably worried about being able to remember a course. It is usually not as big a problem as you might think, although everyone running agility has, at one time or another, forgotten where they were going in a ring! Novice and starters courses are usually very simple since once obstacle tends to follow another. Intermediate-level courses are a little more complex, and advanced-level courses are the most intricate.

One good way to remember a course is to break it into sections. Remember familiar jumping sequences and the shapes of the dog's path. For example, if there are three jumps in a pinwheel configuration, do not think of it as three jumps, but rather as a pinwheel. If, when the obstacles are taken correctly, the dog's path looks like a figure eight, remember the figure-eight path and not the five individual jumps. By breaking a twenty-obstacle course into four sections of five obstacles, you actually only have to remember four things! As you become more familiar with agility, you will find certain sequences repeated. This will also make remembering the flow of the course easier. Try naming familiar sequences so that you can spot them more easily. A turn back into a tunnel next to the dog walk is often referred to as a "turn-tunnel" sequence, because those are the commands to be used.

Planning

To plan an effective strategy and memorize the course, you will need to walk a course more than once. The first time through, see if you can find the numbers and get a feeling of the path's flow. Next, walk it as if you are the dog, and try to see things from the dog's point of view. What will he see coming off of each obstacle and out of each tunnel? Keep in mind the angle at which the dog will be jumping.

Next, walk the course and plan your handling strategy. Where will you cross? What kind of cross will it be? Try walking a sequence different ways to see what feels better and in case you cannot get to where you think you can. It never hurts to walk an alternative plan in the event that things do not go exactly as predicted. Handlers running multiple dogs often use different handling techniques for each dog on the same course. What is the best way for one dog is not necessarily the best approach for another. Part of the strategy of running agility is to know the best way to get a specific dog around the course.

When you have decided on your handling approach, walk the course and pretend to be watching the dog. Find whatever necessary markers you will need for your crosses so that you do not need to take your eyes off of the dog. Use your peripheral vision to negotiate your way around the course. Finally, make use of the remaining walk time (if there is any) to practice running the course with your imaginary dog until you can do it without having to concentrate too much. You do not need to run physically, but proceed through the course uninterrupted in order to accustom yourself to the flow.

STUDYING OTHER RUNS

If you know what to look for, watching other dogs run the course can give you invaluable insight that will help your run be more successful. If you have a big dog, it is more helpful to watch other big dogs running the course. However, information can still be learned by studying any dog navigate the course before you. If you are running a small dog, watching almost any run will be helpful.

As you sit ringside, take notice of what dogs are looking at as they move around the course. What common off-courses do you see? Is there a certain jump that is being knocked down more often than others? Can you determine why? Is it an awkward distance or a strange angle? Are handlers rushing at that point on the course? Are dogs jumping into the sun?

Pay attention to different handling strategies. Notice which ones seem to give the dog the most information about where he is going next. Take notice of where the judge is standing and moving. If you are planning a very different handler path from the other exhibitors, you might want to mention this to the judge before the class begins. While judges usually try to stay out of the handler's way, sometimes they have not planned for a unique handling path, and a word of caution would be appreciated.

Study handler errors and dog errors, and see if you can analyze why things did not work. If you repeatedly see a handling technique fail and you had planned to do it, think again. Perhaps there is a better way to do it. On the other hand, if you see a new handling technique that is working very well, but you did not get a chance to walk it that way, it is risky to try it unless it is a skill with which you are very comfortable. Do not be afraid of being creative. If you plan a course for your dog and you feel comfortable with it, do not change it just because you do not see anyone else running it that way.

WARMING UP

Handlers and their dogs are provided one single bar jump on which to "warm up." The warm up is the time to get in sync with your dog, wake him up, warm up his muscles, focus his attention, and get him used to the jumping surface. The warm-up jump is not a time to train your dog. You are not going to teach him anything he does not already know at the practice jump! Since there are many people trying to warm up on one jump, your time is limited. You need a warm-up plan that will only take a minute at the most.

Before you get to the practice jump, begin getting the dog ready to go into the ring by encouraging him to relieve himself and letting him run a little (on a leash or flexi). Using a motivator, spin the dog in both directions to help stretch him. Other stretching can be done by getting your dog to bow on command, stand on his hind legs, and sit up and beg, among other stretching exercises for dogs. Play with the dog to wake him up and sharpen his reflexes. If it is very hot, you may want to wet him with a hose under his belly, chest, and legs. Do not wet the top of the dog's back, as this usually seals in the heat of the beating sun.

At the practice jump, each dog works best with an individual kind of warm up. Try different things to see what is best for your dog. At some point, the dog should jump extended over the jump, be asked to collect his stride, and be asked to jump and turn sharply. If your dog is taught to lie down on contacts, you might want to practice a jump followed by an immediate lie-down command. Personally, I try to re-create a certain part of the course that I am about to run. I set up an angle that the dog will face or a cross that I plan to make. This is as much a warm up for my timing as it is practice for the dog.

Some dogs, usually lower-energy dogs, do better with several, very short sessions over the jump, while others do well with one longer warm-up session. The practice jump is also a good time to remind your dog about a stay at the start line. It is important to be courteous to other exhibitors who are waiting to use the jump. I usually ask a person waiting when they are scheduled to be in the ring, and if it is before me, I relinquish the jump to them and return to it when they are done. Un-entered dogs are never permitted to use the practice jump.

AGILITY AS A PARTNERSHIP

Agility competition is fun and addicting. Many people who start with no intention of ever competing sooner or later find themselves waking up before dawn to drive to trials that are hours away. Competition can be exhilarating and is a chance to test your training skills against standards and other teams, and to gain recognition through titles and achievements. However, competition is not for everyone and every dog. If you do not feel the urge or derive the pleasure of attending dog trials, do not do it! It is not a requirement, and there is nothing wrong with simply training and running your dog in your backyard or in agility classes. Agility is first and foremost a partnership meant to enhance the relationship between you and your dog.

Earning a MACH! Master Agility Championship.

A TRUE Partnership. Photos by Marian Hummel.

THE BORDER COLLIE IN AGILITY

CHAPTER **27**

Breeds of dogs that were developed to herd excel in the sport of agility. Border Collies, Shetland Sheepdogs, Corgis, Belgian Tervurens, Belgian Sheepdogs, Belgian Malinois, Bearded Collies, Australian Shepherds, and many others have repeatedly taken high honors in serious agility competition. Their speed, athleticism, and trainability, developed initially to control livestock and take commands at a distance, have given them skills that are well suited to the sport of agility.

Dogs from working Border Collie lines are unique and require a different type of training and understanding than any other breed of dog. Most dogs work for praise and rewards and to avoid corrections. This is not true of the working Border Collie! Amazingly, these dogs work for the pleasure they derive from working. They work to work. Training dogs that view their work as a reward requires an entire new set of rules.

In an effort to better understand the mind of the herding dog, particularly the Border Collie, I decided to study sheepherding. What started as an innocent exploration has now blossomed into a compulsive passion, and at this writing, I own forty-one sheep! The more I have worked my dogs on sheep and in agility, the more I see how one sport affects the other.

Sometimes I borrow commands from herding and use them in agility (like the "lie down" for up contacts). Understanding how the herding dog views the world around him has helped me see why a dog's herding instinct may cause confusion in agility.

Herding dogs seem to be born with the instincts to gather, hold, drive, and predict where livestock will move next. Of all the herding breeds, Border Collies appear to have the strongest herding instincts, and some Border Collies have more than others. While the herding dog still requires training, the mannerisms of crawling, stalking, and circling are instinctive. It is not surprising to see a Border Collie circling wide out around a jump that he was directed to take or slowly creeping down the plank of a dog walk as he stalks the target placed there by his handler. I have even witnessed Border Collies stalking and circling a single jump as if it were a sheep and then biting at the base of the jump ("gripping" in herding terms) in an effort to get the jump to move. When this happens, I advise the owner of the dog to let this dog work sheep so that the dog can understand where it is appropriate to use his natural herding skills.

When you watch the Border Collie as he gathers sheep, you can begin to appreciate why it is difficult to get this dog to run ahead of you in straight lines over a series of jumps. His natural movement is to run in an arc and curl back toward you. I have worked very hard to be able to send my Border Collies in straight lines—something that the sporting dogs do very naturally.

Border Collies are all about movement. They notice very slight movements easily and react to them instantly. They want things to run so that they can stop them from running. When handling a Border Collie on the agility course, your position and movements must be accurate and timed correctly. Some handling maneuvers work better than others on dogs with this degree of sensitivity.

It is not uncommon to see a handler attempt to turn a Border Collie using a sharp "shoulder pull," only to find that the movement ends up sending the dog away instead of toward him or her. See Fig. 27-1. To those who are unfamiliar with herding, it appears as if the dog is not obeying the shoulder movement. What is actually happening is that the herding dog is reacting to the sharp turn of the handler's shoulder by kicking out away from the handler, in an attempt to stop his movement. As the dog sees it, he must get in front of the sheep, called heading (in this case, the handler) to stop the movement, and in order to do this, he must first make a big arc away from the sheep (in this case, the handler). This is an instinctual behavior that any herding Border

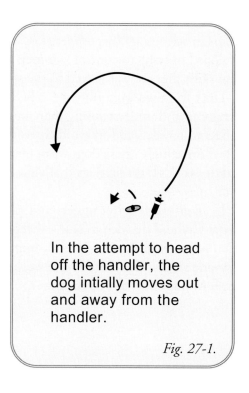

In the attempt to head off the handler, the dog intially moves out and away from the handler.

Fig. 27-1.

Collie would make if sheep were to suddenly turn, and it is very difficult to change through training.

Rear crosses require a dog to move toward the handler as he is sent ahead of the handler. For dogs that are difficult to pull with a shoulder, these rear crosses need a lot of practice until the Border Collie begins to recognize the shoulder pull as the beginning of a rear cross.

Many handlers with "herding" Border Collies rely heavily on front crosses to turn their dogs. Front crosses are effective with these dogs, because when you front cross you are turning toward the dog, who instinctively wants to come to your head and will immediately change his direction. Not all Border Collies have the strong, herding instinct. Herding-related problems in agility are not as serious for Border Collies with less herding instinct.

Our good agility dogs are highly driven and come to an agility competition with an intensity rarely seen in practice. This same intense state of mind follows the dog onto the sheep field. It is an advantage to be able to train your dog when he is in this intense

zone; however, it is often difficult to re-create this intensity in practice. If your dog is intense on sheep, the training and control you teach on sheep is likely to transfer to the agility ring. I have borrowed the lie-down command from herding and use it in agility for the up contacts with many dogs, and for the down contacts with some as well. Training "lie down" on sheep when the dog is in high drive helps you gain control and be able to enforce a lie-down under agility trial conditions.

In addition to allowing me to teach control, herding helps build a dog's confidence. When a dog realizes that he can control other animals, his self-esteem is boosted. This self-confidence adds to his speed and willingness to work away from the handler.

Herding and agility both require the dog to focus on more than one thing at a time. Simply put, in agility the dog must listen and know where his handler is while also looking for obstacles. In herding, the dog must listen for commands, know where his handler is, and not take his eyes off of the sheep. Success in both activities relies on the

The athletic Border Collie makes a sharp turn out of a tunnel and drives towards the dog walk.

dog's ability to multitask. As the dog gains proficiency in one sport, it is readily transferred to the other. Dogs that make direct eye contact with their handlers in agility miss jumps, weave poles, and contacts. Dogs that watch their handlers on the sheep field lose their sheep!

In my experience, herding helps a dog's performance in agility, but the reverse is not necessarily true. Agility can make a herding dog too fast on sheep and too quick to respond to commands. In herding, dogs are working with livestock; it is not desirable to have livestock frightened or moved too quickly. The great herding dogs are calm, quiet, and stealth like in style. They can be fast when necessary but then return immediately to a calm pace. It is difficult to get the same dog to move with continuous speed and lightning reflexes in

agility, and then calmly and cautiously while herding. I am still working on it!

The working Border Collie is different from every other breed of dog. The reward for the sheepdog is the opportunity to work sheep. Most will work sheep in adverse weather conditions, even if they are injured. Males will work sheep running next to a bitch in heat! The drive to herd is so strong that the only thing the dog views as a correction is when he is not permitted to herd. For many Border Collies, the reward for agility is to be able to run agility. While they may be seen tugging on toys, and occasionally eating treats, their real motivation is the adrenaline rush they get from running, jumping, and turning over agility equipment. It is not uncommon for the Border Collie to repeatedly do the wrong piece of equipment, even if you let him know it is wrong, because to him, the act of running and doing is, in itself, a reward. The trainer who understands how the Border Collie thinks will know how to change the undesired behavior.

Let's look at what happens when the dog is wrong in herding. If the dog takes an incorrect flank (goes in the wrong direction), he is corrected verbally with a "no," and he is stopped (usually with a lie-down command). Then the flank command is repeated. Eventually, the dog figures out the proper direction in which to move, if he is going to be permitted to continue working the sheep. The same training approach can be applied to agility. If a Border Collie heads for an off-course obstacle, stop him instantly from working with a lie-down command, then redo the sequence. In agility, you must be sure that you have given the correct command and signal before blaming the dog

for the off-course mistake. Only when you are certain that the mistake was not caused by your own error should you correct the dog with a stop (lie-down) command.

Border Collies are quick to pattern behaviors. If you run a short sequence, they remember it and will repeat it easily without thinking. This can make it difficult for handlers to solve problems, as the dogs end up doing a sequence correctly because they have been patterned to do it, not because they understand the handler's commands. When you are training a Border Collie, try not to repeat things in the same order. Not being repetitious will require the dog to pay attention and not rely on a previous patterned sequence.

Excited Border Collies often have trouble staying at the start line of a course as the handler leads out. If a Border Collie breaks a start line to begin the course, there are very few corrections that are effective. The best approach is to remember how the Border Collie thinks and use it to your advantage. The dog hopes that, by breaking the start line, the handler will begin running and the fun will commence. This should never be allowed to happen. If, when the dog breaks the start line, you do not begin running, the dog will change his behavior because he will not be getting what he wants. What to do with start-line stays and training techniques is explained in Chapter 11, *The Start of the Course,* "Stays at the Start Line", page 90, but here is an overview of how it all works:

Leave your dog at the start. Command "stay," and lead out. At any point that the dog gets up, freeze! Do not move. Do not say anything to the dog. Do not look at the dog. Eventually, the dog will wander back to you as if to say,

"Aren't you going to run?" At this point, slowly walk the dog back to the start line and begin again as if nothing bad happened. It should only take a few repetitions for the Border Collie to realize that when he moves first, you do not move at all!

As mentioned earlier, Border Collies are all about motion. This can work for you and against you in agility. It is an advantage to have a dog that notices your every movement when you are running a course together. It is not helpful to have a dog that focuses on all the movements made by other dogs and people outside the ring!

Teach your Border Collie to focus on only your movements as you stand outside a ring. This is most easily accomplished by getting the dog to play tug with a toy. The game of tug can be exciting enough to hold your dog's attention while other things go on around him. It is up to you to make it exciting. Never have your young Border Collie

Noticing handler's movement, this dog is turning.

on a leash outside the ring watching the other dogs run agility. This teaches your dog to focus on movement that does not involve you. If your dog does not like to play tug, teach him. Food will never be enough of a motivation to take the dog's focus off of movement. After all, he's a Border Collie—not like any other breed of dog. He could go for days without eating and still work if he had to.

It is no secret that Border Collies are the number-one large breed of dog in agility today. In England, there are so many Border Collies competing that they have had to make a separate venue called the ABC class; ABC stands for Anything But a Collie! As more and more handlers turn to Border Collies to derive the thrill of running a fast dog in agility, the more important it becomes for people to understand the mind of this special herding dog. Border Collies are not easy to train until you understand them, but they sure are a lot of fun!

Soaring over the triple jump; Border Collies would do this all day long!

CHAPTER **28**

THE VALUE OF AGILITY

The sport of agility brings together people of all ages, from all different walks of life, and allows them to share quality time with their canine companions of all kinds, sizes, and shapes. On the agility playing field, all are welcome and invited to test their brain power, skills, and athleticism.

All breeds of dogs are capable of running agility successfully, because agility is a natural game that makes sense to dogs. Handlers and dogs form lasting friendships with other fanciers whom they otherwise would never meet and spend time with.

In agility, dogs compete against other dogs of approximately their same height. All dogs in the same class run the identical course for the day. If the jump bars stay up, contacts are touched, the obstacles are performed in the correct order, the handler does not make physical contact with the dog, and the dog is fast enough to complete the course under the standard course time, the dog and handler will be successful. If the standards are met and dog and handler manage to post the shortest time on the course, they will win. Dogs and handlers are never judged on style, only on performance; therefore, no judge can prevent a winning team from taking home the blue ribbon. Exhibitors enjoy knowing that they have a fair and equal chance of earning agility titles, but oddly enough, titles and winning are not really what agility is all about!

Anyone involved in the sport has had many experiences on course when things did not go exactly as planned, yet the dog and handler leave the ring panting with excitement, invigorated, and looking forward to the next round. What happens in the agility ring is really more about a moment in time and a point of exhilaration—literally a few seconds—when canine and human work and play as one. Once your team has felt the thrill of a great agility run, it will become painful to stay away from the sport!

These awesome experiences in agility have helped both species overcome depression, fears, obesity, and loneliness. Dogs that end up in shelters because of their bounding energy find a positive outlet in which to focus their drive. People who never before saw a reason to run and exercise now find themselves working to become fit so that they can keep up with their dogs; some have even stopped smoking! Shy dogs and people become gregarious and outgoing and can even be found barking or shouting as they get caught up in the excitement of the agility ring. Agility truly changes the lives of dogs and people.

For some dogs, agility is an important job. My Border Collies, true working dogs, are very serious and intense about their performances in the agility ring. Executing obstacles in the ring in response to handler cues gives these dogs a sense of accomplishment and pride as they perform their "job" of the day. Because dogs were originally bred to work with man and there is little work left in the world for dogs to do, agility fills a need. Other breeds of dogs view agility as a game and will literally pull their handlers into the ring for a chance to play with their favorite human. At the very least, agility serves as a training ground for any dog to learn to obey off leash and work as a team member while developing a powerful relationship between himself and his human.

Strong relationships of any kind are built on trust and honesty. The secret of any outstanding agility team is that both the human and canine members of the team have faith in each other. The dog must trust that the handler will clearly communicate where to go next on the course. In return, the handler must trust his trained dog to perform as he was taught, working at top speed and at great distances. When this trust is demonstrated in the agility ring, it is truly magical. To watch a dog plow through weave poles, while his handler runs twenty-five feet in another direction to set up for the next movement, is breathtaking.

From another perspective, the dog must trust that, if his handler's instructions are in error, he will not be corrected for moving in the direction he thought his handler wanted. While it is easy to teach dogs to do the agility equipment, developing the skills and relationship needed to negotiate a course of obstacles takes time and patience. In my opinion, it is well worth the time, for the end result is a canine partner for life.

I hope you have enjoyed reading *Agility Start to Finish.* The writing of this book has been an emotional experience for me. As you can tell, I am passionate about agility and its value for people and dogs. Agility is a great deal more than dog training, competition, or even having fun with your companion. It is a sport that builds understanding, appreciation, and communication with dogs in a natural way.

In the past, dogs were always expected to learn "human" language. Now, through agility, dogs have been given the opportunity to teach people how to speak "dog." I wish you all the best as you strive to become fluent in this new language.

GLOSSARY

Back Weave: The fault incurred when dogs mistakenly take a few weave poles in the wrong direction.

Bounce Jumps: Describes jumps that are set so close to each other that the dog cannot take a stride between them and must take off upon landing, in effect "bouncing" between the jumps.

Buja Board: See Wobble Board.

Channel System Poles: A special type of Weave Poles constructed so that the poles slide to the side thus creating an unobstructed channel path through which the dog can pass without bending; used to teach Weave Poles.

Contact Obstacles: The general term given to the dog walk, A-frame and seesaw.

Contact Trainer: A device resembling a much scaled down version of the dog walk and A-frame used by some to practice contact training. Its smaller size allows for more repetition, especially in limited space.

Critical Points: A specific spot on a course that requires the handler's physical presence in order to direct the dog.

Cross: Anytime the dog is moving from one side of the handler to the other.

Delayed Gratification: Getting the dog to realize that he must do what you want before he can earn his reward; a step in teaching "touch" and contact behaviors.

FAST: "Fifteen And Send Time" is an agility game in AKC agility which involves point accumulation and distance handling.

Flank, Flanking Command: A command used in sheepherding to tell the dog which way to circle the flock of sheep (clockwise or counter-clockwise.)

Flattening Out: Refers to the dog's arc and body position over a jump. The dog takes off early before the jump, and instead of arcing high over the top of the bar, he skims it.

Food Tube: A training tool in which food can be placed, but the dog can only access the food when the handler opens the tube. It prevents the dog from cheating and self rewarding.

Four Ways: Refers to the four possible ways that any obstacle can be performed. They are the run-by right, run-by left, call-to and send.

Front Cross: A movement in which the handler goes from one side of the dog to the other. This is accomplished when the handler is ahead of the dog and rotates towards the dog.

Fun Match: A match or fun match is a practice trial that does not count towards any titles. A club must hold an "A Match," which is a type of match, required before the club is permitted to host a sanctioned trial.

Gamblers: A competitive game class in USDAA that involves point accumulation and handling at a distance.

Handler Restrictions: Any situation in which the handler's movement and placement is physically limited. This can be due to natural restrictions, like poles and fences, or can be created by judges by strategically positioning obstacles that limit the places a handler can run.

Heading: The natural tendency of some herding dogs to run to the front of their handler in an attempt to stop the handler's motion.

Independent Performance: The ability of a dog to perform an obstacle without the handler in close proximity.

Inside Arm: The hand and arm closest to the dog.

Jumpers: A competitive class offered in several venues in which contact obstacles are excluded. In AKC, it is Jumpers with Weaves and the Weave Poles are always included.

Lead Arm: The arm that instructs the dog which lead to land on. If the handler uses her right arm the dog is to land on his right lead; if the handler uses her left arm, the dog is to land on the left lead.

Lead-Out: A handling strategy in which the handler leaves his dog in a stay at the start line and moves ahead on the course a few obstacles in order to gain a handling advantage.

Leash Stirrup: Making a loop in a leash by the dog's collar such that the handler can step into it and thus encouraging the dog to lower his head and body into a down position.

Line of Approach: The imaginary line extending approximately six feet long from the first weave pole that depicts the path the dog should take to enter the poles correctly.

Lure: Refers to the action of artificially creating the desired behavior by leading or moving the dog via the help of food or other motivator. The dog is not purposefully executing the behavior but is just "following the food."

Moving Drop: The behavior in which a dog will lie down on vocal command only while moving. (The handler must continue to move as the dog drops.)

Off Course: The fault incurred when a dog performs an obstacle out of sequence.

On the Flat: The area of the course in between the obstacles. Also term used to describe movement on the ground with no obstacles.

Outside Arm: The hand and arm farthest from the dog.

Pairs Relay: A competitive class in USDAA in which one dog and handler team runs the first half of the course, exchange a baton, and a second team runs the second half.

Pinwheel: A configuration of three jumps with all three jump ends pointing into the center.

Pivot Point: The point on the seesaw where the board starts to move.

Proof: A test of a dog's understanding.

Qualifying, Qualify: Refers to completing the minimum standards of an agility competition class, thus earning a "qualifying score."

Rally: An AKC event similar to obedience where the dog and handler perform a course and various obedience exercises as directed by descriptions on signs.

Reverse Flow Pivots (RFP): A handling technique used to sharply adjust a dog's path, changing his direction for a brief moment and then returning to the original direction.

Rock Back: Refers to the dog shifting his weight back from his front end onto his rear end, such as before entering the weave poles.

Serpentine: A jumping pattern where the jumps (or other obstacles) are set end to end in a line. The dog is required to slice jump in a weave pattern. For example, the dog jumps away from the handler over the first jump, towards the handler over the second jump, and away from the handler over the third jump. A serpentine is also sometimes referred to as a "grapevine."

270: A jump sequence of two jumps where the dog covers 270 degrees of a circle (3/4 of a circle) as he goes from the first jump to the second jump.

180: A jump sequence of two jumps where the dog covers 180 degrees of a circle (1/2 of a circle) as he goes from the first jump to the second jump.

Shaping: Adjusting the shape of the dog's path in between obstacles.

Single Stride: One stride.

Slicing: Jumping a jump on a sharp angle.

Snooker: A competitive Game class in USDAA that involves individual strategy and planning to accumulate points.

Spread Jumps: The Double, Triple, and Broad jumps, all which require a dog to stay in the air longer to clear the wide expanse of the jump.

Standard Course Time (SCT): The maximum amount of time permitted for a dog to run an agility course. Anything longer incurs time faults.

Standard Agility Course: A course that includes contact obstacles (dog walk, seesaw, A-frame) and a table along with the jumps, weaves, and tunnels.

Stride: The distance covered in forward motion at a canter or gallop, consisting of a coordinated series of steps that brings the legs back to their original position.

Sway Bridge: A small bridge that moves as you walk over it.

Threading-the-needle: A situation on course where the handler must direct the dog past many off-course obstacles on his way to the correct obstacle.

Threadle: A jump pattern the same as a serpentine but instead of asking the dog to weave back and forth over jumps, the dog is sent over a jump and is then called through the space between the first two jumps so that he can jump the second jump in the same direction he jumped the first jump.

Vertical Distance: Refers to the distance between the handler and dog as the dog continues forward and straight ahead of the handler.

Walk Through: When a handler walks the course without the dog to plan his strategy.

Weave-A-Matic: A special type of weave poles constructed so that the poles tilt to the sides thus creating a "V" through which the dog can run without bending. Used to teach weave poles.

Wings: The structures placed next to the standards of jumps that add width and thus create additional challenges and handler restrictions. They can be solid, fence like, large, small, and creatively decorated.

Wobble Board: Also called a Buja Board. This is a flat board (usually 3' by 3') with a ball attached in the center on one side. When placed with the ball side down, the board wobbles as a dog walks on it.

APPENDIX I

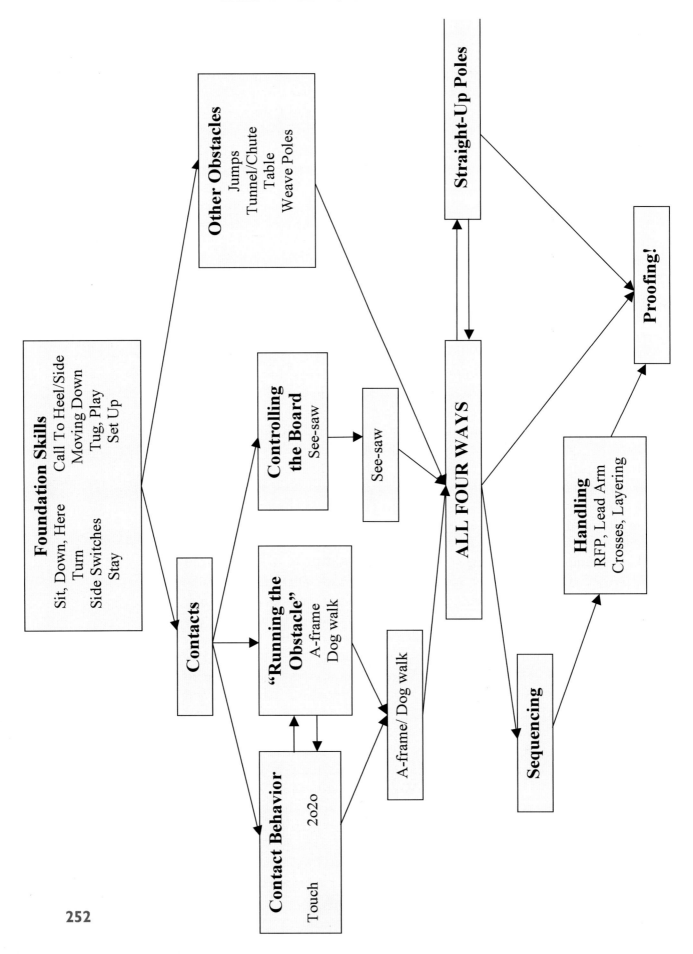

APPENDIX II
AGILITY PROGRESS SKILL CHART

Directions:
Every time you work a skill on a particular obstacle, color in a small portion of the appropriate box. This helps you keep track of how much you have worked that skill on each obstacle. A trained dog has the entire chart completely shaded in.

	Call-To	Send	Run By Right	Run By Left	Angled Approach	Front Cross	Rear Cross	Peeling Off	Contact Behavior	Proofing
Dogwalk										
A-Frame										
See-Saw										
Open Tunnel										
Chute										
Table										
Tire										
Single Jump										
Double Jump										
Triple Jump										
Panel Jump										
Broad Jump										
Weave Poles										

AGILITY REFERENCES AND RESOURCES

NATIONAL ORGANIZATIONS

American Kennel Club (AKC)
www.akc.org/events/agility/index.cfm
Organization which sanctions a variety of canine conformation and performance competitions. Offers local and national agility competitions. Participation is restricted to purebred dogs of breeds recognized by the AKC.
Purpose: *"Advance the study, breeding, exhibiting, running and maintenance of purebred dogs."*

Australian Shepherd Club of America (ASCA)
http://www.asca.org/Programs/Agility/index.htm
A breed specific organization allowing all breeds and mixed breeds to participate in agility competition.

Canine Performance Events, Inc. (CPE)
www.k9cpe.com
Agility specific organization which sanctions local and national agility competitions. Participation is open to all dogs, regardless of breed or pedigree.
Basic Philosophy: *"…for the dog and handler to have FUN while competing for agility titles"*

Dog on Course in North America (DOCNA)
http://www.docna.com/
This venue was established in 2005 and offers agility for all dogs, regardless of breed or pedigree.

North American Dog Agility Council (NADAC)
www.nadac.com
Agility specific organization which sanctions local and national competitions. Participation is open to all dogs, regardless of breed or pedigree.
"Where safety and fun mean everything."

Teacup Dog Agility Association (TDAA)
http://www.k9tdaa.com/
A competitive venue adapted for small dogs. Participation is restricted to dogs measuring less than seventeen inches regardless of breed or pedigree. *"The purpose of the Teacup Dogs Agility Association is to provide a competitive venue for dogs of small stature without regard to breed or pedigree."*

United Kennel Club (UKC)
www.ukcdogs.com/agility.htm
Organization which sanctions a variety of canine conformation and performance competitions. Though a breed registry, participation in UKC agility is open to all dogs, regardless of breed or pedigree.
Philosophy on Agility: *"… that all handlers, regardless of physical abilities, and all dogs, regardless of breed and physical structure, should have the opportunity to participate and experience success in agility."*

United States Dog Agility Association (USDAA)
www.usdaa.com
(972) 487-2200
Agility specific organization which sanctions local, regional, national, and international agility competitions. Participation is open to all dogs, regardless of breed or pedigree.
Motto: *"Promoting Competitive Excellence in Dog Agility"*

INTERNATIONAL ORGANIZATIONS

Agility Association of Canada (AAC)
www.aac.ca
Canadian venue which promotes inclusive, competitive agility at the local, regional, and international level. All dogs may participate, regardless of breed or pedigree.

Federation Cynologique Internationale (FCI)
http://www.fci.be/
This organization sanctions international championship competitions. In the United States, it is affiliated through the AKC.

International Federation of Cynological Sports (IFCS)
www.dogsport.ru
This organization sanctions international championship competitions. In the United States, it is affiliated through the USDAA.

AGILITY EQUIPMENT

Affordable Agility, Inc.
www.affordableagility.com
(800) 254-9441
Quality agility equipment for training. Goal of keeping agility equipment affordable.

Agility of Course
www.agilityofcourse.com
Quality agility equipment for training, lightweight, affordable, and easy to use.

Clean Run Productions, LLC
www.cleanrun.com
800) 311-6503
Largest agility magazine, books, videos, training supplies, clothing, course designing software, and resource center.

J & J Dog Supplies
www.jjdog.com
(800) 642-2050
Competition agility, obedience, and other dog training equipment and supplies.

M.A.D. Agility
www.madagility.com
(717) 543-5693
Competition and training quality agility equipment. Special requests honored. Equipment rental for trials available.

Max 200 Performance Dog Equipment, Inc.
www.max200.com
(800) 446-2920
Complete line of state of the art competition and training quality agility and obedience equipment. Agility equipment rental for trials available.

NTI Global
www.ntiglobal.com/dogagility/
(800) 947-7767
Wide selection of tunnels, tunnels accessories, trial mats and some other equipment. Free shipping!

Rocket Tunnels
www.rockettunnels.com
(800) 464-0112
Wide selection of competition and training quality tunnels and accessories.

MAGAZINES

Agility in Motion
www.agilityinmotion.com
Video agility magazine available on DVD.

Clean Run
www.cleanrun.com
(800) 311-6503
Largest agility magazine.

ABOUT THE AUTHORS

DIANE BAUMAN

Obedience titles, tracking titles, herding titles, agility accomplishments, and even breed championships — the list goes on and on. Regardless of the venue, Diane competed, won and titled. She made history with unusual breeds, rescued dogs and also with the ever-popular Border Collie. The walls of her training facilities in northwestern New Jersey are covered with championship ribbons, trophies and awards from her thirty year career as a competitor and trainer.

Unless directly asked, she is unlikely to tell you about the awards. It's simply not important to her. What is important to her is to make a difference in someone's life. She is the consummate teacher.

Devoting hours to rehabilitating and training hundreds of rescued dogs throughout the years, she has touched many lives —both human and canine. Some dogs go to pet homes, some join her family, and others get matched with eager students seeking Diane's knowledge to teach newly adopted canines the skills needed for obedience, herding, agility or tracking.

With the help of her husband, Robert Potter, DVM, Diane maintains two large indoor and outdoor training facilities currently outfitted with 41 sheep, two goats, eight dogs, one cat, three agility courses and an obedience venue. Her students, who travel from as far away as California, can take private lessons or attend one of the many seminars on problem solving, obedience and agility.

Unlike many agility enthusiasts who profess that Border Collies are the "agility dog of choice," Diane is interested in training all breeds for the agility ring. She feels that learning and exploring the dog universe makes one a better teacher. According to Diane, "every new breed of dog you work with is like learning a new language. Some are more difficult than others."

Always looking for new challenges, Diane's insatiable quest for knowledge helps raise the bar for herself and her students. The proof is there. Many of her students have gone on to become instructors, famous trainers and competitors in the world of canine competition, something she is very proud of.

It is rare that a winning athlete can also be an outstanding instructor and mentor. Diane's passion to impart her tried and true methodologies has made her one of the dog world's most respected professionals. She is, first and foremost, a teacher.

Diane can be reached at diane@dianebauman.com.

CAREER HIGHLIGHTS:

Member of the 1998, 1999, and 2000 AKC World Agility Team Championships ...with her MACH 3 American Cocker Spaniel "Torville" winning Gold in 1998 and Silver in 2000.

Third competitor in history to achieve a MACH of any breed (Master Agility Champion) with her American Cocker Spaniel "Torville."

First MX (Master Excellent) and MXJ (Master Excellent Jumpers) titles ever on an Afghan Hound that also had multiple High In Trial awards in AKC Obedience!

Four tracking titles with a Golden Retriever, Keeshond, Papillon, and Cocker Spaniel.

Attained four OTCH's (AKC Obedience Trail Championships) with a Pomeranian, Pekingese, Keeshond, and Golden Retriever, accumulating 16 perfect scores of 200 in obedience.

Earned Top Herding Dog in AKC Agility JWW in the US (in 2004) and achieved 4 MACHs with her rescue Border Collie "Luca."

JESSICA AJOUX

Jessica Ajoux loves agility. She was fortunate to discover the world of agility early, at the age of fifteen to be exact. While she quickly developed aspirations of world competition, she had the challenge of balancing the new found passion with her educational priorities. She first competed with her dog, Mocha, in Southern California during a dynamic time when new concepts and innovating training techniques were pushing the sport forward like never before. Agility was exploding in concept and popularity and she was riding the wave of progress.

In 2003, Jessica left California for New Jersey when she enrolled at Princeton University. Trying to find a way to stay in touch with the world of agility competition, she soon had the fortune of meeting dog enthusiast and agility competitor Jane Jeter, who introduced her to new viewpoints and disciplines, and ultimately to Diane.

Jessica describes her meeting with internationally renowned trainer Diane Bauman as "life changing." She spent hours watching her train and picking her brain, discussing training techniques, trends, philosophies and theories. She was able to get back into the ring by running Diane's Border Collie, Luca, and Jane Jeter's Cocker Spaniels. Since Jessica graduated in 2007 with a degree in Psychology, she finally has her own dogs to train and compete with. Jessica has also served as an official USDAA judge since 2004 and travels around the country judging trials. With Diane's help, Jessica has grown into an experienced trainer, competitor and teacher.

ABOUT THE PHOTOGRAPHERS

BOHM MARRAZZO PHOTOGRAPHY

The majority of the photographic images shown throughout this book are the result of the collaborative work of partners Linda Bohm and Gerard Marrazzo of Bohm Marrazzo Photography located in Montclair, N.J. Nationally known for their award winning advertising campaigns, they were the perfect duo to create over 150 images illustrating Diane's teaching methodology.

As an agility competitor herself, Bohm knows just when to capture that special moment that says it all . . . dogs love agility.

M. NICOLE FISHER PHOTOGRAPHY

Photographer M. Nicole Fischer of New York City also combines her passions for agility and photography. Known throughout the agility world for her action photos, Fischer successfully captured the intensity of the competitive canine throughout the book.

When she's not ringside capturing those special images of breeds large and small, you can see her running her beloved Standard Poodle "Mayday" in the ring.

INDEX